Revolution Rock

Revolution Rock

The Albums Which Defined Two Ages

Amy Britton

AuthorHouse™
1663 Liberty Drive
Bloomington, IN 47403
www.authorhouse.com
Phone: 1-800-839-8640

© 2011 by Amy Britton. All rights reserved.

No part of this book may be reproduced, stored in a retrieval system, or transmitted by any means without the written permission of the author.

First published by AuthorHouse   11/11/2011

ISBN: 978-1-4678-8710-6 (sc)
ISBN: 978-1-4678-8711-3 (ebk)

Printed in the United States of America

Any people depicted in stock imagery provided by Thinkstock are models, and such images are being used for illustrative purposes only.
Certain stock imagery © Thinkstock.

Because of the dynamic nature of the Internet, any web addresses or links contained in this book may have changed since publication and may no longer be valid. The views expressed in this work are solely those of the author and do not necessarily reflect the views of the publisher, and the publisher hereby disclaims any responsibility for them.

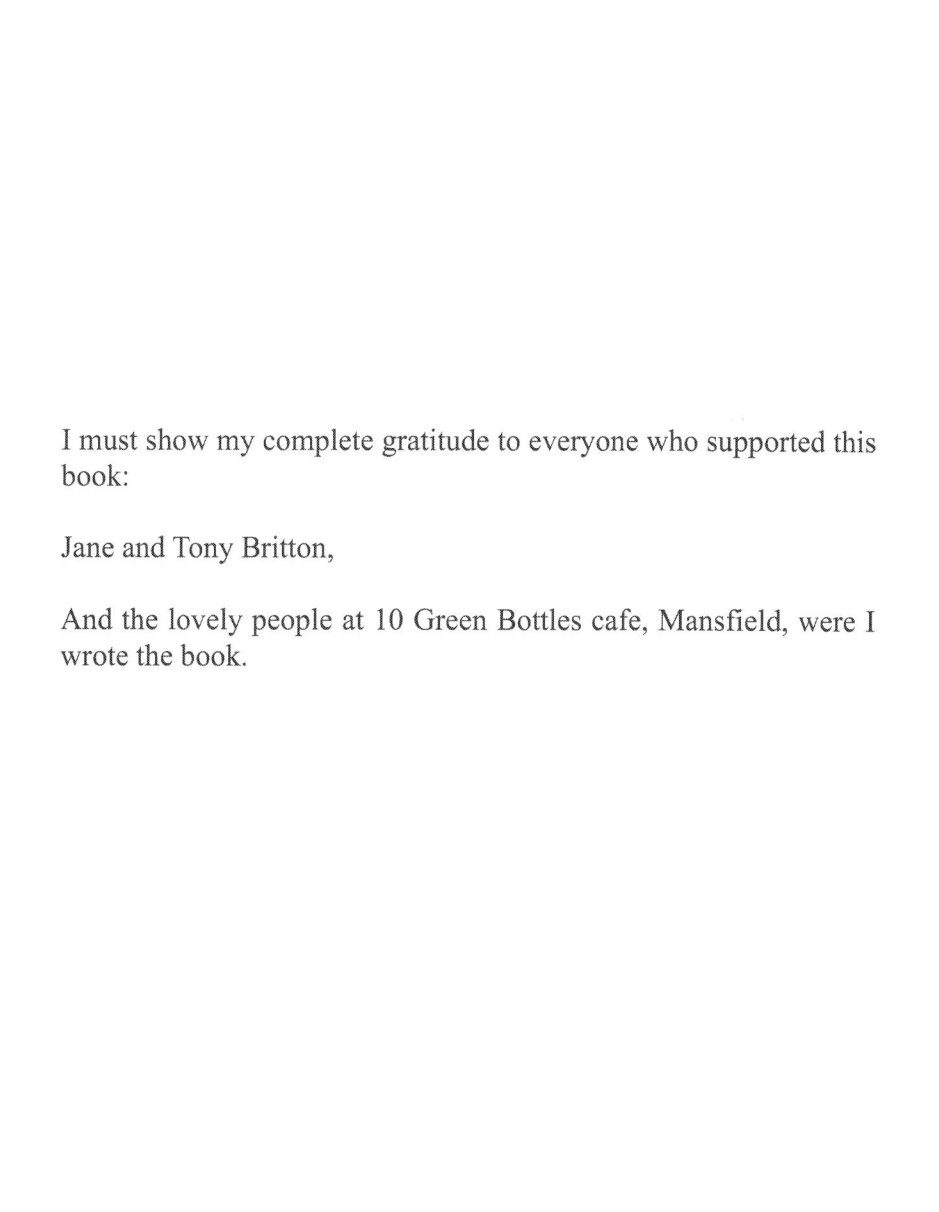

I must show my complete gratitude to everyone who supported this book:

Jane and Tony Britton,

And the lovely people at 10 Green Bottles cafe, Mansfield, were I wrote the book.

INTRODUCTION

For as long as their existences, music and politics have been linked; I have always believed that the political landscape will be reflected in the music of the time.

The past thirty years in British politics are easily divided into two "halves". The first is the Thatcherite age. Thatcher was in power from 1979-1990, but this age of Conservatism also carries into the course of John Majors reign until 1997.

The second of these ages is the "New Labour" age, from 1997-2010. Tony Blair is definitive of this (1997-2007) but it was continued by Gordon Brown (2007-2010.)

I believe Thatcher and Blair to be the most dominant, history defining Prime Ministers of the twentieth century. I also think that they made a lot of terrible mistakes worthy of the kind of fierce dissent it is the duty of rock'n'roll to provide.

This book explores individual British albums released in these history-making years 1979-2009. Most of the albums are classics, either in the traditional sense or the "alternative sense." All of them have had some relevance and some part to play in the cultural landscape of the time; from the gloom of Joy Divisions "Unknown Pleasures" coinciding with the entry of Thatcher into the Prime Minister role to The Cribs "Ignore the Ignorant," taking on the rise of the BNP.

History repeats itself; both Thatcherism and New Labour dealt with recession and war. Also, it is widely felt that New Labour is simply rebranded Conservatism. In these difficult years, British music thrived in many forms, from post-punk to Britpop. These are the albums which define two ages—or one age, inconveniently divided by a name.

PART ONE
THE THATCHER YEARS

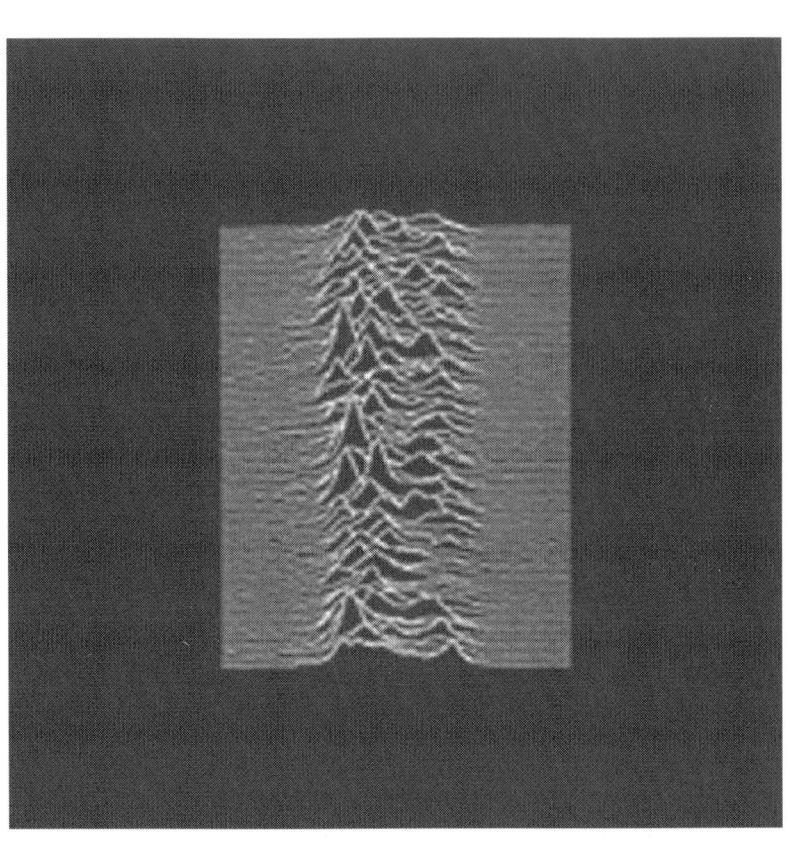

JOY DIVISION—UNKNOWN PLEASURES

On the 4th May, the Conservatives won the general election by a 43 seat majority. There were notable losses from Parliament (Liberal leader Jeremy Thorpe) and additions (MP for Huntingdon in Cambridgeshire, John Major.) But the wider cabinet seemed almost a frippery considering the figure of the new Prime Minister, the first ever woman to take the role, Margaret Thatcher.

Thatcher had been an MP since 1958, when she had been an MP for Finchley. Her first speech was supporting her private members bill. Three years later, she was promoted to front bench as Parliamentary Undersecretary at the Ministry of Pensions and National Insurance in Harold MacMillan's administration. From 1964 she became Conservative spokesperson on housing and land. By 1970 she was shadow transport minister, then education minister, a role in which she was highly controversial; her scrapping of free school milk earned her the nickname "Margaret Thatcher, milk snatcher."

It was another nickname which would come to define her, though. Once she became Leader of the Conservative Party, in 1975, she became a harsh critic of the Soviet Union. As a consequence, the Soviet Defence Ministry newspaper Krasnaya Zvedna (Red Star) gave her the nickname "the Iron Lady," which would become forever associated with her image. So, as this Iron Lady became our Prime Minister, it was a time for music to reflect this ; a new age of musical austerity.

The post-punk genre was already representing this; the debut albums from The Fall and Public Image Limited had already been released. This genre was to reach its peak, though, in June 1979 with the release of Joy Division's classic debut album, "Unknown Pleasures."

The roots of this wonderful album had been planted in July 1976, when Bernard Sumner and Peter Hook, friends since the age of eleven, were amongst the six people who attended the second Sex Pistols show at the Manchester Lesser Free Trade Hall. The next day, Peter Hook bought his first bass guitar. They later recruited vocalist Ian Curtis, without asking him to audition. Bernard Sumner claimed "I knew he was all right to get on with and that was what we based the whole group on."

The bands first gig saw them billed as Stiff Kittens, at the suggestion of Buzzcocks manager Richard Boon, but they instead chose to call themselves Warsaw. However, they would then go on to change this to Joy Division in order to avoid confusion with the band Warsaw Pakt. The name Joy Division evoked the darkest corners of European history, being drawn from the sexual wing on Nazi concentration camps (as outlined in the novel The House of Dolls.)

It would be easy to presume that at this time, Britain would be more concerned with contemporary Europe than with history. June 7th saw the first election for European Parliament—the turnout for Britain was embarrassingly low at 32%. But the Nazi connotation of Joy Division was quickly seized on by an angry press who accused the band of Nazi sympathies. Although they would later admit to being fascinated by fascism, drummer Stephen Morris said that they simply wanted to keep the memories of the sacrifices made by their parents and grandparents during World War Two alive.

The band had other ways of grabbing attention; Ian Curtis shouting at Granada television producer Tony Wilson, "Oi, Wilson, you cunt! You bastard! You put the Pistols and the Buzzcocks on television, what about us?" He responded by giving them their first television performance on "Granada Reports"—and then signing them to his label, Factory.

After this, the band made a rapid ascent, appearing on the NME's cover and recording a John Peel session, but it was not all straightforward; Curtis was finding himself frequently hospitalised with epileptic seizures. This frustrating, malevolent condition was almost reflected in the aggression of the bands acclaimed live shows. The next step was to commit this sound to record.

However, once this album had been completed, under the authority and heavy influence of producer Martin Hannett, the band felt the aggression of their live shows had been lost, initially disliking the more atmospheric feel Hannett had added to the sound. However, they would go on to see that the "Joy Division sound" had truly been created, and "Unknown Pleasures" was adored by the critics. The public also took to the album on an unexpected level. Perhaps the gloom and Gothic edges of songs like "Shadowplay" and the intensley claustrophobic "She's Lost Control," were striking a chord; Thatchers Conservatives were already making some questionable decisions. On the 21st May, the rest of the cabinet backed Thatcher's proposals to sell off parts of nationalised industries. During the year, the government would begin to sell its stake in British Petroleum.

Joy Division's 24 date support tour with the Buzzcocks allowed them to quit their day jobs and further accelerated their support, in particular a devoted following nicknamed "The Cult With No Name," who were stereotyped as "intense young men in grey overcoats."

This sparse, bleak image was perfectly timed. Normal people were struggling in their day to day lives—on 25th May, the price of milk increased by more than 10%. The way the government dealt with this was certainly questionable—on 12th June, their first budget saw chancellor Geoffrey Howe cut the top tax rate from 83% to 60%, but on 23rd July they announced £4billion worth of spending cuts. In other words, the rich benefited while the masses lost out. Such public spending cuts created a world which felt wide and empty.

"Unknown Pleasures," is a classic in every respect, right down to Peter Saville's iconic artwork. But its value at the time was no doubt derived from its relevance in this empty, gloomy Britain.

THE BUZZCOCKS—A DIFFERENT KIND OF TENSION

AND

GANG OF FOUR—ENTERTAINMENT!

By August, 1979, punk was past the peak of its glory years, which are widely considered to be 1976-1977. The scene was viewed as having descended slightly into self-parody, but it was not all over. For example, the beginning of the year had seen Rough Trade put out the debut by Stiff Little Fingers, one of the most angry and important punk bands. But even if punk itself was fading, its musical "next step," post-punk, had just as much to offer. In spite of being seen as more arty and intelligent, it could also sit quite comfortably alongside punk itself. Hence, this particular month was a rather exciting one for British music—there were new albums from the very established and utterly brilliant punk band The Buzzcocks, and from new post-punk band Gang of Four.

Gang of Four were driven, political and, in the moral conscience of the time, potentially offensive. Their song "At Home He's A Tourist," about social alienation, was successful enough to warrant a "Top of The Pops" performance, but the shows producers felt that censorship was necessary—they asked the band to change the line "and the rubbers you hid in your top left pocket," to "rubbish" for fear of causing offence. The band outright refused, causing the appearance to be cancelled. To refuse to compromise like this simply served to show the artistic integrity of the band, but they were far from the first to have this kind of integrity. In fact, nobody had practised this better than the Buzzcocks, whose DIY ethos and spirit of independence made them hugely important.

"A Different Kind of Tension," shows that they had lost none of their intelligence and excitement. With song titles like "Raison d'etre," (the title of a morally existential Jean-Paul Sartre novel, translating into "The Age of Reason,") this was as sharp and interesting as ever. Gang of Four showed similarities—a spiky, well-constructed sound, a Northern background (Gang of Four are from Leeds, the Buzzcocks from Manchester) and an openness to a range of themes. "Entertainment!" covers so much that it is hard to know were to begin. The Great Man Theory? That's covered on "Not Great Men." Guerilla warfare in Central America? Just flick to "5:45." Want their take on the commodification of leisure? That's the theme of "Return the Gift."

Some of the songs on "Entertainment!" are particularly timely—largely, "Naturals Not In It," and "Ether."

The theme of "Ether" is Special Category status prisoners in Northern Ireland. Issues in Northern Ireland had been dominating the news for some years now, and on 27th August two major events occurred. One was the massacre of eighteen soldiers killed in two booby trap explosions near Warrenpoint close to the border with the Irish Republic . . . this came just hours after the death of the Queen's cousin Lord Mountbatten after a bomb exploded on his boat in Northern Ireland. The IRA immediately claimed responsibility, issuing a statement saying, "This operation is one of the discriminate ways we can bring to the attention of the English people the continuing occupation of our country." Mountbatten was far to easy a target—his boat was left unguarded in the public dock in Mullagmare were it was moored; the village was just twelve miles from the Northern Ireland border and near an area known to be used by IRA members as a refuge.

So, "Ether," was a very relevant song. The albums other aforementioned key lyrical moment, "Natural's Not In It," covers the Marxist concept of alienated labour. This theory can largely be found in Marx's manuscripts of 1844, and refers to the separation of things which are in natural harmony—including socially alienating people from aspects of their human nature. (Guttungswen, usually translated as "species-essence" or "species—being.") For Marx, this alienation is a systematic result of capitalism.

As Thatcher's government celebrated capitalism and brought in the age of laissez-faire, this was as relevant as ever. It was also the perfect time for intelligent, angry music—be it from the new in the shape of Gang of Four, or the established in the form of The Buzzcocks.

THE SLITS—CUT

On 14th September, the government announced plans to regenerate the London docklands with housing and commercial developments. It was an age of regeneration which apparently did not have a place for the working-classes. Eleven days later, Margaret Thatcher opened the new Central Milton Keynes Shopping Centre, the largest indoor shopping centre in Britain, after its final phase was completed six years after the development of the huge complex first began. The "spend, spend, spend," aspect of a greedy political culture had truly established itself.

The UK's first female Prime Minster should have been a step towards liberalism, not a more right-wing age. Feminism had always been a left-wing culture; were was it to go now? As Thatcher's attitude was decidedly masculine, perhaps the best way feminism could react was to embrace the seperateness of women to men, something managed by the all-female, teenaged punk band The Slits. Right from their suggestive name onwards, the band—Ari Up, Tessa Pollitt and Viv Albertine—is about what is different about women from men, without buying into any unpleasant ideals or stereotypes.

Albertine, the guitarist, was at the heart of the band, and she was very conscious of developing a more feminine guitar style in contrast to the male punk guitarists, determined to do something a little different. And she certainly succeeded—what really sets "Cut" apart is the reggae feel to the guitar work. (The Specials debut and The Clash's 'London Calling' were not released until later in the year—The Slits were slightly ahead of it all.) "New Town," in particular, has a strong reggae feel, further distinguished by Ari Up's unique lyric about the new towns which appeared across redeveloped Germany following the fall of Nazism and the end of the war.

The Slits most famous song, however, is probably that classic slice of feminism, "Typical Girls." Predating riot grrl by fifteen years, it is a reaction against everything girls are told they should be. "Typical Girls/ worry about spots and fat and natural smells . . . who invented the typical girl? Whose bringing out the new improved model?" However, the most striking line is probably "typical girls/ are cruel and bewitching." This is not feminism peppered with aggression; it is feminism which tells us all to be nicer to each other. As the most significant woman in the country seemed to lack any sense of altruism, perhaps the most rebellious thing a woman could do was simply be nice.

Of course, The Slits were to punk to be fully "nice"—"Love Und Romance," for example, is everything you would expect from a feminist punk band, taking a sledgehammer to traditional notions of romance with shouted lines like "call you every day on the telephone/ and break your neck if you aint home!"

"Cut", on the whole, is an incredibly accomplished album, especially considering the youth of its creators, who were just fifteen. Ari Up was described by the producers as "feral". The album cover art, of the band semi naked in a tribal context, reinforces this, while continuing the theme of the band promoting, rather than denying, their femininity.

As Thatcher forced us to rethink feminism, The Slits did a very fine job. Later in the year, Rough Trade would release the debut album by feminist band The Raincoats. Clearly, this was a school of thought no longer just for academia, but pop culture as well.

THE FALL—DRAGNET

Nowadays, The Fall are so established and seem to have been around for so long that its hard to imagine that they were ever a new band. (They will come to dominate this book somewhat.) By the time Thatcher had come to power, however, they had released only one album, "Live At The Witch Trials."

The follow-up to this album, Dragnet, was released in October 1979; their final album with Step Forward before signing to Rough Trade, the label which they are most closely associated with. Recorded in three days and just eight months after its predecessor, it feels slapdash, but in a wonderful, oh-so-typically Fall sort of way. Their prolific nature certainly added to their unique sound. They were also beginning their now-notorious regular turnover of band members—only Mark. E. Smith and Marc Riley remained of members from the debut album, and Riley had switched his role from bass to guitar. Riley had concerns about single-handedly replacing original guitarist Martin Bramh, so suggested that nineteen year old guitarist Craig Scanlon should also join (Fall fanzine The Psued, issue #2) This album also saw the arrival of bassist Steve Hanley (also nineteen) and drummer Mike Leigh.

Two years after The Clash's "Complete Control," "Dragnet" stretches out the idea of satirising the music industry.

The bands live shows are the spark behind this album—"Printhead" and "Your Heart Out," actively reference these shows. In a further expansion on this, the album itself is almost live, with a muddy but still effective style of production which was intended as a deliberate contrast to the sharp, clean sound of their debut.

We have already talked a little about the genre of "post punk." The Fall are another such band given this label. Post punk as a concept is difficult to pin down—is it just a matter of era, or is it an actual sound? Many of the post punk bands have only minor points in common; it tends to be notified by its originality. It can be political, but sees things as less black and white than other, polarising movements which potentially lead to extremism. Extremism, as it happens, was something which still ran strong—on 30th October, National Front leader Martin Webster was found guilty of inciting racial hatred.

The National Front had been a disturbingly prominent voice in the political landscape for a few years now, as people turned to extremism to deal with dissatisfaction with the mainstream. With people struggling to know were to turn in an age which lacked clarity, the muddy sounds on "Dragnet" were perfect for the age. The beautifully minimal, monochrome cover art also seemed darkly fitting—a butterfly trapped in a spiders web, about to be caught. No way out—with Thatcher just five months into her term, and political terms lasting four years, that was no doubt how many members of the British public felt at the time. As if Martin Websters actions were not discomfiting enough, the UK embraced further deplorable actions when the unethical Chairman Hua Guofeng became the first Chinese leader to visit Britain.

The Fall had only just begun, but already seemed perfectly relevant—which, as we shall go on to see, they would continue to be right up until the present day.

"2-TONE: MORE THAN A RECORD LABEL, A WHOLE NEW CULTURE." THE SPECIALS—THE SPECIALS AND MADNESS—ONE STEP BEYOND

November, 1979 saw bank rates reach an all time low of 17%. On the first of this month, the government announced £3.5billion of public spending cuts and an increase in prescription charges. The nation felt unbelievably deprived; the best move that popular culture could make was produce a movement which reflected the grim realism of this was also being a respite. This was difficult; was it even possible? Happily, yes, it was, something reflected in the emergence of "2-tone,"—a record label but also a whole culture of its own.

The label was started as a branch of Rough Trade by Jerry Dammers, of the label's most important act, the brilliant The Specials. The fact that this was more than a label was instantly apparent as its artwork and imagery—created by Dammers, with the assistance of Horace Panter—was to become of central importance. The "logo" was a fictional man named Walt Jabsco, based on a photograph of former Wailers member Peter Tosh, dressed in a black suit and tie, white shirt, pork-pie hat, white socks and black loafers.

This appropriation of Tosh's image was not the only inspiration Dammers and his bandmates drew from Bob Marley and The Wailers. They also took their phrase "the concrete jungle" and recycled it to reinforce how relevant it was in the increasingly difficult, modern, urban world.

The Specials eponymous debut is just that—special. In a feature on the band, broadcaster Mark Lamarr says "how lucky we were to have the perfect template of what a band should bring. Every generation should have one."

The album draws on the past—cover versions of "Monkey Man," Dandy Livingstones "A Message To You Rudy," and a rewrite of Lloydie and the Lowbites "Birth Control!", "Too Much Too Young," which is vastly superior and far wittier than the original song which inspired it. But, as Lamarr points out, it all sounded so new.

After all, the sense at the time was that we needed something new. The world looked tired and unsatisfactory. Thatcher had been in power for just six months, but was already losing popularity—a 21st November MORI poll put the Conservatives five points behind Labour with a 45% share of the vote. Rarely had public opinion of anybody dropped quite so rapidly—no wonder popular culture leant towards anti-Thatcherism.

Of course, it takes more than one band to make a cultural movement, and 2-Tone had plenty more to offer, signing The Selector, Madness, and The Beat. The acts had to sign a contract which gave them the freedom to leave after just one single; yes, this was unusual in the music industry, but I think we have established that 2-Tone was not an ordinary record label. Most of the acts took advantage if this contract—The Beat formed their own label, Go Feet Records, whilst Madness would go on to sign to Stiff, the label more closely associated with them.

The links to Stiff are there from the start; one of its most important acts, Elvis Costello, produced the two key 2-Tone albums of the time, the Specials debut and Madness' One Step Beyond, another great album (the track "The Prince," is one of the 2-Tone genre's most defining moments.)

The multicultural feel of 2-Tone was also important as it contributed to its wider anti-racism message—in his list of things which made The Specials great, Mark Lamarr includes, ". . . opening barely formed minds to racial tolerance, their constant defiance of the ever present National Front,"—and this was to become an integral part of 2-Tone, which is what makes it so strangely ironic that's acts such as Madness would develop a fanbase within the National Front faction.

Just as this key moment in musical history was occurring, so were key moments in political history. On the 13th November, miners rejected a 20% pay increase and threatened to go on strike until they got their desired pay rise. This was simply a threat, and on the straightforward matter of pay—the struggle which would go on to occur between Thatcher and the miners was more expansive, more complex, and more history-defining. Both culturally and politically, something truly important had begun.

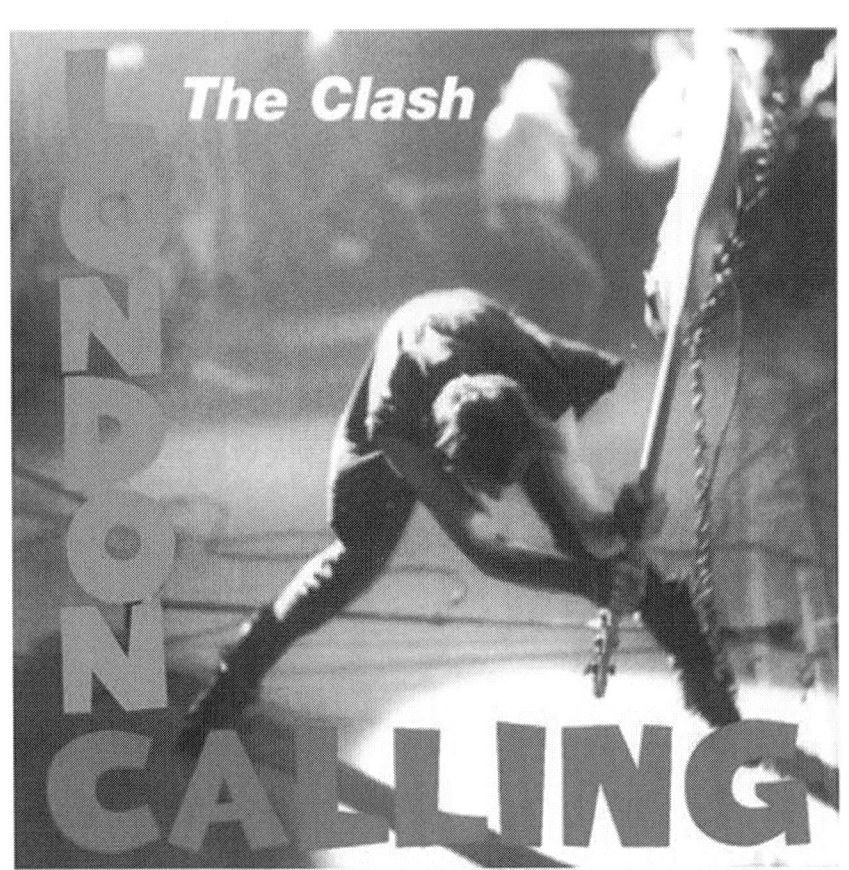

THE CLASH—LONDON CALLING

1979 had not, it is fair to say, been a politically promising year. As it drew to a close, economic strife and Thatcher's rock solid support for the free market left the public feeling disillusioned. Political music, in its most dissenting, anti-capitalist, anti-establishment form, had a huge role to play. The Clash, one of punks most articulate acts, were needed more than ever—lucky, then, that they released their landmark album, the brilliant classic "London Calling," at this time.

Whilst people's "favourite Clash album," varies, it is "London Calling," which tends to earn the high place in those greatest-albums lists, and not without good reason. A mix of sounds, this album takes the Clash's original punk sound as a template and elaborates on it with layers of ska and reggae, making it sound fresh, modern and relevant to the 1979 listener.

Its opening title track has been overplayed and I do not rank it as one of the bands finest moments, but it serves its purpose as an opener very well, its clear cut guitar line giving way to the line, "London calling to the far away towns/ now war is declared/ and battle come down," like a call to arms.

As ever, the lyrical content on this album is broad, interesting and worthwhile in the Thatcherite age—"Lost In The Supermarket," is Joe Strummer's imagining of Mick Jones' childhood growing up in a basement, but could also be read as a comment on consumerism, "The Guns of Brixton," (the first track to be either written or sung by Paul Simonon) discusses an individuals paranoid take on life, whilst "Spanish Bombs," is a thought-provoking piece on The Spanish Civil War. With "Clampdown," meanwhile, they produced one of their greatest moments, particularly with its lyricism on people who forsake the idea of youthful idealism, urging young people to fight the status quo. The message of this is that by doing so, we can fully change the world: "Kick over the wall, cause governments to fall, how can you refuse it?/ Let fury have the hour, anger can be power, do you know that you can use it?)

As ideals in Britain were changing (the move to independence for Rhoedsia was another step in us beginning to see the concept of "empire" for what it really was), the liberal voice of The Clash was something to emphathise with; far more so than the authority of the government, who were continuing to take some divisive steps. On 20th December, they published the Housing Bill, which would give council house tenants the right to buy their own homes from the following year. When history wishes to treat Thatcher with affection, it always points towards this bill. But was it really such a good thing? Council housing was supposed to be for the poorest sections of society; this wave of people buying their own council house changed the social landscape forever, the legacy is still there in many areas.

The key aspect of "London Calling," is that the experimentation keeps it exciting. For "The Card Cheat" they recorded everything twice, to "create a sound as big as possible." "Wrong Em Boyo," is contemporary ska, whereas "Guns of Brixton," and the track that gives this book its title, "Revolution Rock," are out and out reggae. It may not have been a particularly great age in terms of the wider world, but occasional news stories kept it exciting—on 16th November, Anthony Blunt was named as the fourth member of the Cambridge Spy Ring. The Cambridge Spy Ring had been one of the most exciting stories in the news in recent years—the "Cambridge Five," being a ring of spies recruited in part by Russian talent spotter Arnold Deutsch in the United Kingdom, who passed information to the Soviet Union during World War II and into at least the 1950's.

On the whole, anger was something which prevailed in the UK, not excitement. The Thatcherite era made a king out of marketing and advertising (something documented on "London Callings" "Koka

Kola") we seemed to be being told—and sold—what to think. The Clash were everything this was not.

The twelfth track on "London Calling," "Death or Glory," is Joe Strummer looking back on his life to acknowledge the complications and responsibilities of adulthood. The Clash's earlier albums meant that he had already created a lot to be proud of in his life. But "London Calling," remains the peak of the bands career. Timely, innovative and gloriously dissenting, it is everything that any classic album ever should be.

THE DURUTTI COLUMN—

THE RETURN OF THE DURUTTI COLUMN   Jan 1980

Even though Thatcher came to power in 1979, she is largely linked solely to the eighties. The entrance into this new decade, uncomfortably, meant that the unofficial age of Thatcherism had truly begun.

Typical Thatcherism events occurred as soon as the decade began. Her hostility to trade unions and the working classes meant that her time in power often saw her battling against those who had taken strike action. On 2nd January, workers at British Steel went on a nationwide strike over pay called by the Iron and Steel Trades Confederation, which had some 90,000 members among British Steel's 150,000 workforce, in a bid to get a 20% pay rise. This was the first steelworkers strike since 1926 (in what had been a momentous year of national strikes.)

Strikes have had an important part to play throughout history—sometimes inspiring wider movements which have left a legacy of cultural relevance. A particularly good example of this are the Parisian wildcat strikes on 1965, which inspired the school of left-wing political thought known as Situationism. Thus, as the steelworks strike raged under a disagreeable, right-wing government, it was the perfect time for an album infused with Situationism to appear and inspire.

The Manchester band The Durutti Column drew both their name and this album title from a Situationist International poster series entitled "The Return of The Durutti Column." Signed to the Factory label, and produced by Martin Hannett, on paper the most obvious act to make comparisons to are Joy Division—and, in frontman Vini

Reilly, we had another complicated, troubled genius. But the two bands, although both brilliant, are really quite different.

Whereas Joy Division had originally been unsure about Hannett's production, The Durutti Column revelled in it. Reilly says of him, "he more or less got sounds for me that no-one else could understand that I wanted. And he understood that I wanted to play the electric guitar but I didn't want this horrible, distorted usual electric guitar sound and he managed that." Reilly was right to want such clarity in his guitar sounds, as he is frequently named as the most underrated guitarist of all time. His style is very much in the classical, flamenco style, precise and intricate. When combined with the strength of his songwriting, this made for an incredible debut album. Reilly explains this sound by saying "I had a lot of classical training when I was young, guitar and formal training—the scales I write with and the techniques I use are classical techniques and scales—a lot of minor melodic and minor harmonic scales, which generally aren't used in pop music. Usually its pentatonic."

This, then, was post punk, but not as we knew it. It is a wonderful album, but will perhaps always be overshadowed by its artwork. As acolytes of Situationism, Factory were inspired by Guy Debord's "Memoreis," a book with a sandpaper sleeve (to "destroy the other books on the shelf,") and boss Tony Wilson issued "The Return Of The Durutti Column," with a sandpaper sleeve also. Reilly says he was "mortified." However, he was equally thrilled to have reached the stage of creating an album, after two years under The Durutti Column name (he had previously come to attention with punk band The Nosebleeds.) He says, "I didn't know this was going to be an album . . . Martin had to physically get me out of bed to get me to the studio—that's how little I believed it would happen. I was still doing late night petrol station shifts. I was even more amazed when Tony presented me with a white label. I was completely baffled. 'What, this is really going to be an album? You must be insane! No-one's going to buy this!"

The strike action in Britain showed that such a defeatist attitude was not present in all fields—but it may as well have been as on 14th

February, Thatcher announced that state benefit to strikers would be halved, and three days later it was announced 11,000 jobs would be axed from British Steel.

It would have been easy to disregard strikes at this point. Luckily, the Situationist stylings of The Durutti Column were there to remind us what they had achieved through history.

STIFF LITTLE FINGERS—NOBODYS HEROES   March 1980

The previous year had seen the release of a hugely important record—Stiff Little Fingers "Inflammable Material," the first release on the Rough Trade label (Rough Trade had previously only acted as a record store) which charted at no. 14—the highest charting release ever for an independent label. Not only did this make history, but its material was perfect for the age, songs like "Alternative Ulster," and "Suspect Device," distilling the sound of the Troubles in Northern Ireland.

Following up such a landmark record could not have been easy. Such controversial, politicised acts are also faced with the problem of how the public will react to them—although "Inflammable Material," had shown that they could react rather well.

The truth is, people were ready for the media and popular culture to get political. The 25th February saw the first episode of the satirical sitcom "Yes, Minister," broadcast by the BBC.

Dissent could also be found in the most unlikely of places—on 25th March, the British Olympic Association voted to defy the government and send athletes to the Olympic Games to he held in Moscow, USSR, in the summer.

On the whole, then, a follow-up to "Inflammable Material," had come at the right time, and whilst not quite as aggressive as its controversial predecessor, it still had plenty of worthwhile comments to make.

The song from this album which became the best-known is the angry commentary of "Tin Soldiers," which looks at the naivety of young men who join the army before realising what they have got themselves into—a cycle of exploitation and horror. "He joined up to get a job and show he wasn't scared/ swapped mascara for army cap/ he thought he's be prepared," sings Jake Burns in an unusually subdued fashion before the song kicks in with typical vengeance and vehemence. "He joined up for just three years it seemed a small amount/ but they didn't tell him that the first two didn't count/ at the age of seventeen he did as he was told . . ." it continues. By the time the protagonist is twenty-one, he is "in Catch 22," and "still marches to their tune." As the song closes with the lines "Tin soldiers/ they take away your name/ Tin soldiers/ they treat you all the same," we find ourselves truly considering how little military practice has changed over the years.

Life for people in any profession in Britain was looking bleak. Economic strife meant that the 26th March budget raised tax allowances and duties on petrol, alcohol, and tobacco. This seemed like a rather small event, in spite of how many it affected, when the next day a terrible disaster hit the news—the Alexander Keilland North Sea accommodation platform for oil workers collapsed, killing 123, when a massive wave hit one of its legs causing it to break and fall into the sea. There seemed to be a lot of these kinds of industrial disasters of late—as if this kind of work was not already blighted by enough misery.

In fact, as many people continued in difficult professions in a society with no desire to reward them, with seemingly no way out, you did not have to be a soldier to empathise with "Tin Soldiers." The theme of being drawn into a profession which you come to hate, feeling trapped by it, meant that Stiff Little Fingers had created something people all over the country could truly identify with.

THE CURE—SEVENTEEN SECONDS

On the 1st April, 1980, the steelworkers strike was called off. It was by now fully apparent that the valiant strikers would not get what they wanted. It may have been April Fools Day, but nobody was laughing on this date. Nearly a year into her time in power, one of the key things which defined Margaret Thatcher—her hostility to trade unions—had been well and truly established. The failure of the steelworkers strike stood almost as a warning to anybody that even attempted to fight for their worker's rights. The 11,000 steelworkers who lost their jobs were not the only ones hit by uemployment—unemployment as a whole in Britain stood at 1, 500,000, the highest it had been in two years. In short, it was all doom and gloom. The timing, then, of The Cure album "Seventeen Seconds," was perfectly timed in providing an appropriate soundtrack. Over the years, The Cure—still new at this stage[1]—would almost become the laureates of immense misery, and whilst "Seventeen Seconds," was is not quite as bleak as some of their later albums, such as "Pornography," and "Disintegration," it still shows their potential for capturing a sense of isolation, the key feeling in the anti-society, Thatcherite nation.

The most famous song on "Seventeen Seconds," and still one of The Cure's most popular songs, is "A Forest," almost an exercise in How To Write A Goth Song. Its minimal beat and panicked lyric of "lost in a forest/ all alone," is the distillation of the loss, confusion and isolation of the public into (really quite brilliant) sound.

---

[1] They had already released the albums "Three Imaginary Boys" and a compilations, "Boys Don't Cry." Boys Don't Cry had been released in Feb 1980 but as it is largely material from "Three Imaginary Boys" it is not included in this book due to the time frame of the material.

This was what "news" was based around—the every day misery of the masses. However, this changed on 30th April with the Iranian Embassy Siege. A six—man terrorist team calling itself the "Democratic Revolutionary Movement for the Liberation of Arabistan (DRMLA)" captured the Embassy of Iran in Prince's Gate, Knightsbridge, taking 26 hostages. Such news events as this, which looked at Britains part in the wider world, forced us to contemplate the global political stage, but this did not change the bleak situation of our own socio-political landscape. But there would be no such dramatic attempts at "liberation" action from us—we had quickly learnt from the steelworkers strike that there was probably little point. As the working class stumbled through life with difficulty, the emergence of The Cure meant that we had one of the bands who were perfect for the dark side of the 80's.

THE TEARDROP EXPLODES—KILLIMANJARO May 1980

If there was one thing that Thatcherism prized above anything else, it was privatisation, something which constantly increased throughout Thatcher's time in power. On the 1st May, British Aerospace was privatised, just one in a long line. It was not easy to notice this as other issues dominated the news, such as the ongoing Iranian Embassy Siege, which did not end until the 5th May when the SAS stormed the Iranian Embassy Building, killing five out of the six terrorists and freeing all the hostages.

These kinds of momentous events warranted new musical movements to soundtrack them appropriately, but there did not seem to be anything since the unifying fires of punk had died down. What seemed more frequently occurring now was movements or scenes in individual cities or regions.

One such city was Liverpool, which as not been so musically thriving since the days of The Beatles and the Cavern Club. The scene was so rife with characters, that a band called "The Crucial Three" comprising all is most important figures, never even released a record, but still became shrouded in legend. Along with Pete Wylie and Ian McCulloch, one of these characters was Julian Cope, who would go on to form The Teardrop Explodes. Signed to the Zoo label (as were Echo and the Bunnymen) they quickly became an important part of this exciting new scene. As the UK economy slid into recession and unemployment reached a postwar height of 1, 600, 00, the psychedelic stylings of the band, along with Cope's star quality (a mixture of arrogance, faint craziness and teen idol good looks) were a perfect blast of escapism. Their first single to be released on Zoo, February 1979's "Sleeping Gas," showed a band of enormous potential.

Maybe having a scene as self-contained as the Liverpool scene was not so bad. Far-reaching things of late only seemed to be problematic, particularly in the international affairs which concerned Britain. On 17th June, Secretary of State for Defence Francis Pym revealed to the House of Commons that US nuclear cruise missiles would be located at RAF Greenham Common in Berkshire and the disused RAF Molesworth base in Cambridgeshire. Two days after this, in something of a twisted sequel to the Iranian Embassy Siege, gunmen attacked the British Embassy in Iraq; three unknown attackers were shot dead by Iraqi security forces.

In spite of the apparent smallness of the Liverpool scene, The Teardrop Explodes were not as self-contained as a band usually is, undergoing several line-up changes during the recording and touring of their brilliant debut album "Killimanjaro," an album which yielded such classic hits as "Reward" and "Treason," note-perfect pieces of songwriting which distil a new kind of anger born out of arrogance, rather than dissatisfaction.

Public anger, in the meantime, had hit a high—the previous year, anti-National Front campaigner Blair Peach had been killed by police at a demonstration. On 27th May, 1980, an inquest into her death ruled a verdict of misadventure, sparking a public outcry.

"I can see a course of action leading to a chain," sings Cope on "Treason." As events unfolded and unsavoury politics repeated itself, this was a lyric fitting to all at the time.

"LOOKING THROUGH THE FOG OF GLOOM"
ECHO AND THE BUNNYMEN—CROCODILES
AND
JOY DIVISION—CLOSER

What a terribly bleak month July, 1980 was. The working classes needed to put up a fight for what they deserved (on the 8th July, miners threatening to strike demanded a 37% pay increase, ignoring pleas from Margaret Thatcher to hold down wage claims) and unemployment had hit a 44 year high of nearly 1, 900,00. (the following month, it would increase to 2, 000,000, the highest it had been since 1935, with economists warning that it could be up to 2, 500, 000 by the end of the year.)

The albums released in July 1980 certainly reflected this mood—key releases included Echo and the Bunnymen's debut "Crocodiles," and Joy Divisions, "Closer", both infused with gloom and darkness.

"Closer", in particular, had a terrible shadow hanging over it. Two months previously, frontman Ian Curtis had hung himself; blighted by depression as a consequence of both his severe epilepsy and the shockingly high doses of barbiturates he was prescribed to help combat the symptoms. "I just feel like I'm being sucked into a big whirlpool and there's nothing I can do," he had told bandmate Bernard Sumner. And "Closer" is certainly the sound of being sucked into a big whirlpool, the punk stylings of "Unknown Pleasures" swapped for haunting, imposing atmospherics which demanded something of the listener. Produced again by Martin Hannett, the feel of the music is almost funereal. The scene is set by opener "The Atrocity Exhibition," inspired by a JB Ballard book that Curtis loved, but the intensity deepens throughout, hitting its peak on the two downtempo closing tracks, "The Element," and "Decades."

As this was obviously Joy Divisions final album, perhaps it was time to pass the baton of gothic gloom. Even though Ian Curtis was obviously irreplaceable, Echo and the Bunnymen's "Crocodiles," showed that they certainly had potential to be the new kings of dark and moody. The NME described the album as being "scattered with themes of sorrow, horror and despair, themes that are reinforced by stormy animal/ sexual imagery." American critics expressed a similar viewpoint—Creem described "Crocodiles" as "moody, mysterious fascinating," whilst Rolling Stone described how "McCulloch trips out on his worst fears; isolation, death and emotional bankruptcy."

In spite of this, McCulloch himself was ambitious and arrogant, which could be reflected in the music—in his book "Rip It Up and Start Again," Simon Reynolds described McCulloch's vocals as having "precocious authority." He also points out the line "stars are stars and they shine so hard," from the track "Stars are Stars," which shows how the band felt no embarrassment in their desire to be famous.

The mood of heavy gloom present on both "Closer" and "Crocodiles," is also reflected in both of their album sleeves. The photo used as the sleeve for "Crocodiles," was taken of the band by photographer Brian Griffin in woodlands in Hertfordshire late at night. Initially, the band had wanted to use burning stakes, but given the possible KKK connotations they decided to opt for moody lighting instead, which works just as well—Creem said "the cover art suggests four boys dazed and confused in a drugged dream, a surreal where-are-we landscape. The Bunnymen's images are of loneliness, disconnection, a world gone awry."

This is only faintly disturbing when compared with the hauntingly prophetic sleeve of "Closer"; designed by Peter Saville for the album months before Curtis' suicide, it depicts a Genoa tomb.

So, in every respect—sound, lyrics, even cover art—music in July 1980 was brilliant but bleak, tapping into the mood of a dissatisfied nation. On 11th August, Margaret Thatcher visited the Harold Hill area of North London to hand over the keys to the 12, 000th council tenants to buy their home under the right to buy scheme—and was jeered by neighbours of the family as she did so. After all, she was bringing more misery on the whole than not; it was the sounds of gloom which truly captured public feeling.

SKA CONTINUES!

THE SPECIALS—MORE SPECIALS

AND

MADNESS—ABSOLUTELY

The releases of debut albums from Madness and The Specials the previous year (and accompanying events such as the momentous 2-Tone gigs) had shown that the ska revival was a force of musical brilliance. But could it maintain its potency? Yes, is the autumn of 1980 was anything to go by, as Madness and The Specials issued their follow-up albums.

What had made 2-Tone so great in the first place was the way it encouraged people to actively get involved and make a stand (particularly on the issue of racism) and people were most certainly starting to do this—the 21st September saw the first CND rally at RAF Greenham Common. It seems slightly ironic, then, that one of the key tracks on "More Specials" was entitled "Do Nothing." *"I'm just living in a life without meaning,"* sings Terry Hall in droll fashion on the chorus. As we wandered through the landscape of Thatcherism, Hall certainly had the knack for capturing this (the following year the band released the single "Ghost Town", which is viewed by many as the most definitive song of the age in capturing Thatcherism's recession-hit landscapes)

Madness, meanwhile, adopted a more fun take for "Absolutely." Its biggest hit, "Baggy Trousers," is an entertaining look back on school days. But his makes them no less relevant—they became the biggest selling band of the ska revival. Important in 1979—now we could see that the ska revival was still important in 1980.

THE FALL—GROTESQUE (AFTER THE GRAMME)

3rd October, 1980, saw the Housing Act come into effect. This allowed council house tenants of three years standing in England and Wales the right to buy their home from local authority at a discount. Just like when the Right to Buy scheme had first been announced, all to often Thatcer's supporters used this in her defence—so it is important to see the wider picture of what her government was doing, particularly were the economy was concerned. The 23rd November, 1980 saw the economy in recession and the government's monetarist policy to tackle inflation being blamed for the downturn—but they continued in much the same way, announcing further taxation rises and spending cuts. The previous month, even Thatcher's own MP's had warned her that her economic policy was responsible for the current recession and rising unemployment, but she stood firm by her policies—in fact, this warning had simply resulted in her famous "the lady's not for turning" speech.

In this environment, the anger and conscious counter-culture feel of postpunk thrived, with excellent debut albums from Killing Joke and The Residents making their mark on the world. In spite of these strong debuts, post punks finest album in these months came from the already-established The Fall, who were now on their third album, the excellent "Grotesque (After The Gramme)." Their were some departures from their previous two albums, "Live At The Witch Trials," and "Dragnet"—Marc Riley played organ on several tracks, and their was a new addition to the line-up in the form of fifteen year old Paul Hanley. After all, as post punk expanded with a wealth of new bands, The Fall had to show that they were still different.

There were changes in the political world as well as in the musical world. On the 15th October, seventeen months after being ousted as Prime Minister by the Conservative victory, James Callaghan resigned as Labour Party leader after four and a half years. On the 10th November, Michael Foot was elected as his replacement.

Whilst this was obviously a key political change, it did not seem like any great leap forward as Conservative power held firm. More momentous signs of progress were to be found in music, particularly with The Fall—"Grotesque" is considered far more outward looking than its predecessor, with Mark. E. Smith's new found lyrical maturity being particularly striking. The lyrics are sometimes idiosyncratic to the point of being widely misunderstood—"The NWRA," is often wrongly thought to stand for "The North West Republican Army"—in fact, it stands for "the north will rise again." Other such titles include "WMC-Blob 59," (WMC being an abbreviation for working mens club) and "C 'N' C-S Mithering," a reference to cash and carries, specifically two warehouses near Manchester. This song as a whole is a brilliant state-of-the nation address ("In Lanchashire they're A/ In King Nat Ltd Empire/ Kwik Save is there/ The scene started here/ Then was America/ Then was America/ We went there/ Big A&M Herb was there/ His offices had fresh air/ but his rota was mediocre") which takes a darker turn ("five hundred girl deaths/ A Mexico revenge, its stolen land/ they really get off on 'don't hurt me, please/ rapists fill the tv's") before looking inwardly to the industry ("A circle of low IQ's/ there are three rules of audience/ my journalist acquaintances, go soft, go places, on record company expenses/ I lose humour, manners become bog writers, don't know it/ the smart hedonists, same as last verse, allusions with/ H in electronics, on false stage histronics/ Corpse mauling dicks pose through a good film.")

The nation is also addressed on "The English Scheme": ("O'er grassy dale, and lowland scene come see, come hear, the English Scheme/ the lower-class want brass, bad chests, scrounge fags/ the clever ones tend to emigrate/ like your psychotic big brother, who left home/ for jobs in Munich, Holland, Rome, he's thick but struck it rich.") Such a cynical viewpoint of Britain—which is accelerated by the end with the lyrics "Down pokey quaint streets in Cambridge/ cycles over distant spastic heritage . . . if we was smart we'd emigrate"—was fitting for such a currently bleak nation. On the 28th

October, Margaret Thatcher announced that the government would not give in to seven jailed IRA terrorists who were on hunger strike in the Maze prison in the hope of winning prisoner of war status. But then again, she would never give in to anything, no matter how wrong or at fault she was.

The musical world was also bleak—on 8th December, John Lennon was shot dead in New York, a terrible loss to the music world. In this age, the cynicism of The Fall, sometimes twinned with paranoia (conspiracy theories and on "New Face in Hell", gothic horror on "Impression of J. Temperance" and nightmarish artwork by Mark. E. Smiths sister Suzanne) was perfectly timed.

"THE GESTATION OF GOTH—PART ONE"

THE CURE—FAITH

AND

ECHO & THE BUNNYMEN—HEAVEN UP HERE

The beginning of 1981 saw a wave of changes, but the most significant of these occurring on the 25th January with The Limehouse Declaration, in which four Labour members of Parliamentt—Shirley Williams, Roy Jenkins, William Rodgers and David Owen—announced plans to form a separate political party, The Social Democratic Party. The following day, a further nine Labour MP's declared their support for them. Owen and Rodgers were sitting MP's, Jenkins had left Parliament in 1977 to serve as President of the European Commission, whilst Williams had lost her seat in the 1979 General Election. The four of them's decision to leave the Labour Party was based on policy changes enacted at the January 1981 Wembley Conference which committed the party to unilateral nuclear disarmament and withdrawal from the European Common Market. It is difficult to agree with their theory that the Labour Party had become almost Trotskyist, but then again anybody seemed far-left compared with the current government. On the 18th February, they sounded a further death knell or the working classes when they announced plans to close down a further 23 mines. On the 17th March, the governments budget was met with uproar due to further public spending cuts.

Whilst the term "goth" had yet to be applied to the style of music which now has the label, it was a perfect time for it to thrive—hence the spring releases of two bleakly Gothic albums, The Cure's typically depressing "Faith" and Echo and The Bunnymen's "Heaven Up Here." The NME described "Heaven Up Here" as darker and more passionate than its predecessor, "Crocodiles," whilst Record Mirror said that it was "an anatomy of melancholy, resplendent with the glamour of doom."

Considering the climate, doom seemed a fitting mood. Three issues dominated the news. The first was recession and general financial issues—on 9th March, thousands of civil servants held a one-day strike over pay, and on 2nd April, the iconic Birmingham based bus operator Midland Red closed down its headquarters with the loss of some 170 jobs. The second was the IRA—on 16th January, Northern Ireland civil rights campaigner and former Westminster MP Bernadette McAliskey was shot and injured by suspected Loyalist paramilitaries at her home in County Tyrone, Northern Ireland, and on the 10th April hunger striker Bobby Sands was elected MP for South Tyrone. Abhorrently, the third dominant issue was racism. On 28th March, Enoch Powell warned of "racial civil war," in Britain. On the 3rd April, clashes between Asians and the National Front resulted in 80 injuries. As further racial unrest sparked riots in Brixton, the despicable Powell warned that Britain "had seen nothing yet," with regards to racial unrest.

With such a negative collection of issues clouding the news, the mood of the gothic was once again the ideal music for the time.

"THE GESTATION OF GOTH"—PART TWO"

SIOUXSIE AND THE BANSHEES—JUJU

AND

BAUHAUS—AT THE CONTROLS

The end of April had seen unemployment pass the 2, 500, 000 mark for the first time in nearly 50 years. Misery was something felt by the masses; the early signs of the gloomy gothic movement were given the perfect background to fully extend—and two consummate goth albums, the debut by Bauhaus and the fourth album by Siouxsie and The Banshee's, were not only timely but brilliant.

The mood of such music was deep and penetrating; often marked out by a theme of death. Bauhaus best-known song even went so far as to combine death with classic horror—it has the title "Bela Lugosi's Dead."

For it is death which uncomfortably defines the spring/summer period of 1981. On 5th May, after his 66 day hunger strike, Bobby Sands died in The Maze prison. One by one, his fellow hunger strikers died—Francis Hughes on the 12th May, and both Raymond McCreesh and Patrick O'Hara on the 21sy May. Bauhaus were perfect for capturing the dark, deathly mood, but a more established band like Siouxsie and The Banshees could do an equally fine job—their fourth album "Juju", ranks as one of their finest moments. This is largely in part to the new addition of John McGeoch on guitar—an excellent guitarist whose style has been highly praised by former Smiths Morrissey and Johnny Marr. Marr described McGeochs work on the album opener, "Spellbound" as "really clever" whereas in 1997 Morrissey named the song as a favourite of his, saying, "they were one of the great groups of the late 70's, early 80's . . . Siouxsie and The Banshee's were excellent."

Gothic sounds were maintaining the critical acclaim that they had begun to win earlier in the year because so little seemed to be changing as the year progressed. The problem of racism continued to rage—on 2nd July, four members of an Asian Muslim family (three of them children) were killed by arson at their home in Walthamstow in a racially motivated attack. Racial tensions also manifested themselves in a series of riots. The 3rd July saw hundreds of Asians and skinheads rioting in Southall—two days later, the Toxteth riots broke out in Liverpool, were the first use of CS gas was made by police. The same day saw less serious riots occur in Wolverhampton, High Wycombe, Handsworth and parts of Lecister, Coventry and Derby. The next few weeks would see riots break out all over the country. On the 15th July, police in Brixton raided properties owned by blacks in search of petrol bombs which were never found, causing further clashes. Whilst goth music is seemingly an all-white genre, it still captures something of the injustices of racism by celebrating and giving a voice to the maligned outsider. By rising up and giving themselves a voice, that is just what victims of racism were doing.

Of course, it was not just victims of racism that were dissiatisfied with the government. Anger over the unemployment issue drove 100,000 to march in the TUC's March For Jobs in Trafalge Square on 30th May. Alternatives to the government were desperately needed. On the 16th June, the Liberal Party and the SDP formed an alliance, the SDP-Liberal alliance, but as they were to the right of Labour they were not an ideal alternative to the Conservatives.

Seemingly with nowhere to turn, the people of Britain seemed to be in a dark place. Gothic had never sounded so right.

BOW WOW WOW—SEE GO JUNGLE! GO JUNGLE! GO JOIN YOUR GANG YEAH! CITY ALL OVER SO APE CRAZY!

1981 was just news on a loop, the same things happening over and over, with just a change in names or location each time. The lives of the Irish hunger strikers continued to be lost—the death of Micheal Devine on 20th August took their total death toll to ten. As with everything, Thatcher was quick to shirk any responsibility transferred to her government, giving a speech which denied responsibility, instead blaming IRA leaders for the deaths.

The issue of racism had also dominated the news. Music had tried to provide a voice of protest, but it was often overlooked—the same day as an anti-racism concert by The Specials, more than 80 arrests were made during clashes between white power skinheads and black people in Coventry, where the National Front were planning a march. What if, then, music took a stance that was implicitly political in its own way, but a little more fun? Step forward Malcolm McC;aren's Situationist project Bow Wow Wow, who were here to provide pure pop escapism.

McClaren "stole" Adam Ant's backing band—Matthew Ashman, Leigh Gorman and Dave Barbarossa—to form a new group, then recruiting fourteen year old Annabella Lwin after hearing her singing in the local dry-cleaning shop were she had a Saturday job. The band were perfect to represent what McClaren wanted—a musical tangent of a youth-sex based wider project, and ideal promoters of Vivienne Westwood's latest line of pirate inspired fashion. For this project, the answer to the current recession was to "wear gold, and dress like a pirate"—feeling rich was the best rebellion the poverty hit masses could put up against the government. A government we would have to put up with for a long time, even if at times we were led to believe otherwise. On 18th September, David Steel told delegates at the Liberal Party Conference to "go back to your constituencies and prepare for government," after most opinion polls showed the SD-Liberal Alliance in the lead.

However, Steel was being hopelessly optimistic—the Conservatives remained in power, them themselves not changing much. On the 14th July, they had appointed a new chairman, Cecil Parkinson, who was in the same vein as traditional Conservatism. (His track record for success was also not flawless—in the 1970 general election, he had lost out as a candidate for Northampton, but six months later a by-election saw him win the seat for Enfield West. When this constituency was abolished four years later he was elected for the new South Hertfordshire constituency.)

Music had a duty to be anti-establishment; and Bow Wow Wow certainly fulfilled this. The underage sex element often felt unsavoury (other tangents of this "sex gang children" movement included the film "The Mile High Club" and the magazine, "Chicken") with Lwin posing naked for a recreation of Manets "Le Dejuener Dur L'Herb", and McLaren urging the other band members to draw straws as to who should take Lwin's virginity. (When the task fell to Ashman, he refused to undertake it) But their lyricism could be sharply anti-establishment in other ways. Their song "W.O.R.K (NO Nah NO! NO! NO! My Daddy Don't)" runs "demolition of the work ethic takes us to the age of the primitive" in a song which journalist Simon Reynolds describes as "taking the Situationist fantasy of perpetual play and updating it for the microchip era."

The bands biggest hit, though, was "Go Wild In The Country," a call to arms for the youth of the day to forsake the MacDonalds lifestyle in favour of getting back to nature; a high point of an album that reads like an anthropological study, with shades of The Golden Bough, Totem and Taboo, Levi-Strauss and Jung.

At times a questionable concept, Bow Wow Wow were everything the establishment were terrified of—a glorious dividend of a political ideal (Situationism) in a time that really needed it.

THE HUMAN LEAGUE—DARE   Oct 1981

On 12th October, British Leyland announced the closure of three factories—a move which would cost nearly 3,000 people their jobs. The unemployment problem in Britain seemed to be expanding every day, stoking the wrath and dissent of the nation. On the 15th, Norman Tebbitt told his fellow Conservative MP's "I grew up in the thirties with an unemployed father. He didn't riot. He got on his bike and looked for work and he kept looking until he found it." Looking to the past like this, and presuming people could just get work if they looked hard enough, just showed how horribly out of touch the government were with their public—no wonder a 23rd October MORI poll put them in just third place with 27% (the SDP-Liberal alliance topped the poll with 40%, and Labour were second on 31%)

The grimness and greyness of the real world led people to seek escapism in glamour—the most representative album for this from the time is the Human League's brilliant third album, the classic "Dare." Their style of synth-based electro was becoming the dominant musical style—this month also saw the release of New Order's debut album "Movement." Comprising the surviving members of Joy Division, the sound of New Order heavily capitalised on the use of strings on "Closer."

But nobody was doing it as well as The Human League. Their frontman Phil Oakey was a born star, but backing singers Susan and Jackie turned the "everyman" concept into "everywoman," having been randomly selected in a nightclub to join the group. There is something of the fairy-tale about this story—just what people needed to hear. On 24th October, a CND anti-nuclear rally march attracted over 250,000 people. The voice of dissent was strong, both in this matter and on the employment issue (on 1st November, British Leylands workforces began a strike.) But The Human League provided another type of respite—stories of the everyday mixed with the glitz and glamour of escapism.

THE DURUTTI COLUMN—LC   Nov 81

As recession blighted the country, capitalism still somehow managed to thrive in an environment that by rights should have slowed it down. On 13th November, the Queen opened the final phase of the Telford Shopping Centre in Shropshire, nearly a decade after development began on what was now one of the largest indoor shopping centres in Europe.

A week after this, a report into the Brixton riots pointed the finger of blame at social and economic problems which affected not only Brixton, but much of Britain. So the nation had economic issues, but somehow we still managed to fund huge shopping centres. Weird, that.

In this landscape of rioting and capitalism, music provided subtle alternatives—particularly from the unassuming figure of Vini Reilly, who in this month released The Durutti Column's second album "LC", a record every inch as brilliant as its predecessor, making further use of Reilly's incredible guitar abilities with intricate, precise songs. The most moving moment on the album is Reilly's tribute to Ian Curtis, "The Missing Boy." "I don't believe in stardom/ machinery in action," runs the chorus, twinned with a verse on "some accident of beauty." Reilly had bonded with Curtis when both of them were plagued by depression. Reilly was believed to be suffering from anorexia nervosa and was shockingly frail—lines in "The Missing Boy," such as "try to capture/ as the light begins to fail/ shapes to compose/ shadows of frailty," have seen it suggested that the song could be about himself as much as Curtis.

But, whilst obviously everyone's problems were not in the same field or on the same level as Curtis' and Reilly's, misery was such a prevailing mood that far to many could identify with the sentiment here. December saw the first case of AIDS diagnosed in the UK, which would come to be the defining scare-story of the 80's. But this still affected few—it was in politics were peoples misery was truly felt. Thatcher's slide in popularity was becoming ever-more obvious—on 26th November, the Conservative majority was overturned in the Crosby by-election, which had been won by Shirley Williams for the SDP. A 19th December MORI poll not only gave the SDP-Liberal alliance the support of up to 50% of the electorate, but also showed that Thatcher was officially the most unpopular post-war Prime Minister. What we really needed was for Thatcher to have a great nemesis who could put up an impressive fight, but this was not to be found in opposition leaders. Instead, this emerged on 8th December when Arthur Scargill was made leader of the National Union of Mineworkers. He had secured 70% of the vote. One of his main policies was to give more power to union conferences rather than executive meetings, on the ground that the former was more democratic. This had great implications for the NUM—every region, even quite small ones, had one delegate, and the larger regions only a few more (Scotland and South Wales had two delegates each, Yorkshire had three.)

With his background in the Yorkshire Left (a group of left-wing activists in the Yorkshire region of the NUM), and having been involved in the mass picket of Saltely Gate in Birmingham during the previous miners strike, Scargill was clearly a force to be reckoned with.

The beautiful, wallflower's music from the likes of The Durutti Column was welcome respite from the harshness of Thatcherism. But, in the real world, we needed someone that could match her—Scargill was set to be the truly momentous thorn in her side throughout her rule.

THE FALL—HEX ENDUCATION HOUR

The role of the "Camus bands" (The Fall, named after a novel of his, and The Cure, whose song "Killing An Arab" was inspired by his novel The Stranger) was to be crucial far into the future, but in particular the early eighties. Camus influence aside, these acts appear to have little in common, they did both provide an ideal soundtrack to what would come to be known largely as the year defined by the Falklands War.

The year opened with the Welsh Army of workers claiming responsibility for the bomb explosion at the Birmingham headquarters of Severn Trent Water. It was another explosive event in a world that needed The Fall—their art-school posturing and serious intelligence may have been what their critics held against them, but intelligence was becoming a rarer and rarer thing. One particularly entertaining example of this is Mark Thatcher, the Prime Ministers son, who failed miserably at school and in January of this particular year managed to disappear in the Sahara during the Paris-Dakkar rally. (He was found safe and well six days later.)

The Fall's latest collection of refreshingly intelligent material, Hex Enducation Hour, included songs like "Winter" and "Winter No. 2." Never before had there been such an appropriate time to sing songs of winter, as the lowest ever UK temperature of—27 Celsius had been recorded earlier that year at Braemar in Aberdeen shire.

Several years after Callaghan's winter of discontent, this looked set to be one in a much more traditional way. It certainly was not a repeat of Callagahan's time, as miners voted against strike action and accepted the National Coal Board offer of a 9.3% pay rise. This did not necessarily mean a satisfied nation. Unemployment continued to be a problem, with figures recorded at 3,000,00, whilst the riots at St. Paul's in Bristol showed deepening racial tensions.[2]

The defining moments of the year truly began, however, when the Argentines landed on South Georgia Island[3], precipitating war. This uncomfortable climate was almost reminiscent of the air of paranoia during the Cold War. The previous day, an Argentine scrap metal dealer had rasied the Argentine flag in South Georgia island. As this was a British colony this was a hugely inflammatory action.

However, the Falklands conflict at times invited misguided patriotism, perfectly coinciding with the Fall album track, "Who makes the Nazis?"

The domination of the Falklands over the news does not mean that there were not other long-running events being called to attention. The IRA were still at force, bombing and sinking the Glasgow-registered coal ship St. Bedan after driving a hijacked boat into Lough Foyle. The events of the previous year with the "Gang of Four" had, however, ceased as Roy Jenkins won the Hillhead by-election in Glasgow for the Social Democrats, who surprisingly still headed most opinion polls.

There were changes within the Fall also; "Hex Enducation Hour" was the first album to feature both Karl Burns and Paul Hanley in an unusual, two-drummer line up. They captured the cold, bleak sounds of back home by partly recorded in Iceland (hence the song "Iceland") and partly in a disused cinema in Hitchin.

Opening song "The Classical" hints sets the scene perfectly, with such sharp lyrics as "Hey there, fuckface," laughing in the face of censorship. The release coincided with Mary Whitehouse's legal case against the National Theatre over alleged obscenity in the play "The Romans in Britain." Tellingly, she lost the case. Freedom of expression through artistry reigned—a good time, then, for The Fall.

---

[2] 30th Jan, 1982

[3] Located in the Falklands

The darkness and edginess was further exemplified on the song "Deer Park", with the refrain referencing Colin Wilson. A somewhat oblique reference, Wilson was a writer on the occult and existential philosophy. The Fall had already showcased existential philosophy through their mere name, but the public ahd little to relate to here. Now wonder Motown records would later say of the Fall uspon hearing this record "I see no commercial potential in this band whatsoever." But in the Thatcherite world of buy, buy, buy, this makes this a refreshing, timeless piece of work.

THE CURE—PORNOGRAPHY

"Pornography" is frequently cited as one of the darkest albums of all time. If this statement is to be agreed with, then it certainly came along at the right time. The nation was getting darker, and at a younger and younger age. On 1st April, 1982, a 12 year old unnamed Birmingham boy became one of the youngest people in the UK to be convicted of murder after he confessed to murdering an eight year old boy. Murder, death and general tangents of darkness were key subjects for the Goth movement, even though the definition of goth was broadening as managers and record labels sought to promote "positive goth." By recording such a famously dark album, the Cure were almost reacting against this.

In the same vein as The Cure, the ever-provocative, post-punk band Killing Joke also released their third album, brimming with their consistent themes of warfare. Both bands were tapping into the atmosphere as the Falklands war accelerated. On the 2nd April, Argentina officially invaded the Isles. It took just two days for the British Falkland Island government to surrender, placing its islands in Argentine control. The following day, Royal Navy task force set sail drawing up to a 200 mile exclusion zone around the Falklands. The drama continued as by the end of the month, the Royal Marines had captured South Georgia. The fighting and turmoil should have, by rights, turned opinion against the government. In fact, it appeared to have quite the opposite effect, with the Conservatives returning to the top of opinion polls with 43% of the vote. Thatcher was growing increasingly cold and almost descending into a self-parody of her "Iron Lady" persona; on the 2nd May, she ordered that the British nuclear submarine Conqueror sink the Argentine cruiser General Belgrano—even though it was shown to be turning *away* from our shores. Years later, when showing people around no. 10, she would still proclaim with excess pride, "this is were I was sat when I decided to sink the Belgrano." The Sun newspaper, who had a daily readership of 400,00 and thus enormous influence, famously reported the story with the victorious, dehumanising headline "Gotcha." This level of reprehensible thought in the masses meant that sensitivity was the preserve of the counter-culture; it was certainly something associated with the Goth movement. This sometimes has its critics complaining that it is to separate, to self-absorbed, but this is not necessarily true—in fact, its sensitivity enables it to see the bleak truth of the world. The opening line of Pornography, is "it doesn't matter if we all die." This is almost Robert Smiths epitaph to the world and certainties within it, a world with little left to live for. As the month from Pornography's release date progressed, so did the military conflict. The HMS Sheffield was damaged by an Exocet missile and sank six days later. In a display of old-fashioned militarism, Royal Marines and paratroopers from British Task force landed at San Carlos Bay on the Falkland Islands and raised the Union Jack. There was then the explosion of the HMS Antelope and the Battle of Stanley, and the deaths of 48 UK servicemen, killed when two supply ships were bombed by Argentine air strikes. The conflict did not end until the formal surrender of June 14th. But the scars, mental and physical, were there for those returning, echoing "Pornography"s line of "I will never be clean again." War was not clean. It felt like a sickness. "I must fight this sickness/find a cure," run further lyrics from "Pornography." It would appear that conflict was not a "cure."

Music was not just defined by gothic miserabilia. The Hacienda, the nightclub offshoot from Factory records, also opened this year, its very name evoking hedonism and sheer pleasure. But it was to be the existential nature of "The Camus bands" which defined this year most aptly.

ECHO AND THE BUNNYMEN—PORCUPINE

The beginning of 1983 in some ways acted as an epilogue on from the naval activity of the previous year, also being defined by water. On 6th January, Danish fishermen defied the British governments prohibition on non-UK boats entering its coastal waters. A fortnight later, the ban on non-British boats in British waters was lifted as the EEC's Common Fisheries policy came into effect. Water also gained impressive visual status when red rain fell, caused by sand from the Sahara desert in the droplets. This watery atmosphere was effectively captured in the lyrical visuals of Echo and the Bunnymen's third album "Porcupine"—even though they themselves had been suffering something of a creative drought. They had been rehearsing for five days a week at their Liverpool rehearsal room The Ministry, but still struggled to write new material, something probably not helped by the fragmenting nature of the band. (Les Pattison had grown cynical, Pete de Frietas was involved with the band Wild Swans and Will Sargeant had recorded a solo album.) They were working in a nation were disillusionment was all-prevailing, as unemployment stood at a record high of 3,224,715. The Bunnymen's answer to this lack of motivation was to mix the familiar with the unfamiliar, recruiting former producer Ian Broudie once again but also recording at London's Trident Studios, the first time they had recorded in London. The process of this, was, however, painfully slow. De Frietas said that "Porcupine was very hard to actually write and record . . . Heaven Up Here was pure confidence, we did it really quickly, we had a great time doing it—but this one was like we had to drag it out of ourselves." However, tension and difficulty must have suited the band, as "Porcupine" is more acclaimed than "Heaven Up Here"—it also earned the band their first big hit with "The Cutter", a plea against government cuts towards those hit the hardest by unemployment. "Not just another drop in the ocean," sings McCulloch with an almost pained anguish, as those struggling had been forgotten, made faceless by the government. It is also the beginning of the "watery" soundtrack . . .

The visuals and album art of Porcupine also tie into this, particularly in the video for "The Cutter." Filming of this took place on and near the frozen Gullfoss waterfall near Reykjavik (considering the Fall's recording process the previous year, Iceland was developing into a musical muse of a nation.) McCulloch says of the dangerous process "if we had slipped there was nothing for hundreds of feet below us." This type of uncertainty was a reflection on emotions in the UK—as was Iceland's frozen wastelands, a reflection on the dearth of jobs back home. The journalist Dave Rimmer wrote that "Iceland does seem an appropriate location for this group. Its isolated, cold, bleak, and fits perfectly with the moody image they've attracted to themselves." McCulloch himself will vouch for this bleakness, saying that "I found the material from it really heavy to play—like, really oppressive. That's the only reason I didn't like the album. The songs were great but it didn't make me happy." But now was not the time for happy. Now the time to be ignored in a world that took the focus away from society. On 24th April, Peter Tatchell lost the Bermondsey by-election to the Liberal Simon Hughes. People joked that a liberal vote was next to apathy—here, it was born of the uncertainty captured in "Porcupine."

THE DURUTTI COLUMN—ANOTHER SETTING AND IT-PULP

26th May 1983 did not suggest that frailty or being a wallflower could ever be popular or interesting ideals, as opinion polls suggested that the iron, strident Conservative Party were looking set to be re-elected with 51% of the vote, 22 points ahead of Labour. This was confirmed on the 9th June, when they won with a majority of 144 seats over Michael Foot, whose highly divided and weakened Labour Party earned just 28% of the vote. The new Labour Party members of Parliament would, however, go onto be hugely influential—Tony Blair for Sedgefield in County Durham and Gordon Brown for Dumferline East in Scotland. Musically, both established acts and new bands were giving a voice to the opposite of successful politicians, the "awkward outsider," with the release of the Durutti Column's third album and Pulp's debut. The Durutti Column seemed set to always carry the "underrated" label—something Pulp would also live with until 1994 with the release of "His 'n' Hers." The sharpness and wit of frontman and lyricist Jarvis Cocker's lyrics is created by the fact that they were a whole new kind of political—more socio-political—ideal for the changing climate. For there were changes. Yes, the Conservatives were still in power, but the centre left was changing. On 12th June, Foot resigned as leader of the Labour Party. It was expected that Neil Kinnock, the MP for Iswlyn South Wales and shadow spokesman for education would succeed him—but the successor would not actually be confirmed until autumn. For those who did not support Thatcher, this was awkward—would Labour be a viable alternative or not? The persistent issues of uncertainty were raised again, perfectly captured by the "indie" awkwardness of Vini Reilly and Jarvis Cocker.

The centre left changes were not just in the Labour Party. Roy Jenkins also resigned as the leader of the SDP and was replaced by David Owen. They were struggling to live up to their early promise of popularity anyway, as no-one stood in the Conservatives way—surprising, given Nigel Lawson's 7th July announcement of £500 million of public spending cuts. There may have been surprisingly few voices of dissent, but what was there was powerful and strong. Later in the year (October 22nd) over a million people demonstrated against nuclear weapons at a march in London. An even more powerful voice of dissent was to not be against weapons, but to use them—as the IRA made their prescence known again. On 5th August, 22of its members had received sentences totalling 4,000 years from a Belfast court, but they were undeterred, as the 25th September saw the Maze Prison Escape: 38 IRA prisoners armed with six guns hijacked a lorry and escaped in the largest prison escape in British history. One guard died of a heart attack and twenty others were injured.

Violence established itself in other ways too—football hooliganism was a problem, one which authority sought to crack down on, convicting seven men of taking part in a fight near Wolverhampton Wanderers stadium.(All of the men in question were members of the Subway Army, a football firm associated with the club.) The "alpha male" figure was clearly still a dominant one—but musicians such as Cocker and the famously fragile (most musically and physically) Reilly were a showcase for the fact that the counterculture could always have the alternative to whatever the mainstream ideal was. The "superstar frontman" was also on the rise, for example with the release of U2's third album "War". In contrast to the likes of Bono and his apparent belief that he was the one to change the world, Reilly and Cocker seemed almost like the anti rock stars. It somehow lends their left wing principles a larger dose of integrity than those of bigger bands. And now was a time in which we saw high principles (the SDP voted against a merger with the Liberals) and horrible low, misguided principles which we are still paying for—Social Services Secretary Norman Fowler privatised the NHS cleaning and catering services.

The previous year, the Cure had sang "I must fight this sickness/find a cure" and "I will never be clean again." How darkly prophetic. Those with a sickness clearly would never be clean again . . .

THE FALL—PERVERTED BY LANGUAGE

December 1983 was an eventful month, dominated by IRA activity. On the 4th, an SAS undercover operation ended in the shooting and killing of two IRA gunmen. Anyone who thought that the war against the IRA was being won was very much mistaken, as a fortnight later a PIRA car bomb explosion outside Harrods injured 90 and killed six (three members of the public and three policemen.) A second bomb exploded on Oxford Street on Christmas Day, but with no injuries. Such a dramatic month meant that it was probably the right time for another Fall album, but by this stage the Fall were doing something slightly different to the strident post punk of previous albums and showing, with "Perverted By Language", their more accessible, almost mainstream side. As were the movements they were soundtracking—it was also in this year that Gerry Adams, president of Sinn Fein, was elected MP for Belfast West, but declined to take up his West Minister seat as he refused to swear an allegiance to the Queen. (His influence on the IRA would go onto be profoundly influential in the peace process.)

Whilst his newly mainstream role in clear, perhaps it is best not to exaggerate the supposed "pop" nature of "Perverted by Language" to much. It is still very much a Fall album. This slight change in direction, however, is often attributed to the addition of Mark. E. Smiths new American wife Brix to the line-up, as she appears responsible for the tightening up and smartening up of the band (even in their visual appearance—small wonder she would go onto become a fashion expert with her own boutique in London.) What Brix brought to the Fall is not so much a mainstream sheen as an extra dimension of beauty, particularly on "Garden" and "Hotel Bloedel", on which she sings whilst her husband is transferred to violin and spoken-word. In the month in which openness was being let into everything—the House of Lords voted to allow television broadcasts of its proceedings—it was also being let into the Fall. There is plenty of "traditional" Fall on here, though—"I Feel Voxish" "Smile" and the frantic, doom-laden "Neighbourhood of Infinity"—alongside lyrics on such mundane subjects as returning rental videos late on a track which John Peel picked for his "Desert Island Discs" and allegedly found so great that he fainted upon hearing it.

It is worth noting that in this month, William Golding won the Nobel Prize for literature as the panel claimed his novels "with the perspicuity of realistic narrative art and the diversity of universality of myth, illuminate the human condition in the world of today." In this case, if there was a Nobel Prize for lyricism then Mark. E. Smith would surely be a worthy winner.

THE SMITHS LP

Whilst 1984 was not shaping up to be quite like George Orwell's novel, the year still began with political intrigue and backstabbing when the 23 year old Foreign Office Clerk Sarah Tisdall was charged under the Official Secrets Act. She had anonymously sent the Guardian newspaper photocopied documents detailing when American cruise missile nuclear weapons would be arriving in the UK, outlining the tactics that defence minister Micheal Heseltine would use to present the matter in the House of Commons. In spite of the lack of any actual threat to national security, the government still quickly bought legal action against the government which required them to reveal their source. The Guardian successfully argued that it was protected by section 10 of the Contempt of Court Act 1981 from revealing this, but Justice Scotts judgement was rapidly overturned, due to the Attorney Generals appeal that although the documents themselves were harmless, a civil servant showing the capability of leaking them might leak other documents which could pose a greater threat to national security, thus leading to Tisdalls six month sentence. Now was an interesting time for the rarely used Official Secrets Act to come into play; one of the greatest songs of the year opens with the line *"All men have secrets for years/Here's mine, now let it be known."* This was the song "What difference does it make?", by the latest darlings of Rough Trade, The Smiths. The Smiths had already shown potential to be one of the most important bands of the decade (which they would go onto to fulfill) with the earlier singles *Hand in Glove/ Handsome Devil* and *This Charming Man*. The Smiths are in many ways the perfect band, with a tightly wound and talented rhythm section in Mike Joyce and Andy Rourke, but it is Morrissey and Johnny Marr who are the real heart of the band, two of the most talented people in the history of British music.

The Smiths are all to often written off as depressing, but at the time they were seen as an injection of Wildean wit and delightful whimsy into a a formerly bleak Manchester music scene swarming with pseudo-depressives trying to fill the aching void left by the death of Ian Curtis.

This does not mean that the Smiths were inoffensive. The song "Handsome Devil" had already attracted a lot of attention to them due to its controversial lyrical content, which allude to sexual relations between a teacher and student *("A bird in the bush is worth two in the hand/I think I can help you get through your exams")* complete with sado-masochism *("I crack the whip/you skip/but you deserve it")* and salacious foreplay *("Whom will swallow whom/when were in our scholarly room?")* The press was in outrage, and the fact that Morrissey was dangerously misquoted as saying "I don't mind singing about molesting children . . . it makes a change" did little to help this. Similar themes on "This Charming Man", a song about a young rent boy aided by a Wildean figure, added fuel to the fire, but those with any sense could see that these were pieces of light wit about consenting figures, not justifications of abuse. But music at its best has always been inflammatory—for example, in the punk years in which Morrissey had been a part of the Nosebleeds along with Vini Reilly and Billy Duffy later of the Durutti Column and The Cult respectively.) Considering the era of mixed values, the mix of joy and controversy provided by the Smiths was ideal. On the negative side, the government (famously hostile to trade unions) had prohibited GCHQ staff from belonging to any trade union, but on the positive side the old Left were re-establishing themselves, as the "rebel" Tony Benn won the Labour Party's nomination for the Chesterfield by-election, eight months after losing his seat as MP for Bristol in the General election—although over a month would have to pass by before we knew whether he was successful.

However, to see the Smiths as simply the soundtrack to good times would be as much of a mistake as to write them off as depressing. The debut also included the horrifying account of the Moors Murders, "Suffer Little Children." Morrissey had been a child himself as the time of the murders, in that area, and felt lucky to have not been a victim but also haunted. He defended the song by saying that the murders were a part of history which should not be swept under the carpet. Regardless of what the individual thinks of "Suffer Little Children", it cannot be denied that social realism can be an important part of fine lyricism. Clearly, a band of true relevance had been borne.

NEW MODEL ARMY—VENGEANCE

On the 1st March, the Left finally found out that they had a minor victory that they had been waiting for—Tony Benn had won the Chesterfield by-election and was returning to Parliament. The next day, opinion polls showed that five months after Neil Kinnock had become their leader, Labour came top of a MORI poll with 41% of the vote against the Conservatives 38%. The Conservatives grip may have apparently been weakening, but they were still in power and with another election not due until June 1988 voices of dissent were still required—this could be found in some of the new bands appearing. Perhaps a band named after Oliver Cromwell's English Revolutionary Army, the New Model Army, could fulfil this.

Dissent was also to be found, amongst ordinary people, on a mass scale which would earn an important place in British history. On March 12th, the miners strike began, pitching the National Union of Mineworkers against the government. Thatcher's fixation with Adam Smith-inspired free market economics extended to free market reform of the nationalised industries—this included plans for the closures of most of Britain's remaining coal pits. But British miners were a formidable section of society. Not prepared to back down. Thatcher may have been a strong leader, but the miners had their own strong leader in the National Union leader Arthur Scargill. This was clearly going to be something of a battle. On the 9th April, more than 100 pickets were arrested in violent clashes at the Cresswell colliery in Derbyshire and the Babbington colliery in Nottinghamshire. The miners were not the only ones disagreeing with Thatcher over various issues—in the same month that the strike began, the EEC summit broke down with disagreement Britain's biggest rebate, with Thatcher threatening to veto any expansion of spending plans. And the counterculture was certainly disagreeing . . .

New Model Army's debut album "Vengeance" was released in April 1984, the time period captured in Orwell's novel. But whilst the clocks were not striking thirteen, there were other events of fear and doom—for example, the shooting and killing of WPc Yvonne Fletcher by a lone gunman during the 1984 Libyan Embassy Siege. (11 others were shot, but survived.) In the wake of this, Britain cut off diplomatic relations with Libya, warning its seven Libyan diplomats to return there. "Vengenace" perfectly captured the tense mood, with its political, often humanitarian messages. "1984" was obviously an anthem for the time, "No Mans Land" gives a humanised voice to soldiers in a style highly reminiscent of the First World War poets Wilfred Owen and Siegfried Sassoon, whilst "Spirit of the Falklands" attacks Thatcher and her decisions in the Falklands conflict through the medium she seemed immune to, sensitive emotion. "a Liberal Education", meanwhile, hits hard with its opening lines of "Take away our history/Take away our heroes/ And leave us with nothing" and closing lines "Nobody respects you for your weakness." Dissent was not dead; it was just getting more articulate.

Echo & The Bunnymen — OCEAN RAIN

ECHO AND THE BUNNYMEN—OCEAN RAIN

On 2nd May 1984, the Liverpool International Garden Festival opened, creating a world of prettification in the city. This did not reach the whole of the cities population, as the definitive Liverpool band of the eighties and purveyors of realism and misery, Echo and the Bunnymen, released their fourth album "Ocean Rain" on the 8th May. The songs had been written the previous year and at the beginning of 1984 were recorded, mainly in Paris with a 35 piece orchestra. The other sessions took place in Bath and Liverpool, but the romance of Paris is captured in the lush, multi-layered strings, a slight departure for the band. Familiarity still infused some aspects of the band, most of the album being written in Liverpool, and previewed in their sixth session for John Peel's show.

Whereas "Porcupine" had something of a watery atmosphere, Ocean Rain departs from this somewhat and has the subtle atmosphere of "the night", with songs like "Nocturnal" and the eerily Gothic "The Killing Moon." "The Killing Moon" is a darkly sensual piece of music, recorded and self-produced by the band at Crescent Studio in Bath, but it took their home city to perfect it, with Ian McCulloch re-recording his original vocal in Liverpool. In all fairness, this is not just the typical McCulloch perfectionism—he had caught a cold before recording the original. This dark, nocturnal theme extends into the cover art, a fulfilment of the bands desire to continue the elemental themes of their previous album covers. Designed by Martin Atkins and photographed by Brian Griffin, it depicts the band in a rowing boat within the dark confines of Carnglaze Caverns, Liskeard, Cornwall. In his 2002 biography of the band, Turquoise Days, Chris Adams says it is a "perfect visual representation of arguably the Bunnymens finest album." Fantastical imagery through Gothic mediums was also to be found in the literature of the time, with the release of Angela Carter's "Nights at the Circus" and Iain Banks

"The Wasp Factory", stories of people out of the ordinary which fit perfectly into the confusing quest for identity in a Thatcherite society which left people unsure of themselves. Echo and the Bunnymen are aware of the mood of darkness that they managed to capture on the record, with guitarist Will Sergeant saying that "we wanted to make something conceptual with lush orchestration . . . something with a twist. Its all pretty dark. "Thorn of Crowns" is based on an Eastern scale. The whole mood is very windswept—European pirates, a bit Ben Gunn, dark and stormy, battering rain; all of that." Transferring darkness to an imagined European World could be seen as a way of projecting it away from the Thatcherite Britain the band were based in. As the country grew more complicated, so did the bands music—as well as drums, De Frietas played xylophone and glockenspiels, Sergeant distorted his solo on "My Kingdom" through a valve radio, and bassist Les Pattinson used an old reverb machine. However, reviewer Max Bell claimed that "this time vocalist Ian McCulloch has tempered his metaphysical songs with a romantic sweetness." It was an album understood in its own environment—Ian Broudie claimed that "Ocean Rain" stood out for me as unique and special album the first time I heard it. It captured a great band at a perfect moment and has a lasting, timeless quality which still reverberates in every song." Overseas, however, it was harder for critics to understand why bleakness was a key part of British culture at the time, with Rolling Stone saying that the album was "too often a monochromatic dirge of existential imagery" which "to much tortured soul gazing" missing the point that it was just this which made it relevant. At the end of the month (the 9th) fighting at Orgreave colliery between police and striking miners left 64 injured, with Arthur Scargill arrested and charged with the obstruction the next day. Soundtracking this bleakness by distilling it and wrapping it up in lush beauty meant Echo and the Bunnymen were perfect for their time. In an episode of classic 80's sitcom "The Young Ones", Thatcher-loathing sociology student Rik announces he is going to write to his MP. When told, "you haven't got an MP, you're an anarchist," he responds, "well in that case I shall write to the lead singer of Echo and the Bunnymen."

Seems a fair alternative . . .

BREWING UP WITH BILLY BRAGG

It was not the best of summers. British unemployment was at a record high of around 3,260,000 under a Prime Minister with a laissez-faire policy which easily translated as "not caring." There was still political music, but the art of the "protest singer" seemed faintly archaic, someone who belonged to 1960's America as opposed to 1980's Britain. Who, then, could truly capture the voice of an angry, disillusioned, working-class Britain?

A search for somebody to fulfil this role in the summer of 1984 would not have been fruitless. Billy Bragg is a singer-songwriter who means very word he creates, something reflected in his consistent political activism. He had been "on the scene" since 1977, touring London pubs with his punk.pub rock band Riff Raff, and come to true prominence in 1983 with his debut solo album, the sparse but brilliant kitchen sink drama of an album, "Spy Vs Spy."

A follow-up album from Bragg could not have come soon enough considering the climate. On 7th June, 120 people were arrested when fighting broke out outside the houses of parliament during a mass lobby by striking miners. On the track "Its Says Here", on Bragg's timely second album "Brewing Up With Billy Bragg", he attacks the tabloid press belief in "a large dose of law and order/ and a touch of the short sharp shock." "It Says Here" is generally an attack on the tabloid press as a whole, with their bias and right-wing leanings ("Theres to sides to every story/just remember that the paper is Tory.") Considering the dehumanising "Gotcha!" coverage of the Falklands, many may have empathised. Tabloids were, after all, disreputable—the amoral Robert Maxwell had just bought the Daily Mail for £113.4 million. Bragg was seemingly an ideal voice of reason for the time, a genuine working-class figure for an era that seemed anti-worker—on 26th July, the Trade Union Act prohibited workers from striking without a ballot.

Bragg's songs are so effective because of experience. He is a committed activist and uses his Army experience to great effect on anti-Falklands songs "Like Soldiers Do" and "Island of No Return", were "Brewing Up" describes a tank being idecinary bombed. Not just a voice of dissent then, but the human voices for issues which seemed to otherwise lack one.

LLOYD COLE AND THE COMMOTIONS—RATTLESNAKES

Autumn was not progressing well. On the 6th September, a MORI poll showed that the Conservative support had a lead over Labour. At the end of the month, the High Court ruled that the miners strike was unlawful. As had so often occurred in the twentieth century, it seemed that the right to fight for one's rights did not exist. The landscape was bleak; luckily music had on its side a voice of escapism who could back up this escapism with a blistering intelligence.

This was Lloyd Cole, a former student of literature and philosophy. But rather than abandon these upon graduating, his music was both literary and philosophical in a way which was sometimes considered pretentious. Academia is an important subject for Cole—on opener "Perfect Skin" he sings about "My IQ . . . academia blues." But there is a wider, more traditional story to "Perfect Skin", a wonderful piece of typical eighties indie. It is the story of his affection for a sexually enlightened weathergirl who "at the age of ten looked like Greta Garbo." The theme of girls who evoke Hollywood's past is continued on the title track, with a girl who "looks like Eva Marie Saint in On the Waterfront." But this girl is also more than an edgily pretty face—she also "reads Simone De Beauvoir." Many see this line as typical Cole pretentiousness, De Beauvoir being the wife of Jean-Paul Sartre and a complex philosopher in her right. But is this pretentiousness, or a celebration of women? De Beavoir was a feminist unafraid of sexuality—see her work "Must We Burn De Sade?" as an example of this. Couple this with the "sexually enlightened" heroine of "Perfect Skin" and it seems that maybe Cole is something of a new kind of feminist himself. The nation may have been being led by a strong woman, but one in denial of sexuality—a part of womanhood. In writing "Rattlesnakes", Cole had created something of a "Femal Eunuch" set to music. With Thatcher seeming to believe that the path to strength was a denial of femininity, Cole was a refreshingly appreciative view of the enlightened, intelligent woman.

The Wonderful and Frightening World of... The Fall

"THE WONDERFUL AND FRIGHTENING WORLD OF THE FALL"

Working class Britain was a wasteland. Factory and mine closures hit certain parts of the UK hard. One of these areas was Durham. No wonder the Bishop of Durham, David Jenkins, was keen to attack Margaret Thatchers social policies. Many from such towns no doubt wished to attack her in the same way, but lacked a platform or the words. Of course, words were not the only form of attack this month . . . on 12th October, the Provisional IRA attempted to assassinate the British cabinet in the Brighton Hotel Bombing. Thatcher escaped uninjured, but Norman Tebbitt was trapped under the rubble (his wife Margaret was paralysed.) Five people, including MP Anthony Berry, were killed. The musical world and its hatred of Conservatism were largely unsympathetic, with Morrissey famously saying that the great tragedy of the bombings was that Thatcher had not been killed. The public, however, simply accelerated their support, with the latest polls putting the Conservatives nine points ahead of Labour with 44 per cent of the vote.

Public fear of the IRA in England meant that its victims were seen as objects of sympathy, regardless of who they were. The fact that the government were letting down the nation was apparently irrelevant, even after the events of the miners strike had led to a £200,000 fine for the NUM (There was an additional £1,000 for Scargill for contempt in court—but how could he have shown anything other than contempt considering the circumstances? This was another example of expected servitude to so-called superiors from the true heart and blood of the nation, the workers.) Could music tap into the feelings of the nation? Concerning this wave of fear, then yes. The Fall manage to take this mass wave of feeling and distil it into their own small world on "The Wonderful and Frightening World of The

Fall." Their world was, as ever, changing—Paul Hanley left the band around this time, thus ending their "two drummers" period. This is an album which shows a band being truly self-aware—after all, they really were (and still are) wonderful and frightening. Rather than attempting to see the two as one and the same by merging them, that split the album into two halves "wonderful" and "frightening." But both moods run right through it, down to the sinister artwork by the Danish artist Claus Castenkoild. Uniting wonder with fear was not to difficult—although this kind of fantastical fear was miles away from the mundane uncertainties of Britain.

THE SMITHS—HATFUL OF HOLLOW

The closing of the year did not indicate any improvements in a bleak, Thatcherite Britain. On the 19th November, the number of working miners increased to around 62,000 when nearly 3,000 formerly striking miners returned to work. This may have fundamentally been seen as a good thing, but could there have been more of a fight—had they given in to easily? Their work was, after all, demanding and dangerous—they were surely worth more than they were working for.

Work and its perils was a theme which appeared on the Smiths collection of BBC sessions released at this time, "Hatful of Hollow." "I've never had a job . . . because I am too shy," sings Morrissey and "I was looking for a job and then I found a job/ and heaven knows I'm miserable now," on "Heaven knows I'm Miserable Now." No matter what the themes were, to have warranted a BBC sessions album at this stage in their career was some clue to their importance. Their cynicism was appropriate for the time—Thatcherite privatisation continued its ascent with the privatisation of both BT and the Trustee Savings Bank, and the miners battle continued as Arthur Scargill was fined £230 and ordered to pay £750 for his role in the Orgreave riots. The struggle at home was distracted from by concerns for other nations, with the runaway success of the Band Aid single.

"Hatful of Hollow" was on a much narrower, more personal world, something reflected in the sound, as some of the songs have a far more delicate, intimate feel than the original recordings (This Charming Man, in particular, feels light as air due to Marr's refined guitar work.) This intimacy is also reflected in lyrical romanticism and wit; debut single "Hand in Glove" features on this collection, with its lyrics of "we may be hidden by rags/ but we've something they'll never have" and "its not like any other love/its quite different because its ours . . . everything depends upon how near you stand to me," are almost fairy-tale Romantic, bought back down to Earth by "the sun shines out of our behinds." Its not all tongue-in-cheek cynicism though. Closer "Please Please Please Let Me Get What I Want" in a thing of minimal beauty. "Haven't had a dream in a long time," it runs. Neither had the British working class; certainly not since 1975 . . .

THE SMITHS—MEAT IS MURDER

"Hatful of Hollow" may have cemented the Smiths reputation, but they still had to fulfil the task of "second album proper." What they delivered was far darker than the debut, a sharp shock to the musical world. The world seemed to be in a giving, optimistic mood in terms of the music that was selling, given "Band Aids" success at the end of the previous year. But this was the beginning of a new year; one which did not promise positive change. Thatcher was still in power, but still widely disliked. The academic, intellectual world could never really take to her, even in traditional institutions which could never really be associated with the working class—on 29th January, she became the first post-war prime minister to be refused an honorary degree by Oxford University. Education itself was becoming a more liberal field, but it had not always been this way—one of the most moments on "Meat Is Murder" is "The Headmaster Ritual," Morrissey's attack on the school system he was out through, dismissing his teachers as "spineless bastards." "Spineless bastards" were everywhere. On 16th February, Clive Ponting resigned from the MoD after breaching section 2 of the Official Secrets Act 1911 concerning the leaking of documents relating to the sinking of General Belgrano—in other words, everyone was reminded of a whole new level of spinelessness in the sinking, the anomalies of which the government had clearly wanted keeping under wraps. The senselessness of the Falklands almost had echoes of Vietnam, something people would have been reminded of by the Vietnam artwork of "Meat is Murder." However, many of the "conflicts" on this album are more personal than political, for example the ethereal "How Soon is Now?" First heard on "Hatful of Hollow", "How Soon is Now?" is the quintessential study of teenaged angst, but more intelligent than many other self-pitying songs on this theme. It opens with the lines "I am the son/I am the heir . . . of nothing in particular." This is an allusion to George Eliot's *Middlemarch* (To be the son of a Middlemarch merchant is to be the heir of nothing in particular") although many listeners misheard it as "the sun/ the air", turning it into a song about the elements. No such scientific drudgery in this hymn of loneliness, though, with is chorus of "I am human and need to be loved" and famous lines of "Theres a club if you'd like to go/you could meet somebody who really loves you/ so you go and you stand on your own/ and you leave on your own/ and you go home and you cry and you want to die." These lyrics were recently voted the second greatest of all time (after U2's *One*.) This lies, no doubt, in their relevance to the figure that will never be extinct—the awkward, lonely teenager. In the modern world, this figure does have more of a voice than they would have had in the Thatcherite world which placed the value of the individual on their actual monetary value, something captured by the cash register sounds on "Meat is Murder", and album marked out by sound effects, such as the helicopter on *Rusholme Ruffians*—and even more disturbing sounds on the title track. This track is a piece of musical propaganda as much as any political protest song of the past, and decidedly more effective as dedicated listeners everywhere converted to vegetarianism. The song places an enormous amount of guilt on meat eaters with rhetorical, aggressive questioning ("Do you care how many animals die?") with dark descriptions of slaughter ("heifer whines could be human cries"). At times, the descriptions are alarmingly effective—the "screaming knife" could make anybodies blood run cold. But why, in 1985, should vegetarianism be relevant? The decision to become a vegetarian is one which considers ethics and the well-being of a weaker creature. Thatcherism had bought with it something of a social Darwinism, full of selfishness and lack of regard for others. Anybody symbolic of the era would not have given meat eating another thought. But Morrissey's lyricism is forceful—he uses traditional techniques of rhetoric, like modal verbs ("This beautiful creature must die.") Anybody who hears this song will certainly *think* about the issues raised whether they agree with them or not. Selfless and self-sacrificial, vegetarianism is everything Thatcherism is not. I am a vegetarian myself; I find that it is never left-wingers who find this difficult to comprehend. This about more than a food product, but being utilitarian, thinking *beyond* the individual which Thatcher placed so much importance on. All this aside, is "Meat is Murder" a good album? Yes, of course it is. The harder, darker edges the Smiths added to their sounds and themes did not hurt them. However, with the bleakness of the real world, many would have craved the witty humour of their debut. But it would be their next album, their sheer masterpiece, which would do this . . .

BILLY BRAGG—BETWEEN THE WARS EP

By the 3rd March, the miners strike was officially over. But it had earnt a place in history as one of Britain's greatest strikes. The voice of the miners had been well and truly earnt. This was not something unnoticed by our great political songwriter, Billy Bragg on his EP "Between The Wars", released four months after the strike officially ended. The title track of this is a poetic narrative with the feel of a kitchen sink novel, its protagonist a miner working in the era between the wars. In this song, then, Bragg gives a voice not just to the miners of the 80's strike, but miners through history. This kind of old-fashioned working class politicism is evident elsewhere on "Between the Wars." Even though he is a great lyricist himself, Bragg has a knack for picking out the right words of people form the past to apply to the present, something clear on the song "Which Side Are You On?", lifted from a 1946 pro-striking poem by Florence Reece. I have reprinted the poem here, to show how relevant it was to the eighties in spite of its age:

This government had an idea
And parliament made it law
It seems like it's illegal
To fight for the union any more

Which side are you on, boys?
Which side are you on?
Which side are you on, boys?
Which side are you on?

We set out to join the picket line
For together we cannot fail
We got stopped by police at the county line
They said, "Go home boys or you're going to jail"

Amy Britton

Which side are you on, boys?
Which side are you on?
Which side are you on, boys?
Which side are you on?

It's hard to explain to a crying child
Why her Daddy can't go back
So the family suffer
But it hurts me more
To hear a scab say Sod you, Jack

Which side are you on, boys?
Which side are you on?
Which side are you on, boys
Which side are you on?

I'm bound to follow my conscience
And do whatever I can
But it'll take much more than the union law
To knock the fight out of a working man

Which side are you on, boys?
Which side are you on?
Which side are you on, boys?
Which side are you on?

The title alone was timely as the nation were deciding "whose side they were on." And it appeared that in the political realm they were on Labour's—after beginning the year with a lead of up to eight points, the MORI poll of March 19th put them four points behind Labour, who now had a forty per cent share of the vote. Labour's rise in popularity resulted in Britian's first black council leader, as the Guyana-born Bernie Grant was elected leader of the Labour-controlled London Borough of Haringey. In 1963, Grant had took up the government's offer to let people from the colonies move to the UK to do blue-collar work. By the mid-60's he was a member of the Socialist Labour League, and became a Labour councillor in 1978. (It was not just the rise of the Labour Party that resulted in his election as a councillor, however, but the split in the party over the fight against Conservative 'rate capping.'

A black councillor would have been unimaginable in the past, but the fact that many other things were unchanging kept Bragg's music relevant. No matter what the issue of the day, it was as if there was always a reason to need Billy Bragg.

THE POGUES—RUM, SODOMY, AND THE LASH

On the 25th June, police had arrested thirteen suspects in connection with the Brighton Hotel Bombing of 1984. The wounds from the bombing were still raw and there was a wave of discrimination against the Irish echoed in the "Islmaophobia" which followed the attacks of September 11th, 2001. This makes the Pogue's second album "Rum, Sodomy and the Lash", full of nods to their history, all the braver—and more interesting.

"Rum, Sodomy and the Lash" is exciting before the first note even kicks in. For a start, there is that provocative title, taken from a quote by Winston Churchill—"don't talk to me about naval tradition its nothing but rum, sodomy and the lash!" Then, there is the Theodore Gericault artwork. When the music does kick in, it does not disappoint, with "The Sick Bed of Culcuhainn", on a figure from Irish mythology, (a central figure in 'The Ulster Cycle', a sort of Irish equivalent of the Arthurian legends.) In this story, Culcuhainn is taken ill when he is attacked in a dream by two women with horsewhips and needed to spend a year in his sickbed as a result—before descending into a fantastical tale of spirits and battle. The fantastical and the mythical are here blended with historical reality as Shane McGowan sings "Frank Ryan bought you whisky in a brothel in Madrid." Frank Ryan was a member of the IRA who fought on the pro-Republican side during the Irish Civil War and, in 1934, along with Paeder O'Donnell helped to establish the Republican Congress of Anti-Capitalists Organisation.

England as a whole was unprepared to acknowledge the wider history of the IRA, especially with the wounds of recent events—four days after the arrests in connection with the Brighton bombing, Patrick MacGee was charged with the murder of those who had died in the Brighton bombing.

The history of Ireland is further alluded to throughout the album. "Wildcats of Kilkenny" is a parable of the fighting over boundaries between Irishtown and Kilkenny, whereas further use is made of traditional folk songs from Irish history. The arrests of the Brighton bombing were not the only instance of the IRA hitting the headlines in this year. Earlier (7th March) two IRA members had been jailed for 35 years for plotting the bombing campaign across 1981. Irish history had been written long ago;nothing *new* was happening, it was simply continuing in the same vein. Thus, the appropriation of history was hugely relevant.

But the Pogues view of history is not limited to that of their own nation; instead covering so much that it could be an incredibly visceral textbook, sometimes blending the historical with the modern. For example "Billys Bones" runs *"Billy went away with the peacekeeping force/ 'cause he liked a bloody good fight of course/ went away in an old khaki van to the banks of the River Jordan."* Interpretations of this vary when it comes to historical placing—it is sometimes related to one of the three instances of Ireland committing UN peacekeeping forces in Palestine between the wars (prior to the creation of both the United Nations and and the state of Israel.) Following the defeat of the Ottoman empire, Britain claimed this area as a part of its own empire, and the international community to this day is dealing with the consequences. This setting converts the expected meanings of the language within it—for example, there is a reference to "the Holy City" which one would probably expect to mean Rome, but it is in fact more likely to mean Jerusalem.

The themes of international force were still relevant considering recent events in the Falklands, and the use of Eric Bogle's anti-war ballad "The Band Played Waltzing Matilda" also feels relevant due to this, even though the setting is different—"and amidst all the tears and the shouts and the cheers/ he sailed off to Gallipoli." This refers to the ANZAC contribution to Britain's war effort in the ill-fated 25th April 1915 attack on Gallipoli (a section of the Turkish coast along the straits of Dardanelles.) "How well I remember that terrible day/ How the blood stained the sand and the water/ and how in that town that they called Sula Bay/ we were butchered like lambs in the slaughter.") The invasion is one of the great disasters of military history, with the allies suffering some 250,00 casualties and 50,000 dead. The invasion had been the idea of Churchill, then an up-and-comer in government. This song reinforces that even those with a place in history often did the wrong thing, something resonant in 1985.

Another theme of relevance on the album is police brutality, referred to somewhat obliquely on "The Old Man Drag" with its lyrics of "Between the metal doors on Vine Street I was beaten and mauled." MacGowan confirms this is the book "A Drink with Shane MacGowan":

"So he (police detective on Vine Street interviewing MacGowan over the theft of a chair from a pub) beat me seven shades of shit round the cell. Twenty minutes of solid beating. Really heavy. And going "And now your going to have assaulting a police officer added to your charge!" It was a really heavy kicking . . . the heaviest kicking I've ever had in a police cell, and it was over a bloody chair! And this wasn't even his case."

Police brutality was a notorious problem at the time—many people would have empathised with this. But there is a lot of "everyman" imagery on this record (for example, the real-life characters on "Sally Mclennane." Blending them with the mythical and the historical makes for a kind of musical 'Ulysses'—holding a mirror up to history which retreats into a present full of unsung heroes.

THE CURE—THE HEAD ON THE DOOR

The Cure's previous album, "Pornography", had truly reached the excesses of darkness—the captured sound of a band falling apart. That process of falling apart had now been completed, as the original line-up had completely changed. Did this mean that the Cure would deliver a more positive record—or was it possible that they could go even darker? "The Head on the Door" is not as bleak as "Pornography"—but what could be? It may not reach the same depths as its predecessor, but it does not exactly brim with cheer either. By rights, it was a time for things to be more upbeat—unemployment had fallen from 3,178, 582 to 3,240, 947. However, as ever, there was more to the figures than there seemed—in spite of this, unemployment had actually increased in 73 Conservative constituencies. The government were still letting down the public; despair was still being felt on something of a mass scale. The Cure were becoming a reliable band to tap into this, and The Head On The Door was a prefect reflection of this. At the time of "Pornography", times were obviously bleak—now the darkness was hidden under positivity, something this album also succeeds in—at times the melodies are poppy and uplifting, at first hiding a darker lyricism. Opener "In Between Days" sets the scene for this, an apparently cheerful piece of pop music with despondant opening lines—"Yesterday I got so old I felt like it made me want to cry/ yesterday I felt like I could die." Not only is this tinged with darkness, but it also kicks against the supposed "youth and youth only" sense of the goth movement; as the movement itself aged, it was obviously broadening its horizons. The despair and frustration associated with the kind of teenagers who embraced the goth movement were also being felt by adults, stung by a government who had let them down. Thatchers Britains invited this attitude; the unemployment problem had left people trapped in something of a self-contained, claustrophobic world. The video for the Cure's "Close to Me", from

"The Head On The Door", depicts them compressed together in a dark wardrobe, a video which quickly gained iconic status. There was no trickery or mastery involved in this—the video was upon filming just what it appeared to be, five individuals in a small, dark space—almost a symbol for the age.

The Cure's acceleration in popularity with this album was no coincidence—there are two major factors in its success. The first is the significantly more accessible sound than "Pornography." The singles (the aforementioned "In Between Days" and "Close To Me") are fragments of chart-friendly, singalong pop. The second is that deepening disillusion that a band like the Cure can tap into with such effectiveness.

"COMING OF AGE IN THE RIOTS":

THE FALL—THIS NATIONS SAVING GRACE

AND

KATE BUSH—HOUNDS OF LOVE

At a glance, it may be impossible to see what an album by the Fall and an album by Kate Bush could possibly have in common. And, in truth, in terms of sounds they certainly differ greatly. But there are reasons for writing about them together. The fact that they share a release date means that they came out in the same environment, and both manage to soundtrack that environment perfectly, albeit in different ways. But that is not all—they are both the sounds of established acts truly finding their feet to reach the pinnacle of their successes, and both doing so intelligently and interestingly.

The summer of this year had seen the second Handsworth Riot in the Birmingham suburb of Handsworth (the first being in 1981, and the second in 1991.) As previously mentioned (in "Rum, Sodomy and the Lash") heavy-handed policing was thought to be the root, but blame was also attributed to the rise of Asian-owned businesses aggrieving the black British. The area, since improved, was rife with racial discrimination, poverty, unemployment, dilapidated housing and poor social conditions, a symbol of Thatcher's broken Britain. Both The Fall and Kate Bush had pioneered sparse sounds over their careers which reflected the sparse bleakness of such areas. Both acts also reflect the lack of community in their won way. Recording "Hounds of Love" was a solitary process for Bush—stung by the production costs she had run up for her previous album "The Dreaming", she built a 24-track studio near her home in order to work at her own pace, as well as producing the album herself. Whilst the Fall were far from solitary, they had been heavily fragmented over the years. At the beginning of the year, they lacked the brother Paul and Steve Hanley from their line-up—Paul had left the group permanently and Steve was on paternity leave.

Fragmentation was felt nowhere more than Handsworth. Beginning on the 9th September, the riots were sparked by the arrest of a man near the Acapulco Café and a police raid on the Villa Cross pub. Hundreds of people swiftly attacked police and property, almost reverting to primitive animalism with looting, smashing and setting off fire bombs. Maybe the considered maturity of "Hounds of Love" and "This Nations Saving Grace" were not completely appropriate. The damage was immense—two brothers burnt to death in the post office that they ran, two were unaccounted for, 35 injured, and 45 shops looted and burned. But whilst the actions were almost dystopian, the reasons for such dissatisfaction were all to clear—fewer than 5% of the black population to have left school that summer had found employment.

This environment of darkness invited a need for musical escape—but this escape was not necessarily an instant one. "Hounds of Love" may have been Kate Bush's most successful album commercially, but it does not lack the experimentation of its predecessors. It is split into two halves, the first half of "Hounds of Love" combining five "accessible pop songs"—"Running Up That Hill", "Hounds of Love", "The Big Sky", "Mother Stands For Comfort", and "Cloudbusting". These songs are accessible, but also access deeper and darker themes than conventional pop music. Tapping into the nations fearful psyche on the title track, Bush sings "I've always been a coward/ and I don't know whats good for me," whilst "Cloudbusting" is actually an unashamed piece of intellectualism. "Cloudbusting" is a technique pioneered by the Austrian psychoanalyst Wilhelm Reich (1897-1957), famously played by Donald Sutherland in the accompanying video. Reich was an interesting character and Bush's focus on him is worth dwelling on. In 1933 he published his two most notable books, "Character Analysis" and "The Psychology of Fascism". With 1985's racial tension reflecting ideals of fascism, perhaps he was ideal reading for the era. Reich always tried to unite Marxism with psychoanalysis—in Conservative Britain, appropriating somebody who united Marxism with anything was a bold move. Reich influenced the likes of Saul Bellow, William. S. Burroughs and Norman Mailer, as well as shaping innovations such as Fritz Perl's Gestalt therapy, Alexander Lowen's bioenergetic analysis, and Arthur Janov's primal therapy. He would go on to be as condemned as he was adored by violating some principles of psychoanalysis—touching patients during sessions, and treating patients in their underwear to improve their "orgiastic potency." Whilst this is clearly wrong (he justified it by saying he had discovered a primordial cosmic energy, which he called "orgone" and others called God—he built orgone energy accumulators that his patients sat in) it is interesting that Bush would focus on someone concerned with closeness, touch and unity, everything that the world of rioting and Thatcherism neglected. The other major cultural influence in "Hounds of Love" is the title of the second side "The Ninth Wave"—this is a section of the poem "The Coming of Arthur" by Tennyson. Tennyson's nineteenth century was filled with upheaval—he was an appropriate figure to make use of.

"Hounds of Love" entered the UK album chart at number one, knocking Madonna's "Like A Virgin" from the position. "This Nations Saving Grace" only managed number 54. But both albums capture something—the sound of confident acts blossoming into maturity at a time of apparent regression.

PEAKING TO SOON?:

LLOYD COLE AND THE COMMOTIONS—EASY PIECES

AND

SONGS TO LEARN AND SING—ECHO AND THE BUNNYMEN

The Handsworth riots had left a deep scar on Britain. Ending on 11th September, the final casualty toll was 35 injuries and two deaths—and the discomfort of a "told-you-so" attitude from racists. On the day the riots ended, Enoch Powell (seventeen years on from his dismissal for his Rivers of Blood speech) said that the riots had been a vindication of this warning. This mood of darkness meant that acts such as Echo and the Bunnymen had a continued relevance, but having peaked with their first four albums they issued a compilation album, "Songs to Learn and Sing", rather than any new material. Another act who had already hit their peak were Lloyd Cole and the Commotions, who after his important and brilliant debut "Rattlesnakes" issued a follow up "Easy Pieces" in 1985. However, far from being "easy", it was the "difficult second album", which he himself described as a "mistake." This is perhaps to self-critical, but to a point it lacks the quality of "Rattlesnakes." It was released at an eventful time. Neil Kinnock had made a speech at the Labour Party conference in Bournemouth attacking the Revolutionary Socialist League in Liverpool, whilst racial problems still ran rife. On the 28th September, a riot in Brixton erupted after the accidental shooting of a woman by police. One person died, 50 were injured, and more than 200 were arrested.

Further riots erupted in Toxteth and Peckham—Lord Scarman's report blamed them on economic deprivation and racial discrimination. The mood was further darkened by the death of a 49 year old black woman, Cynthia Jarrett, from a fall whilst police searched her council house on the Broadwater Farm estate in Tottenham. And thus another riot was born, the Broadwater Farm riots. These riots included the fatal stabbing of PC Keith Blakelock. The council leader, Bernie Grant, was widely quoted as saying "what the police got was a bloody good hiding," though he claimed this was taken out of context—the full quote being:

"The youths here believe that the police were to blame for what happened on Sunday and what they got was a bloody good hiding."

All the same, he offered an apology to the family of PC Blakelock, but the comments were condemned by the Labour Party leadership—whilst Home Secretary Douglas Hurd dubbed him "The High Priest of Conflict."

It was as though conflict was everywhere. The songs collected by Echo and the Bunnymen for "Songs to Learn and Sing", such as "The Cutter" and "The Killing Moon" may not have been new but still captured the dark mood. Lloyd Cole, meanwhile, used escape as the theme for his own songwriting. The best known song on "Easy Pieces" is "Lost Weekend," on which he sings, *"took a lost weekend in a hotel in Amsterdam."* The thought of hazy lost weekends in such a famously relaxed city was welcome respite from the tense anger of the United Kingdom—but that is not to say that "Easy pieces" as a whole lacks realism. Opening song "Rich" is a perfect lyrical soundtrack to the monetary obsessions of Thatcherite Britain. *"Even Jesus has a price,"* he sings solemnly, *"Money is for taking, yes."* This is further sharpened by the fact that nobody *had* any money. Unemployment had risen in nearly 70% of the Tory held seats in a year, with economists predicting it would remain above the 3,000,000 mark for the rest of the decade. Doubts over Thatcher were understandably rising—it was not *just* the musical acts of 1985 who had hit their popularity peak earliest on.

PSYCHO CANDY

THE JESUS AND MARY CHAIN

THE JESUS AND MARY CHAIN—PSYCHOCANDY

The closing of 1985 was a great time for Scotland, securing a world cup place and unleashing one of their greatest musical acts on the world. There were also flickers of hope for the UK as a whole in the socio-political world, as the CBI called for the government to invest £1billion in unemployment relief, a move which would cut unemployment by 350,000. The latest MORI polls also showed Conservative and Labour support were almost equal at 36%—the future was not clear. How appropriate, then, that this aforementioned great band would make music which famously lacked clarity. This band was the Jesus and Mary Chain, who had already come to attention with "Upside Down", the first ever release for the iconic Creation records. Considering the wave of unemployment, they were perfectly qualified to provide a relevant soundtrack, given that the heart of the band, brothers Jim and William Reid, had spent five years on the dole. This was time well spent however, as it was used writing and recording, as well as constructing the moody gothic image of the band. The early sound was fairly conventional, but the introduction of heavy walls of feedback marked them out. William Reid claimed "we began using noise and feedback (because) we wanted to make records which sounded different." Early live shows continued this route of unconventionality—Jim Reid's guitar was left out of tune, drummer Murray Dalglish's drum kit was limited to two drums, and bassist Douglas Hart's bass had just two strings. To quote Hart, "that's the two I use, whats the fucking point in spending money on another two? Two is enough." This was everything Thatcherite Britain was against—minimalism, unconventionality and a refusal to succumb to spending. However, the Conservative government itself was in as much chaotic disarray as the sounds of the Jesus and Mary Chain—on 22nd November, Thatcher was urged by her MP's to call a general election for 1987, even though the deadline was not until 1988.

By the time "Psychocandy" was released, the line-up of the Jesus and Mary Chain had changed, with Murray Dalglish being replaced by Bobby Gillespie. The band had also courted their fair share of controversy by this stage, with them all being arrested for the possession of amphetamines and Jim Reid having confessed to use of LSD. In the indie world, however, controversy is no barrier to success—"Upside Down" had topped the indie chart and stayed there for 76 weeks, thus making it one of the biggest selling indie singles of the 1980's with sales standing at around 35,000. But, as successful as their music might have been, how appropriate was it for the time? In the political world, Labour leader Neil Kinnock had suspended the Liverpool District Labour Party amid allegations that the revolutionary socialist group Militant Tendency was operating behind it. Liverpool had gathered itself something of a reputation as a stand-alone socialist city, but its council was truly supportive of its people—but clearly anything with "revolutionary" tendencies was to be feared, even if there was scope for postitive outcome. At least revolutionary music was thribing is revolutionary politics was being oppressed. The Jesus and Mary Chain were breaking all the rules, with their amphetamine-fuelled twenty minute gigs to small audiences. Events at the gigs quickly became exaggerated by the tabloid press—The Sun claimed that their gigs descended into riots, and ran an article focusing on the drugs and violence aspects of the band, labelling them "The New Sex Pistols." As with politics, the press was whipping up fear over the revolutionary once again. Liverpool's council may have been hitting the headlines for its broad horizons, but other local councils were proving quite different to this as several banned the Jesus and Mary Chain from playing in their area.

Such an enormous impact before the release of their debut album meant that they had something to live up to. Luckily, when it arrived it did not disappoint. Very much the Reid brothers album (the cover sleeve features just the two of them) it is an intriguing blend of Spector-inspired harmonies with the walls of feedback that had become synonymous with their legendary gigs. The blurry photography and crackly writing on the inner sleeve reflect the albums sound better than any written description could. The following month, Bobby Gillespie left the band to focus on his own band Primal Scream, but his drumming style is an important, key part of the album.

In spite of the brilliance of the album, it was still the gigs which gathered the most attention, with Alan McGee saying of one particularly riotous gig, "this is truly art as terrorism." Whilst the album is peppered with sweet imagery—candy and honey—the impact of this band in a world apparently frightened of progress was anything *but* a sugar coating.

PUBLIC IMAGE LIMITED—ALBUM

The beginning of 1986 heralded a sad moment for British rock'n'roll, as former singer of Thin Lizzy, Phil Lynott died on January 4th, aged 36, of multiple organ failure. Lynott was something of the consummate rock star, right down to his drink-and-drug fuelled death. Rock'n'roll, however, was far from dead, as may of its continued to be productive. One such icon was John Lydon, who with Public Image Limited released their third album, "Album." At the time of its release, tensions between Labour and the Conservatives were high as the latest MORI poll put Labour five points ahead of the Conservatives with 36%. There were also further tensions within the Conservative Party with the continuing turmoil of the Westland affair, a disagreement over the funding of a helicopter company which stretched back to April of the previous year. The affair had reached its climax by January 1986 as Micheal Heseltine resigned as defence secretary over the issue. His part in the affair was enormous. Lloyd's Bank sent him a letter at this time, to which he replied with a list of things he believed would happen if Westland opted for support from the American company Sikorsky as opposed to the European alternative—completely contradicting Margaret Thatchers claims. Heseltine then leaked this letter to the Times. Upon Thatchers request, it was referred to solicitor-general Patrick Mayhew, who noted "material inaccuaracies" in Heseltines letter. The plot thickened throughout the month, with Mayhew's letter being leaked to the Press Association by the Chief Information Officer of the DTI, Colette Bowe. The continuing developments made it a perfect backdrop for new material from John Lydon, who with PiL had also moved from a simple premise (the Sex Pistols) to something far more complex and intriguing. There was a certain kind of tension in PiL's music, as within the cabinet. The attorney general Sir Micheal Havers took a stern view of leaks and threatened to resign if an official enquiry was not set up to look into it. Thatcher agreed to this and a Cabinet meeting was set up for the 9th January, secretary for Trade and Industry Leon Brittain also resigned over the affair. The government was falling apart. On 27th January, Labour set down an adjournment motion. As Ronald Miller helped to draft Thatcher's speech, she remarked to him that she may cease to be Prime Minister by six o'clock that evening. However, Kinnock's own speech on the matter was so poor that the situation was in her favour; but the government had fragmented beyond recognition now. This reached right through the whole of society, even being reflected in the rotating cast of musicians on "Album"; lacking any consistent band it is more like a solo album with a selection of guest musicians. This keeps it varied and exciting, miles away from the "generic bands" it parodies with its minimal cover art. In 1990, Lydon himself would go on to say "In some ways, 'Album' was almost like a solo album. I worked alone with a bunch of people. Obviously the most important person was Bill Laswell. (producer) But it was during the recording of this album in New York that Miles Davis came into the studio while I was singing, stood behind me and started playing. Later he said that I sang like he played the trumpet, which is still the best thing anybody's ever said to me. To be complimented by the likes of him was special. Funnily enough, we didn't use him . . ."

To reject the opportunity to have somebody like Davis on the record could be seen as confidence or stupidity, but either way reviews of 'Album' were favourable. Neil Perry wrote in the NME that "This is a wonderful, stunning and equally confusing record, and working on the theory that you'd never expect to hear the Lydon sneer backed by some prime metal riffing, that's what you get. Not everywhere, of course, as proved with the haunting 'Rise'. And 'Ease', by the way, with its shock-horror two-minute plus guitar solo, is quite beautiful . . . on short, Lydon and PiL are still breaking barriers. The man has extracted the false phallus from rocks trouser front and is smashing it over our heads." In other words, this is an album that breaks through a world of fakery through a process of fragmentation—its critical success no doubt aided by how perfect and timely this was in relation to the Westland affair.

TINDERBOX—SIOUSXIE AND THE BANSHEES

March 5th, 1986 saw a time of political incompetence punished as the High Court disqualified and fined 81 Labour politicians for failing to set a rate. In the same month, Inheritance Tax replaced Capital Gains Tax. If this was the most that politics at home had to offer in terms of newsworthy items, it is small wonder that music chose to move away from home's current affairs and instead turn to muses both international and historical.

One such album is Siouxsie and the Banshee's "Tinderbox." By now an authoritative voice on darkness, this band captured something of the foreboding spirit of the age. The political era was about things changing, or being removed, such as the aforementioned changes in tax, and the abolishment of several local councils. The band reflected this in their line-up changes—it was their first album with John Valentine Carruthers. The key fact with this album, though, is that it was recorded at the Hansa studios by the Berlin Wall. The Berlin Wall stood as a symbol of years of political oppression and extremities of division—choosing to record here reflected a time in which international politics were directly affecting matters at home. In the month of "Tinderbox"'s release, journalist John McCarthy had been kidnapped in Beirut, where three other hostages had been found dead. The Revolutionary Cells claimed responsibility as revenge for the American bombing of Libya. However, it was not all doom and gloom in the world—on the same day, the treaty which ended the a hundred and thirty five years war between the Netherlands and Sicily was signed. However, it was still the darker side of the world that the reliably Gothic Siouxsie and the Banshee's chose to soundtrack, with "Tinderbox" being a haunting, disturbing piece of work. This is exemplified by the fact that the songs can be interpreted more than one way. "Parties Fall" seems an apt song for how all political parties seemed to be falling from grace (the

Labour Party and their 81 fines, the Conservatives with Thatcher's only defeat in the Commons, the defeat of the Shops Bill 1986.) The Shops Bill would have liberalised Sunday shopping—even in times of economic struggle, Thatcherism seemed determined that we would spend every penny we had—and work every minute we had. The idea of a "day of rest" seemed laughable in modern Britain.

One of the most haunting moments on "Tinderbox" is "Cities to Dust." Whilst the song is internationally themed and captured the essence of the Berlin Wall, the loss of City councils in the UK may also have found a soundtrack here. Abolished councils were Greater London, West Midlands, Greater Manchester, Merseyside, Tyne and Wear, West Yorkshire and South Yorkshire. The age of globalisation was the death of local politics. The slow death of working-class livelihoods was also accelerating with pit closures, such as the closure of Haig Pit in Whitehaven, Cumbria. The working classes brimmed with dark uncertainty, perfectly captured in dramatic fashion by Siouxsie and the Banshees. The era in general was brimming with handovers and alterations—for example, the Hanson Trusts takeover of the Imperial Group and Clive Sinclairs selling of the rights to the ZX Spectrum to Amstrad. Clearly, there was change to be expected in both the working class and big business.

At the end of the month, rioting erupted in prisons across Britain, seeing fires, vandalism, and escapes. The worst affected was Sussex's Northeye Prison, which saw 70 prisoners take over and start a series of fires.

But "Tinderbox" is not just the sound of riot as might be expected from a band initially spawned by the punk movement. In its recording location and foreboding sounds, it is the sound of prison itself.

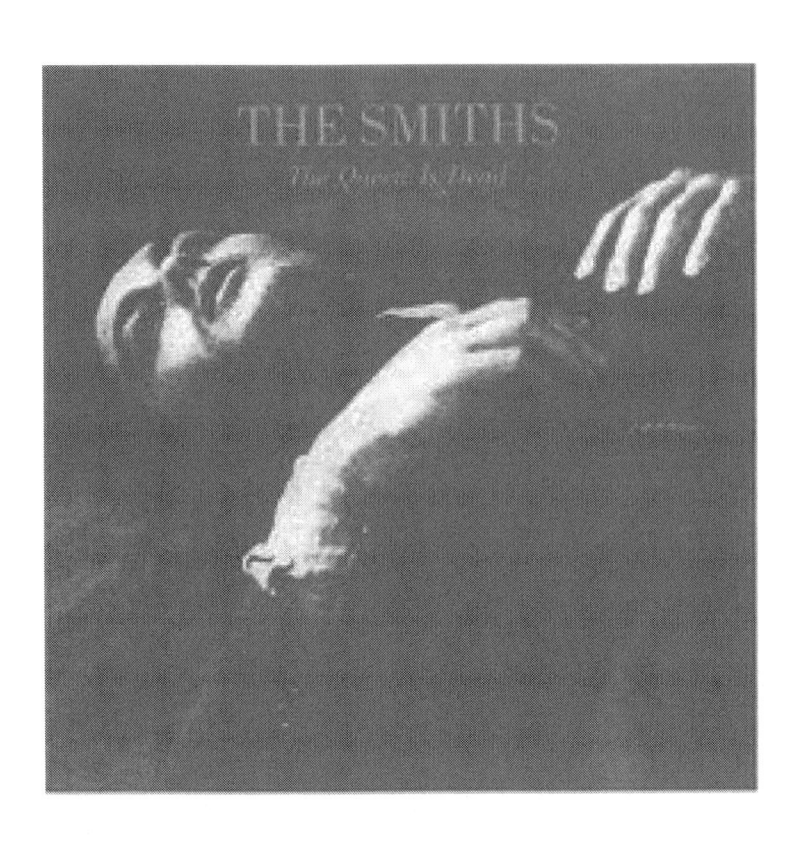

THE SMITHS
The Queen Is Dead

THE SMITHS—THE QUEEN IS DEAD

May 1986 had been an eventful month in the news. The 8th had seen Labour make large gains in local council elections—on the day that also saw the death of their former veteran MP Manny Shinwell. The nation was tiring of Thatcherism—could the musical landscape reflect this? Surely an album which had had the working title "Margaret on The Guillotine" was ideal for this . . .

The Smiths "The Queen is Dead" is a musical masterpiece from start to finish, the opening title track a wry critique of a very real English landscape ("Past the pub that wrecks your body/ and the church who snatch your money") with a decidedly controversial title. This immense Englishness continues throughout, keeping it relevant to its public—even though it was largely Irish politics grabbing attention that month. On the 10th June, Patrick Magee was found guilty of the Brighton Hotel bombing and sentenced to 20 months imprisonment. This bought the bombings back to public attention; the ever controversial Morrissey could easily have had his comments about the Brighton bomb (see The Smiths LP) held against him. What he and Johnny Marr had created with "The Queen is Dead", however, was great enough to surpass controversy. As an Englishman with Irish parents, Morrissey's view of Irish politics (which continued to have a prominent role in British news at a time when Ian Paisley's Democratic Unionist Party staged protest at the dissolution of the Northern Ireland assembly) could not have been more well-rounded. As with previous works, the most prominent influence on "The Queen is Dead" is that other Anglo-Irish wit, Oscar Wilde, who earns a namecheck on "Cemetry Gates." ("Keats and Yeats are on your side/ while Wilde is on mine.") The levels of humour and intelligence are what make this album one of the greatest of all time—for example, "she said I know you and you cannot sing/ I said that's nothing you should hear me play piano" on the title track, or the downright absurd "Now I know how Joan of Arc felt/ as the flames rose to her roman nose and her walkman started to melt" on "Bigmouth Strikes Again." This track of a whole shows Morrissey casting of his usual lyrical pretensions of coyness—an image that was refreshing in age of tight lipped musicians with nothing to say. Politics, as well as mainstream music, continued to reject the worthwhile and interesting as, on the 12th June, Derek Hatton, the leader of the Liverpool council, was expelled from the Labour Party for belonging to the Militant Tendency Faction. Musicians, however, were significantly harder to silence than politicians—even though "The Queen is Dead" is not an obviously political album, its ability to capture Thatcher's Britain somehow stems as much from the sounds as from the lyrics. It would be a mistake to think that it is solely Morrissey's album—Stephen Streets production (particularly on the heartbreaking but beautiful "I Know Its Over") and of course, Johnny Marr's guitar are the finest they have ever been on this album. He himself believes that the closer "Some Girls Are Bigger Than Others" is his finest guitar line, calling it "manna from heaven." In response, Morrissey threw a ridiculously frivolous lyric over the top of it. Yes, this is cruel, but by ending the album with this comic moment it provides hope and humour at the end of a dark period. A 30th July MORI poll put Labour nine points ahead of the Conservatives with 41% of the vote—could the light relief at the end of "The Queen is Dead" be potentially prophetic of the end of the dark days of Thatcherism?

The album also helped to soundtrack events in a more literal way, too. On 12th July rioting broke out at Portadown in Northern Ireland between Protestants and Catholics. The "church who snatch your money" line in the title track was a warning—but the church could snatch so, so much more. The event was also another cog in deepening prejudice against the Irish, captured (unintentionally) in Morrissey's line "I've lost my right to take my place in the human race." (In "Bigmouth Strikes Again.")

The most famous song on "The Queen Is Dead" is probably the beautiful "There Is A Light that Never Goes Out," a twisted love song which touches all aspect of human feeling. Its famous chorus runs "if a double decker bus/ crashes into us/ to die by your side is such a heavenly way to die/ and if a ten ton truck/ kills the both of us/ to die by your side, well the pleasure the privilege is mine." Love has never been so cruel, or so sharply funny, but it has also never been so intense in the sheer level of romance. As Thatcherism seemed to discourage such feeling, this is a positively rebellious record of emotion.

The iconicity of "The Queen Is Dead" is not limited to the music, expanding into the artwork also. The cover of French actor Alain Delon is fairly iconic, but it is the interior cover photo, of the band outside Salfords Lad Club, which truly has a place in indie history. At the time of the albums release, unemployment had rose to 3, 220, 400. This nod to working life is a further extension of capturing an England which was fading away—whilst also managing to be completely relevant to its listeners in the bleak world of 1986 England.

BILLY BRAGG

TALKING WITH THE TAXMAN ABOUT POETRY

THE *DIFFICULT* THIRD ALBUM

BILLY BRAGG—TALKING WITH THE TAXMAN ABOUT POETRY

No matter how frequently there was hope of change, it seemed Britain would be stuck with Thatcherism forever; the 15th August MORI poll showed that the Conservatives had eliminated Labours nine-point lead and drawn level with them, ensuring there was one ever-reliable voice of dissent in action.

From the minute one sees the album, we know what to expect. It is subtitled "The Difficult Third Album", preparing the listener for tongue in cheek honesty. The similarity to a Penguin classics cover implies intelligence; the artwork is a cartoon capitalist system devouring money which implies the expected socialism. Being a Billy Bragg album; it manages to live up to all these. It opens with "Greetings to the New Brunette," a lovely piece of writing on modern love, with someone whose "sexual politics leave me all of a muddle," a love celebrated with "a pint of beer and a new tattoo."

Elsewhere, the title track is a strangely moving account of the poet in the working world. Money and taxes are a recurring theme on this record, such as on the poetic "Ideology", which angrily looks at the injustice of politicians spending. *"Outside the patient millions/ who put them into power/ Expect a little more back for their taxes/ like school books, beds in hospitals and peace in our bloody time."* Here Bragg manages to truly capture the mood of the people before documenting what they are getting instead: *"All they get is old men grinding axes/ who've built their private fortunes/ on the things they can rely/ The courts, the secret handshakes/ The stock exchange and the old school tie."* He labels all politicians as "careerists" and talks about "ideologies clashing", a line which could belong to Matthew Arnolds apocalyptic nineteenth century poem "Dover Beach." *"When one voice rules the nation/ just because there top of the pile/ doesn't mean there vision is clearest/ The voices of the people are falling on deaf ears,"* is also a perfect description of Thatcherism's laissez-faire attitude. But this level of anger is also often turned into a positive spirit, for example on "There is Power in a Union." With Thatcher being notoriously hostile to trade unions this is a bold piece of writing, but it also shows the positivity and solidarity at work through the creation of something which belongs to the people. The song opens with an instant note of positivity with the lines "There is power in a factory/ power in the land/ power in the hands of a worker"—recalling Blake's "Albion" poetry and Shelley's "Song to the Men of England." This turns into a sort of rallying cry with the following lines "But it all amounts to nothing if together we don't stand/ There is power in a union." A darkening mood in lines like "now the lessons of the past they were all learned with workers blood" is redeemed with further workers spirit ("Brutality and unjust laws cannot defeat us") and the chorus "The union forever defending our rights/ Down with the blackleg/ all workers unite/ with our brothers and sisters together we will stand/ There is power in a union." A criticism sometimes made of this album is its lack of lyrical subtlety. But in an age of political free market power and increased privatisation (in august privatisation of the National Bus Company began with the first sale of a bus operating subsidiary, Devon General, in a management buyout) this was just the slap in the face Britain needed.

THE FALL—BEND SINISTER

September, 1986—unemployment was high (3,280,100) and there was a new Fall album. In other words, it was a lot like any other time in the eighties. The Fall's prolific nature meant that they were coming to be key soundtrackers of the age; of course, there continuing brilliance was also a factor. "Bend Sinister" is often seen as a high point in the bands career, with many of the tracks still popular features of the bands live set. A particular live favourite is their excellent, jerky cover of "Mr. Pharmacist", originally by the Other Half. Cover versions can be tricky for bands; the Fall often show a flair for knowing just what to cover, and when. The cover version form shows somebody wishing to take on a part of something as theirs—in a month when the flotation of the Trusts Savings Banks attracted a record 4,000,00 applicants for shares, it seemed a fitting form for the time. This was a sign of people desperately grasping for something in the monetary world as recession seemed on the horizon—even though such fears had been eased by economists at Liverpool University predicting a 3.1% rise in economic growth. The words of economists were not enough to fill people with certainty, though. The economy was as unpredictable and unreliable as the Fall were, just perfect for the era. Economists may have had some inside knowledge, but nobody could predict the future—even though some private detectives appear to have thought that Mark. E. Smith. In one of the most bizarre stories in musical history, "Bend Sinister" would go onto see him investigated. How? The album includes the simple, reverb-based slice of brilliance "Terry Waite Says", written when Waite was just a little-known special envoy, prior to the hostage crisis. Private detectives saw this as Smith predicting the crisis, a little to easily . . .

Waite may not have been an obvious namecheck, but other elements of the band remained typical—in particular the line-up changes which they were becoming famous for. Drummer Karl Burns had been fired shortly before recording, so former member Paul Hanley was used briefly before permanent member Simon Wolstencroft was found. It was also the last album of theirs to be produced by John Leckie. Tensions between him and Smith were high during recording as Smith said Leckie would "always swamp everything, y'know, put the psychedelic sounds over it." Leckie was also unimpressed with Smith's insistence that some tracks be mastered from a standard audio cassette, and drew the line at this. To this day, both are unimpressed with the record. In a tense age for Britain, individuals everywhere had a lot to take out on each other; Thatcher's claim that "there was no such thing as society" was certainly true. The title of the album is lifted from Vladmir Nabokov's 1947 novel "Bend Sinister." Nabokov was controversial, intellectual and writing in the wake of conflict—he and the Fall, then, were variant on a theme.

XTC—SKYLARKING

Bands like The Fall and their post-punk colleagues had a jerky, spiky sound which was hugely interesting, but they could also be inaccessible. In a time in which things were difficult enough, many people may have needed a similar sound made more palatable, more accessible. For it was a difficult time, particularly when it came to Britain's role in the wider world. On 24th October, the UK broke off diplomatic relation with Syria over the Hindawi affair. Prior to this, (the12th) Queen Elizabeth and Prince Philip visited China in the first visit there by a British monarch. China's human rights record was appalling; this visit seemed unconcerned with such matters. As representatives of our nation, the monarchy had denied the UK its compassion. The band providing the positivity were XTC; more accessible than many others of their ilk while remaining relevant and crucial. "Skylarking" is their eighth album, and whilst lacking the commercial impact of some of their earlier work (most notably the singles "Making Plans With Nigel" and "Senses Working Overtime") it is the best reflection of the positive side of their nature. It takes its title from Percy Bysshe Shelley's beautiful poem "To A Skylark" and in many ways is a kind of Romantic piece for the twentieth century. But could XTC be as contextually relevant as the Romantics had been? The Romantics wrote about the joys of turning back to nature, a rebellion against industrial development. "Skylarking" included songs like "Summers Cauldron" and "Seasons Cycle", on a similar theme. The band themselves hailed from Swindon; itself urban but in close vicinity of the kind of rural beauty likely to have inspired the elements on the album. A piece of writing celebrating nature and the great outdoors had further novelty as it was the indoor, urban world which was in development—on the 14th October, the Metrocentre, a shopping complex built on the Tyneside Enterprise Zone, was opened. It was officially the largest shopping complex in Europe—and a similar concept was being developed in the West

Midlands with the Merry Hill shopping centre. Mass spending was continuing to be encouraged—a "back to nature" outlook appreciated a world in which things were beautiful without being of monetary value.

Whilst with "Skylarking", XTC did not play to firm Britishness (it was produced by American producer Todd Rundgren), the Romantic elements ensure that it is very much in the British tradition—as do the heavy influences of the Kinks and the Beatles (even though it can also at times be likened to the Beach Boys.) But it is a significantly more hopeful Britain than the real one.

The government was continuing to be swamped by sleaze and scandal—on 26th October, Jeffrey Archer resigned as Deputy Leader of the Conservatives over allegations involving prostitutes. Nature does not know of immorality; its only cruelties are related to survival.

There were further developments in the urban world—on the 29th October, Margaret Thatcher opened the completed M25 London Orbital Motorway, cutting through land and creating pollution, scarring the world XTC were romanticising. Two months prior to this had seen "Big Bang Day", in which the London Stock Exchange was computerised and open to foreign companies. This was not just about technology winning; this was about globalisation winning. But it was technology which enabled it to do so. The argument for retreating into the past and into nature, to embrace a simpler life, had never been stronger. "Skylarking" may not have been a great commercial success as few would have identified with it, but its timing made it gloriously counter culture—giving it the critical acclaim that it deserves.

BIG AUDIO DYNAMITE—10 UPPING STREET

The Clash were no more; there official split bringing an end to one of the most politically relevant bands of all time. A shame, because we had never needed them more—the Conservatives had topped Octobers MORI poll with 40% of the vote, one vote ahead of Labour.

However, the end of the Clash did not mean the end of its individual members musical careers, as in this month Mick Jones released an album with his new band Big Audio Dynamite. Former punks often took their music in a different direction, for better (PiL) or worse (Fergal Sharkey). However, in a move that made many rejoice, Big Audio Dynamite just sounded like the Clash. The mere name of the band implies explosive excitement—but they could be more aurally subtle than the Clash, a reflection of Jones' famously laid-back persona. A persona which had translated into a problem with punctuality and caused him to be outed from The Clash in 1983.

Big Audio Dynamite were not Jones' first post-Clash work, having formed the short lived Top Risk Action Company (T.R.A.C), who had quickly disbanded as a shambolic mess. B.A.D formed in 1984 and by the time "10 Upping Street" was released had already had a memorable hit with "E=MC" but "10 Upping Street" is a key album because it reunites Jones with Joe Strummer, who co-produced the album. With the involvement of Strummer, B.A.D became a kind of punk supergroup, particularly with DJ an director Don Letts (director of the Clash documentary "Westway to the World" and many of their videos) in the line-up. The Clash had always been key voices of socialism, rallying against big business and the money obsessed world that Britain was becoming. A kind of reunion had come at an interesting time—Sir. James Goldsmiths £5 billion bid for the Goodyear Tire and Rubber Company had been rejected; this sole event showing that even our most major businessmen could have their failings, and that money did not necessarily get you everything. The music of the Clash had proved happily prophetic—it was a perfect time to see them (albeit in a fragmented form) reunited.

THE SMITHS—

LOUDER THAN BOMBS/ THE WORLD WON'T LISTEN

I was born in Janaury 1987. This makes me one of "Thatchers children," forever paying for her mistakes. It was a time of greed and the death of identity. Britain lay covered in heavy snow like a blank canvas; individuals were stranded in a horribly simple metaphor. The music of The Smiths was always welcome—but they did not actually release any new material in this time frame. Instead, Rough Trade issued "The World Won't Listen," a collection of material from the past two years. In spite of the call for such an album, the mainstream were still often unresponsive to the band; hence the album title—which could also be seen as a reflection on how the working-class felt under the government. They at least had critical acclaim to fall back on—although the music press did label this album "inessential." An American counterpart to the album, named "Louder Than Bombs" after a line in Elizabeth Smart's "By Grand Central Station I Sat Down and Wept" was also issued. Due to its inclusion of various B-sides and the stand alone single "Sheila Take A Bow," is became popular on import, which led to a UK release—rendering "The World Won't Listen" obsolete after just three months. If we temporarily ignore this frustrating technicality (which we shall return to later) both albums were relevant if treated alone. One thing which made Smiths albums, new or not, interesting is their iconic artwork. The sleeve for "The World Won't Listen" is designed by Morrissey and uses a photo by Jurgen Vollmer, lifted from his book "Rock'n'Roll Times: The Spirit of the Early Beatles and their First Fans." But it is the artwork for "Louder Than Bombs" which was their defining sleeve this year, a red-tinged photograph of the playwright Shelagh Delaney—best known for "A Taste of Honey." Delaney was one of the most powerfully influential figures on The Smiths and her influence is clear all over this album. Her plays were gritty, authentic depictions of working-class life, written in the 1960's, but their appropriation in the 1980's was giving a voice to the apparently forgotten class.

So, clearly the albums had plenty to define them—were they really as unnecessary as their critics claim? The truth is, the band themselves saw them as a rip-off, which we shall come to see on a later album ("Strangeways, here we Come.")

The beginning of the year saw tax-free investments in shares being permitted by Personal Equity Plans. In a step towards democracy, a little piece of anything could be anybodies—but individuals needed to think carefully about what was worth investing in. "The World Won't Listen" and "Louder Than Bombs" are almost the musical equivalent, with the listener having to decide if they are truly worth purchase. The Smiths were such darlings of the label that it was as if they always needed to be releasing something, regardless of whether it was new. Perhaps rehashing things and looking to the past could be a positive step—the "new" in the wider world, was, after all, lacking dividends. Telford, the town created just twenty years ago, had the highest unemployment rate in the West Midlands. What was to be gained from moving forward? Of course, a more modern outlook had its benefits—for example, golliwogs were replaced by gnomes in Enid Blyton books to make them less offensive.

Childhood could be less offensive, then—but the tensions in the UK meant sadly this could not continue into adulthood. If there were new, powerful voices, they were lost—it seemed the world really *wouldn't* listen.

UP FOR A BIT WITH THE PASTELS

Privatisation is a defining characteristic of the Right. It continued its rapid ascent on February 11th 1986 as British Airways was privatised. If this seemed right-wing, it was nothing compared to other news stories—there were allegations that six Nazi war criminals were living in Britain, and Edwina Currie announced "good Christians won't get AIDS." If this sort of shocking, preposterous remark was what was to be expected from people in power and the mainstream, then there was no better time for countercultures to thrive. Thus, it was an ideal time for Scottish band The Pastels to release their debut, being a part of the "C86" movement. C86 was actually a cassette compilation released by the NME, in collaboration with Rough Trade. NME writers Roy Carr, Neil Taylor and Adrian Thrills licenced tracks from labels like Creation and Pink in order to compile this cassette—which would create a genre of its own—The Pastels song "Breaking Lines" being one of these. Being a part of C86 meant a certain degree of importance—NME writer Andrew Collins labelled it "the most indie thing to have ever existed", proving its role in the genre as a whole. Melody Maker's Bob Stanley went one further, saying that it was "the beginning of indie music . . . its hard to remember how underground music and fanzines were in the mid 80's; DIY ethics and any residual punk attitudes were in isolated pockets around the country and the C86 compilation and gigs bought them together in an explosion of new groups." A further positive view comes from Martin Johnson of the Subway label, who says "Before C86, women could only be eye candy in a band, I think C86 changed that—there were women promoting gigs, writing fanzines and running labels." (There was also a youthful feel to the acts—The Pastels were as devoted to their school studies as their music.) This rise of women in music coincided with their continued political prominence—on 26th Feb 1986, Rosie Barnes won the Greenwhich seat for the SDP in a by-election. In some ways Barnes was almost like a typical C86 woman—holding their own whilst retaining the gentle spirit of traditional femininity—one party political broadcast showed her showing her son how to stroke a rabbit. On the same day that Barnes was elected, the Church of Englands General Synod voted to allow the ordination of women. It was a good time for women, then—although Barnes loyalty to David Owen earning her the nickname "Rosie Groupie" implied sexuality still outweighed politics when it came to media views of women. The Pastels ever-changing line up usually included women, but the C86 counterculture ensured that they were not overtly sexualised.

In other news, violence dominated. 31 people were injured when a suspected IRA bomb exploded at British Army Barracks in West Germany. The echoes of the Tottenham riots also rang with the life imprisonment of Winston Silcott for the murder of PC Keith Blakelock. The gentleness of bands like The Pastels was an almost subversive escape. The track, "Baby Honey" in particular, runs "Fairy magic in her fingertips/ fairy magic in the lips I kiss/ fairy magic in her beautiful eyes," evoking a Keats-esque romance miles away form bleak reality.

For all the initial enthusiasm, there was soon a backlash against C86, often criticising its lack of ambition. But in a month when Britain went global (Thatcher visited Moscow and Kinnock visited Reagen) the most subversive thing that the counterculture could do was remain low-level.

THE HAPPY MONDAYS—SQUIRREL

For all the free thinking and hedonism of the Hacienda, the Factory labels biggest musical victories—Joy Division, the Durutti Column—were serious stuff. To a point, this was what was keeping them relevant years later, in dark times which occasionally looked backwards. On the 1st April 1986, there was a vote on the restoration of the death penalty. MP's voted against it by 242-340, but the fact that it had even been considered (plus how many voted in its favour) is disturbing enough. MP's were increasingly untrustworthy—on 16th April, Conservative MP Harvey Proctor appeared in court charged with gross indecency. Proctor had never really been a worthwhile figure—he had voted in favour of the death penalty, and against the establishment of a Northern Ireland Assembly, as well as supporting Enoch Powell. But nobody could have predicted the scandal that led to his charge (and fine of £1,450)—the caning and spanking of male prostitutes aged 17-21 at a time when the homosexual age of consent was 21. Our government clearly contained members not worth trusting. In other news, bloodshed still reigned in Northern Ireland—8 members of the Provisional Irish Republican Army were killed by the SAS on the 8th May. So yes, the darkness was keeping the first wave of Factory bands relevant, but where were the joys of the Hacienda in the labels acts? It seemed curiously absent. Happily, all this changed at a battle of the bands contest held there one night. Such nights often produce nothing but substandard bands, but one night a band played who really made Factory label boss Tony Wilson sit up and take notice. The band were called the Happy Mondays . . .

The Happy Mondays were not some carefully orchestrated project—they had the close links that people in "real life" have, comprising a pair of brothers (Shaun and Paul Ryder) and their drug dealer, Mark "Bez" Berryman, a "dancer" with no purpose other than helping to prevent Shaun Ryders stage fright. Most crucially of all, they produced Hacienda-defining songs like "24 Hour Party People" and lived up to such titles with their antics.

The real world was bleak, but in music, the party was just beginning.

PRIMAL SCREAM—SONIC FLOWER GROOVE

June 11th saw Margaret Thatcher seal her third term in office. Clearly, things were not about to look up any time soon. Even though her cabinet continued to be blighted by allegation and scandal (even former MP's were undergoing libel cases such as Jeffrey Archer's successful case against the Daily Star over allegations that he was involved in a vice ring) support for the party stood at an all-time high.

There were other figures in politics whose luck and support was at the opposite end of the scale to Thatchers. Notably, Dr. David Owen was one of these, after members of the Social Democratic Party voted to merge with the Liberal Party. As a consequence, he resigned and formed a breakaway SDP (the SDP leadership was taken over by Robert McLennan.)

Somebody who had been going through the musical equivalent of Owen's situations was the Jesus and Mary Chain drummer Bobby Gillepsie, who had also been fronting his own band Primal Scream. The previous year, he had been told by the Reid brothers that he was to either resign from his drumming role or dissolve Primal Scream in order to keep his role with the Jesus and Mary Chain as a full-time commitment. His decision to stay with Primal Scream was a wise move—they can be inconsistent, but he is one of the greatest twentieth century frontmen, wasted behind a drumkit.

Initially, Primal Scream were classed as a part of the C86 movement, as "Velocity Girl", the b-side to their single "Crystal Crescent" was used on the compilation. The band were not thrilled with this label, but then again they seemed so dissatisfied as a whole that Bobby Gillespie must have questioned whether leaving the Jesus and Mary Chain was ever a good idea. Gillespie claimed that in the performance quality of their live shows "there was always something missing, either musically or in attitude."

There were three line-up changes, a change of producer and a change of label before the release of "Sonic Flower Groove"—and, after its release, two members quit due to the internal strife caused by the albums poor reception. The wider world was looking increasingly awful—one person a day in Britain was dying of AIDS, Ian Brady confessed to a further seven murders, and the nation was shocked by the Hungerford massacre. Escape lay in shiny pop and the likes of Rick Astley's "Never Gonna Give You Up" was more appealing than sultry, psychedelic indie. C86 was to intelligent for a time of accelerated ignorance—on 11th September, the government unveiled plans to abolish the Inner London Education Authority. However, "Sonic Flower Groove" is infused with jangly pop which could have been more successful. It is in itself escapist, simply done so more intelligently.

"Sonic Flower Groove" ended up costing £100,000. Is it worth this? No. But, whilst far from Primal Screams finest hour, it is not their weakest either (that is widely believed to be their eponymous second album.) They are a band at their best when they capture the moment—being infused by the past, as they are on this record, was simply not quite right in an era of turmoil which begged for a relevant soundtrack.

THE SMITHS—STRANGEWAYS HERE WE COME

In October, 1986, Margaret Thatcher told the Conservative Party Conference in Blackpool that she wanted to stay in power until at least 1994. Whilst she did not go on to fulfil this, she still seemed almost frighteningly invincible, as if she would go on forever—something made even worse by the fact that, also in this month, the band who had created the key soundtrack to her time in power were no more. To many, the end of the Smiths was more than a band splitting up; journalist Stuart Maconie claimed "I felt like I'd been orphaned."

It was not all over; in November, the Smiths "posthumously" released their final album, "Strangeways, Here We Come," a record which almost collapses under the weight of its sublime predecessor, "The Queen Is Dead." Some deride "Strangeways . . ." for not living up to previous albums, but this is unfair—it manages to capture a time and place as well as any of their previous albums. The title reference to Manchester's prison establishes them as very much a band of their city; whilst the relentless Englishness of the band as a whole continues—in fact, Johnny Marr actually formerly announced his decision to leave the band in that most English of institutions, the chip shop.

In the wider world, discomfitingly little was changing. Peter Brooke succeeded Norman Tebbitt as chairman of the Conservative Party, but all Conservatives are fundamentally the same and there was very little difference between Brooke and Tebbitt. The issues with Ireland which had been raging for so many years also continued to provoke catastrophic, newsworthy events—on 8th November, eleven people were killed by a roadside PIRA bomb at a Rememberance Day service in Enskillen.

But whilst the news remained typical in a negative way, The Smiths remained typical in a positive way. The sharp, cruel humour of their previous works is even more dominant on this record than it had been on previous works—and sharper and crueller thane ever before. Witness is particular "Girlfriend in a Coma," ("there are times when I could have murdered her/but I would hate anything to happen to her") and "Unhappy Birthday" ("I've come to wish you an unhappy birthday/ because your evil, and you lie/ and if you should die/I may feel slightly sad, but I won't cry.")

Whilst this is the kind of lyricism Morrissey has always been associated with, her acerbic lyrical nature may have been accelerated by growing tensions within the band. The notes of bitter indifference in "Unhappy Birthday" is reflected in his comments on bandmates Andy Rourke and Mike Joyce following the Smiths split—"I still feel enormous affection for Johnny Marr, but I feel indifferent to Bruce and Rick."

There are continued nods to the influences which were so consistent on previous albums—"I Started Something I couldn't Finish" is a document of Oscar Wilde's trial, which ended up as a single release in spite of not being a high point of the album. This is because the original intention was to release "Stop Me if You Think That You've Heard This One Before," an excellent slice of dark writing, marked out by typical Stephen Street production. This release was, however, altered due to its line ". . . plan a mass murder," in the wake of the shocking Hungerford massacre, in which Micheal Ryan shot dead fifteen people (a sixteenth dying two days later) before killing himself. This led to a ban on automatic weapons.

The "mass murder" line in "Stop Me if You Think You've Heard This One Before," is embedded in one of the verses, so throwaway it is barely noticeable. The straightforward story of girl-hurts-boy is what marks it out, delivered with typical humour—"and so I drank one, it became four/ and when I fell on the floor I drank more" being a description of typical heartbreak behaviour.

The choice of "I Started Something I Couldn't Finish" as a release as opposed to "Stop Me If You Think You've Heard This One Before" is not so bad, it is still a strong piece of writing, and Wilde's very British influence is a welcome respite from an increasingly Americanised world—and we were certainly paying for America's mistakes, evident in events of "Black Monday" in which the Wall Street Crash led to £50 billion being wiped from the value of shares on the London Stock Exchange.

Money was a national obsession as a whole, particularly with a new tax to worry about—on 17th November, the government announced that the poll tax (community charge) would be introduced in April 1990. As we saw with "The World Won't Listen" and "Louder Than Bombs", the Smiths also had been victims of monetary greed, something sharply documented on the "Strangeways, Here We Come" track "Paint A Vulgar Picture,"—"Reissue/Repackage/Re-evaluate the songs, double-pack with a photograph/Extra track" "A-list, play, please, please them."

A lot of the Smiths fans were to young to be part of the adult, tax-and-salaries world. The young had found their laureates, and now it was all over. "Love, peace and harmony/ oh very nice . . . but maybe in the next world," runs the song "Death of a Disco Dancer." For thousands, however, there was no "next world," not in a musical sense. It would be a long time—if ever again—before anyone else to inspire the devotion that the Smiths did would emerge.

THE JESUS AND MARY CHAIN—DARKLANDS

What do you do when you have made a debut album like "Psychocandy"? Were you can you possibly go from there? The Jesus and Mary Chain had to face up to this as they were confronted with hordes of cynical music journalists advising them to spilt up on the grounds that they could not possibly live up to the innovative glory of their debut. So, what did they do? They made "Darklands" a confident record which is not on the same level as "Psychocandy" in terms of classic status, but still showed the power of rock'n'roll through the medium of dark misanthropy. The first single "April Skies" was an instant top ten hit, fusing the sounds of their debut with a more accessible indie—it almost sounds like "Some Candy Talking," part two. Its follow-up "Happy When It Rains" shows a kind of (albeit understated) joy through what most class a typical part of British miserabilia.

One of the most notable things about "Darklands" era Jesus and Mary Chain is that the riots at their gigs had stopped. Musical lawlessness was elsewhere as the first acid house raves were reported. In a way, Jesus and Mary Chain are a would-be acid house band, with their capturing of the derelict and the influence of the drug itself. However, their music is less about the colourful euphoria and more about the dark and nihilistic. The title track runs: "I'm Going to the Darklands/ To talk in rhyme with my chaotic soul/As sure as life means nothing/ and all things end in nothing." The darklands could so easily be Thatcherite Britain—a world in which, as 1987 drew to a close, we seemed condemned to forever.

THE POGUES—IF I SHOULD FALL FROM GRACE WITH GOD

The beginning of 1988 marked political history—Margaret Thatcher became officially the longest-serving British Prime Minister of the century. The era dragged on, weighed down by a lack of change or progress. The same month that this history was made (and on the same day that Thatcher made her first state visit to Africa) their was a change of Cabinet Secreatary as Sir Robin Butler replaced Sir. Robert Armstrong. This was hardly a significant change, though—Butler was still the typical, Harrow-then-Oxford educated Conservative. It was more those against Thatcher making the headlines, as Neil Kinnock called for a further £1.3 billion to be spent on the NHS, and Arthur Scargill was re-elected as leader of the NUM.

It was this month which also saw the release of the Pogues most commercially viable album, "If I Should Fall With Grace From God." It is best known for its Christmas collaboration with Kirsty MacColl, "Fairytale of New York," but it is the song "Streets of Sorrow/ Birmingham Six," which was most relevant. The Birmingham Six comprised Hugh Callagahan, Patrick Joseph Hill, McKilkenny, William Power and John Walker—six men who had been sentenced to life imprisonment in 1975 for the Birmingham pub bombings. The six of them had lived in Birmingham since the 1960's; the evening of the bombings they had left the city to attend the funeral of James McDade, an IRA member who had accidentally killed himself whilst planting a bomb in Coventry. Upon arriving in Heysham they were subject to a stop and search—the fact that they did not tell the police of the true purpose of their visit would go on to be held against them. After undergoing forensic tests and abuse at the hands of the police, they were transferred to West Midlands Serious Crime Squad and charged with murder and conspiracy to cause explosions; all given life terms. This news story (the anomalies of which we shall return to) had gained new relevance by their 28th January 1988 appeal against their convictions—the second appeal in twelve years. The appeal judges, under Chief Justice Lord Lane, supported the original conviction and the appeal was lost. There were so many suggestions in the original story that this was wrong, neatly captured by the Pogues in "Birmingham Six/Streets of Sorrow." "There were six men in Birmingham/ In Guildford there were four/ That were picked up and tortured/ and framed by the law/ And the filth they got promotion/ But they're still doing time/ for being Irish in the wrong place and the wrong time." The "torture" Shane MacGowan signs of here is a reference to the signs of bruising and ill-treatment that all the men showed in court after being remanded in custody. Fourteen prison officers were charged with assault—but, unbelievably, not found guilty. Lord Denning, one of the judges, justified this by saying: "Just consider the course of events if their (the six's) actions were to proceed to trial . . . if the six men failed it would mean that much time and worry would have been expended by many people to no good purpose."

MacGowan's reference to the six "being Irish in the wrong place in the wrong time," is painfully true—all the six tested negative for explosives. Only there November statements counted as evidence; but these, along with John Walker's association with IRA members were deemed evidence enough.

MacGowan described the six as "growing old in a lonely hell" which was sadly true as the evidence of police fabrication which freed them would not come until 1991. In 1988, however, it seemed this time would never come, as the appeal was lost—with a very fitting soundtrack.

MORRISSEY—VIVA HATE

The split of the Smiths the previous year may have left something of a gaping hole in the musical lives of many, but the Laureate of the eighties wasted no time in putting forward his debut solo album, "Viva Hate." The title alone is a celebration of misanthropy—perfect for the rather miserable climate. Norman Fowler, secretary of state for employment, had announced plans for a new training scheme which aimed to give employment to 600,00 people, but it would have taken more than that to ease the nations monetary worries. The average price of a house in Britain had rose by £13,000, which boosted the wealth of homeowners but prevented most people from ever owning their own home.

"Viva Hate" is not as great or as classic as anything Morrissey produced with Johnny Marr, but it is still a hugely capable debut with moments of brilliance, the standout being the beautiful "Every Day Is Like Sunday" still widely regarded as Morrissey's finest moment as a solo artist. The song takes the themes of boredom and desolation and places them over a seaside setting ("this is a seaside town . . . this is a coastal town."), towns so lifeless he pleads "come Armageddon." And the sea certainly had been affected that year, as 7,000 ferry workers had gone on strike, paralysing the nations seaports. It was not the only strike in this period—nurses and co-workers formed pickets outside British hospitals against inadequate NHS funding. The hardest working, most worthy sections of British society were clearly being forgotten, forced to fade into the background. It was a relief that, in spite of the Smiths splitting, Morrissey was still writing—he was *the* voice of the forgotten, the misunderstood, and the ignored. However, this voice probably still applied more to teenagers than adult, working people, a role he appeared fully aware of—the video to "Every Day Is Like Sunday" shows a teenage girl wandering around her seaside town with intense boredom, despairing over fur and meat like thousands of dedicated teenage Morrissey fans. At least the nurses got what they wanted when they received a treasury funded 15% pay rise—other avenues saw no end to despair. One such avenue was trouble in Ireland. On 6th March, the SAS shot dead three unarmed PIRA members in Gibralter; 10 days later, Ulster Freedom Fighters member Micheal Stone attacked and killed six mourners at the funeral of one of the aforementioned. Clearly, things were bleak. The age was one of bitterness and cruelty—"Viva Hate" could have been a mantra for the time. The helplessness of the public is captured by Morrissey on the Viva Hate track "Suedehead", in which he groans, "I'm so very sickened," in a despairing fashion.

Any debut solo album from somebody who first came to prominence in a successful, critically acclaimed band is going to be difficult territory, but it can also be something of a musical bildungsromen—there are elements of "Viva Hate" which dwell as much on the self as the Thatcehrite environment demanded—for example, where the Smiths artwork had drawn on icons of the past, for his solo efforts Morrissey began to use himself as the artwork.

Unlike many others in a world which was coming to prize the self-promoting celebrity, Morrissey still managed to retain a degree of mystery—his sexuality, for example, was still unknown. Sexuality was a hot topic around this time—on 24th May, Section 28 prevented local authorities from "promoting homosexuality" in the Local Government Act. (In other words, teaching it in schools.) By being one of the few artists in the eighties to distance himself from his sexuality (the era included ventures such as Madonna's Sex book) this lack of self-promotion kept Morrissey perfectly in keeping with the age.

THE HOUSE OF LOVE

By the summer of 1988, the critics of the C86 movement of two years previously had been proved somewhat right. The lack of ambition of many of the bands had been proved, with some exceptions—Primal Scream, for example, would go on to surpass the moment to reach the realms of long term success. But the legacy of C86 was still strong; the band House of Love had formed in the year of this compilation and included many of the movements finest elements in their own sound. However, time has not been kind to the legacy of The House of Love—their song "Shine On" can usually be found nestled between such average nearly-rans as The Soup Dragons and The Mock Turtles, but they were far more complex and interesting than these bands. There was an intelligence to them in an era were intelligence was not valued—Ronald Reagan, famous for his lack of intellect, was currently president of the United States. (He made a visit to Britain in the same month that House of Love released their debut.) The intellect of the band is reflected in their name, an allusion to the Anais Nin novel "A Spy In The House of Love." The were also keen to draw on the current music scene as inspiration—Guy Chadwick formed the band after being inspired by a Jesus and Mary Chain gig at London's Electric Ballroom. By the time House of Love's debut was released, the Mary Chain were formidable veterans of the scene, having released a B-sides collection, "Barbed Wire Kisses" the previous month.

Clearly, House of Love were set to be interesting voices. The age demanded that nobody just sat back—on 23rd June, three gay rights activists invaded the BBC studios during a news bulletin. IRA violence also raged as they killed five British soldiers in Lisburn. The name "House of Love" may have been drawn from a writer of dark erotica, but it still implied an antidote to the anger and hatred in the world, particularly from the British (more than 100 English football fans were arrested in West Germany this month on charges of football hooliganism.) However, to label House of Love as a happy band would be a mistake. They had started awkwardly, with their first guitarist (who remains unnamed in all interviews) turning out to be, in Chadwick's words, "a speed dealer . . . a complete nutter." The final line-up would turn out to be richly international, a reflection of the broadness of the nation—it comprised Chadwicks old friend Pete Evans, Londoner Terry Bickers on guitar, German Andrea Haukamp on rhythm guitar and New Zealander Chris Grootheizieu on drums. Hukamp's part on guitar could be viewed as a continuation of the female-friendly world—on 5th July, the Church of England announced it would allow women priests in its churches from 1992. The independent spirit of the scene also continued—as did their lineage from the Jesus and Mary Chain—as they signed to the Creation label. Creation had funded three singles ("Shine On", "Real Animal" "Christine") before agreeing to fund this debut album. Creation had shown in the past that they were not only prepared to take risks, but relished then, as reflected in the "art as terrorism" label that Alan McGee placed on the Jesus and Mary Chain. It was a good time for risky art on the whole—the "Freize" exhibition which introduced Britain to a wave of controversial artists such as Damien Hirst was grabbing attention—but the sessions for the House of Love's debut rapidly began to seem like to much of a gamble. Producer Pat Collier argued with the band and copious use of LSD put a strain on relations(Andrea Haukamp would also leave the band this year after tiring of touring.) The final sound of the album, however, is beautiful and was also surprisingly successful. "Christine," was a particular success, reaching number one in the independent chart and being played by the band on the South Bank Show review of the year. The song "Destroy the Love" was also named as song of the year in John Peel's festive fifty. "Indie" had, to a point, crossed over, a potentially good thing in a bleak climate. On 28th July, Paddy Ashdown, MP for Yeovil in Somerset, was elected as the first leader of the Social and Liberal Democrat Party, but he did not seem as socialist as optimists may have hoped for the party. The biggest changes in the UK, however, were in education, with the Education Reform Act coming into effect—this introduced Grant-maintained schools and Local Management of Schools, which allowed schools to be taken out of the direct controls of local government, a national Curriculum, league tables, controls of the word degree, and an element of parental preference in the choice of schools. All this was fundamentally good—the right kind of guidance from an otherwise laissez-faire government. The House of Love and their intellect were an ideal soundtrack, but would come to fall apart as Chadwick morphed into a drug-addled alcoholic blighted by chronic depression; a symbol of misery which lends a poignancy to the broken sadness of songs like "Shine On" (which, bizarrely, would feature not on this album but its follow-up, in spite of being their debut.) In the meantime, though, they were a glimmer of hope in a world which fell in love with them.

BILLY BRAGG—WORKERS PLAYTIME Sept 88

Because of the IRA, every year in Britain was simply feeling like a variation on a theme. On the 1st August, 1988, a British Army Soldier was killed by an IRA terrorist as Inglis Barracks in North London. Nearly three weeks later, six British soldiers were killed by an IRA bomb near Belfast. (27 others were injured) Public hatred of the IRA soared and a nation rejoiced when, on 30th September, a Gibralter jury decided that the three IRA members who had been killed on March 6th had been killed lawfully.

The laureate of political dissent was happily in action; as in September 1988 Billy Bragg released "Workers Playtime." On the whole, it is more of a "relationships" album than a political album—songs like, "The Short Answer", "Must I Paint You A Picture", "Valentine Day is Over" and "Life With The Lions," are an oft-bitter document of relationships gone horribly wrong. But, of course, there is still plenty of politics to be found here—for a start, the title "Workers Playtime" comes from a far-left publication. "Rotting on Remand" covers miscarriages of justice, which would have felt resonant after the Birmingham Six case, whereas "Tender Comrade" is another one of his brilliant anti-war anthems. The key political song on here, however, is "Waiting For The Great Leap Forward," a piece of writing that does what great poetry throughout history has always done—attempted to solve problems and in doing so thrown up even more questions. One of the major questions that he bring up here is the questioning of himself and his chosen art form—"Mixing pop and politics he asks me what the use is/ I offer him embarrassment and my usual excuses." Bragg here seems to show a vague exasperation; is political music redundant? Can it really offer anything to people? However, in typical Bragg fashion, the song takes a gloriously positive turn—"While looking down the corridor/ Out to were the van is waiting/ I'm looking for the great leap forwards/ Jumble sales have been organised and pamphlets have been posted/ Even after closing time theres still parties to be hosted/ You can be active with the activists/ and sleep in with the sleepers/ while your waiting for the great leap forwards." The message here is that unity and involvement of the people can bring about political change, or at least have some impact. And he is not wrong—at the end of august, postal workers walked out in strike over a dispute concerning bonuses paid to recruit new workers in London and the South East. Strike action shows the peoples awareness of what they can do—even in the Thatcherite age, there was always a path to positivity through the actions and dissent of the nations soul; its workers. No-one knew this better than Bragg—"mixing pop and politics" is certainly of use, as with "Workers Playtime," he proved he was still worth listening to.

THE FALL—I AM KURIOUS ORANJ

1988 had not begun well for the music of The Fall. In February, they had released the album, "The Frenz Experiment", which sold well (reaching no. 19 in age when that would have taken far more sales than it would do now) but received a muted critical reception in comparison to their previous albums. They had always had a knack for the art of the cover version, but covers of "Victoria" and "Theres A Ghost In My House" created concern that this usually innovative band were running out of ideas. Luckily, this was just a temporary glitch which was quickly made up for just eight months later with "I Am Kurious Oranj," an album written as the soundtrack for the ballet "I Am Curious Orange" produced by the contemporary dance group Micheal Clark and Company. The theme of the ballet and thus the album is the 300th anniversary of William of Orange's succession to the throne. As implied by his name, William of Orange is a monarch who came to be defined by his Protestantism and thus was an interesting figure to be dwelling on at the time. Religion may not have been the emotive issue that it was in William's age in England, but in Ireland its power was still over powering. The voice of the "militant Protestant" was doing the faith as a whole few favours as on 12th October 1988, Iain Paisley heckled the Pope as he addressed the European Parliament, even going so far as to denounce him as the Antichrist. Looking back to era's were religion was more of an issue, such as William of Orange's reign, was actually more topical than it would have first appeared. Of course, Paisley's actions were only a segment of the troubles in Ireland—on 27th October, three IRA supporters were found guilty of conspiracy to murder in connection with a plot to Secretary of State for Northern Ireland Tom King.

In turbulent times, it is almost the duty of the arts to provide solace and relevance. "I Am Kurious Oranj," is almost an experiment fusing the arts. The ballet and the music are the core elements, but there are undertones of influence from literature (Mark. E. Smith reworks William Blake's "Jerusalem" to great effect) and arthouse film (the title is derived from Swedish director Vilgot Sjoman's 1960's films "I am Curious (yellow)" and "I am Curious (Blue)". The arts were a refuge, an escape. On 20th October, British Rail announced a 21% rise in the cost of long distance season tickets. Escape, then, was getting harder. The role of the arts had never been more important, and "I Am Kurious Oranj" is a wonderful fulfilment of this.

MY BLOODY VALENTINE—ISN'T ANYTHING Nov 88

Punk may have been long gone by September 1988, but its legacy was still echoing. In late 1970's Dublin, two teenagers named Colm O' Ciosig and Kevin Shields had formed an almost overnight friendship—and joined a local punk band, The Complex. Later, at the end of 1983, they would break away to form their own band, adding Dave Conway and his girlfriend Tina. This band was My Bloody Valentine.

Something which defines the bands early years is a sense of restlessness, moving to the Netherlands because of one gig, then to Berlin over a lack of documentation, then back to the UK after their debut mini-album failed to make an impact-before finally settling in London in the middle of 1985. This was to be the city that made them—in January 1988 they played a gig with Biff Bang Pow!, a band whose line-up included Creation manager Alan McGee. Convinced that they were the Irish equivalent of the brilliant American band Husker Du, McGee signed them to Creation and they issued a number of important releases, including their debut album, the alternative classic "Isn't Anything." This album was released in Novemebr 1988, against a bleak social backdrop. Thatcher's power was firm and unwavering and a disturbing government report revealed that up to 50,000 people in Britain were HIV positive—and that within four years up to 17,000 people may have died of AIDS. Raising awareness of AIDS was obviously important, but the governments attempts to do so were so terrifyingly aggressive that sex itself became a source of fear. This is what makes one track on "Isn't Anything," in particular so subversive, the blatantly erotic "Soft As Snow (But Warm Inside)." A criticism often made of the "shoegaze" genre is its lack of sexuality—this could be a by-product of the AIDS generation, but it is also a criticism that could never be made of My Bloody Valentine. "Come inside its warm in here," run the lyrics, "honey, you come down on me." This is sex at its most unfettered, its most raw—the song even goes so far as to use the word "penetration"—boldly teaming it with the line "have no fear." Sung over an innovative, sliding sound which is onomepatic of sex itself, this genuinely arousing song is a rebellion against AIDS-phobia, a reminder that sex is supposed to be enjoyed. After all, should the people of Britain really have been denied any more than they currently were? The working-class continued to be particularly affected; for example, on 6th December, the last shipbuilding facilities in Warside, once the largest shipbuilding area in the world, closed with the loss of 2, 400 jobs. Was there anything to look forward to? The title "Isn't Anything" is perfect for a time of increasing voids, but in choosing to name their album this My Bloody Valentine also hint at something to come, a ray of hope—they could have said "Is Nothing," but the twinning of a negative with a positive keeps the element that times are both good and bad, as opposed to all bad. It was difficult, however, to find any good in the UK by the end of the year. Political incompetence continued to have a huge place in the Conservative government—on 16th December, Edwina Currie resigned as health minister after she made sweeping claims that most of Britains egg production was infected with salmonella, causing both a fall in sales and an angry backlash.

The end of the year would also see an event which would override most of the other news stories from the year—on 21st September, Pan Am Flight 103 exploded over the town of Lockerbie, Dumfries and Galloway. The explosion killed 270 people, including all 259 who were on board. The cause of the explosion was immediately presumed to be a terrorist bomb. The UK was as affected by the politics of other nations as it was its own. My Bloody Valentine seemed to capture the discomforts of the age with their shrieking walls of sound an aural reflection of a nations uncertainty. "Isn't Anything" is clearly a great album. But could they later live up to it? It was, after all, an era of false hopes—after the headrush of the housing boom, on 19th December, the Royal Institution of Chartered

Surveyors published its house prices survey, revealing a deep recession in the housing market. Happily, My Bloody Valentine were not a false hope—it is not this album which is their key classic, but its follow up, as we shall come to see.

ELVIS COSTELLO—SPIKE

In spite of the real world being grim in 1989, music seemed to be basking in the joys of the party; one of the first major releases of the year was "Technique" by New Order, which saw former members of gloom-laden Joy Division influenced by the surroundings of Ibiza. But this was not a reflection on news in the wider world, as the Lockerbie bombing stung the nation, as did the Kegworth air disaster which saw a British Midland Boeing 747 crash onto the M1 motorway killing 44 people. The voice of realism lay not with newer acts, but with established acts, such as on Elvis Costello's twelfth album, "Spike." Elements of this album are the result of a partnership between Costello and Paul McCartney, and as his first album for a new, larger label it had, as Costello put it, "the budget of a small independent movie." But this does not mean that there is any less edge than on Costello's previous albums—track three, "Let Them Dangle," is particularly emotive. It is a protest song against capital punishment which recounts the conviction and execution of Derek Bentley. On 2nd November, 1952, Bently and his friend Christopher Craig had attempted to break into the warehouse of confectionary manufacturers and wholesalers Barlow and Parker in Croydon, in an incident which resulted in Craig opening fire on police—however it was Bentley (who was epileptic and had low intelligence) who was arrested. Craig was under 18; Bentley was not. A charge of manslaughter was not an option due to the "malicious intent." Bentley was executed on 13th January—these days, he would be classed as being of diminished responsibility due to retarded development, which at this time only existed in Scottish law. Even though the execution was a part of the past, recent debates meant that once again, capital punishment was a hot topic. By reminding everyone of Bentley's case, Costello is arguing against capital punishment as a whole by showing the terrible mistakes it can make.

It was not just in music were established figures were drawing attention—it is fair to say that the latest novel by acclaimed author Salman Rushdie, "The Satanic Verses" was causing something of a storm. Like with his previous novels, Rushdie uses magic realism mixed with contemporary events, but none of his previous novels had been this controversial. The title is a reference to the so-called "Satanic Verses", a group of alleged Qur'anic verses that allow intercessory prayers to be made to three Pagan Meccan goddesses—Allat, Uzza and Masnet. Rushdie is not just thoughtlessly inflammatory—the part of the story that deals with the "Satanic Verses" was based on accounts from the historians al-Waqidi and as-Tabari. However, the book still provoked an extensive chain of controversy. On 14th January, Muslims demonstrated against it on the streets of Bradford. Then things really moved up on the 14th February, when Ayatollah Khomenei placed a fatwah on Rushdie.

Not since "Lady Chatterly's Lover," had a book dominated the news this way, not even with the House of Lords attempt to block "Spycatcher," the previous year. Other news, however, was consistent with recent years as problems in Ireland continued—the Ulster Freedom Fighters murdered lawyer Pat Finucane, and the IRA bombed the Tern Hill Barracks in Shropshire. Incidentally, Ireland (the Windmill Lane studios in Dublin) was one of four locations used for "Spike,"—the other four were Ocean Way in Hollywood, Southland Studios in New Orleans, and AIR studios in London. Four different bands of musicians were assembled for each—this was clearly a huge-scale, ambitious album. This feels enormously democratic—the gamble Costello was prepared to take on so many musicians is admirable, although he understandably reunited with his former producer, the legendary T-Bone Burnett, to oversee the sessions. These gambles paid off as this album, especially the song "Veronica," saw him "break America." As the arts had proved their power courtesy of Salman Rushdie, for better or worse it was just the right time for Costello to be writing such an emotive album.

NEW MODEL ARMY—THUNDER AND CONSOLATION

Throughout the eighties, New Model Army had been a reliable, articulate voice of dissent—but they had yet to make their "landmark" album. This was to come in March 1989 with the release of "Thunder and Consolation." It was a dangerous time to be as outspoken as New Model Army—the "Satanic Verses" fiasco was showing the power of the arts to provoke on an enormous scale. In the month that the band released "Thunder and Consolation," this reached its height as Iran broke off diplomatic relations with the UK over "The Satanic Verses."

The religious element of "Thunder and Consolation," is of a decidedly different kind—its title is drawn from Quaker Edward Burroughs posthumously released collected works, "The Memorable Works of A Son of Thunder and Consolation." Burrough was a controversial figure. He had been educated in the Church of England, but converted after hearing Quaker George Fox preach in 1652. He then went on to wage a vicious debate with John Bunyan through a series of pamphlets.

Clealry, considering both the name of this album and the name of the band, New Model Army had an interest in this era of history. But there are further reasons why Burrough, in particular, should be important. In 1660, upon the Restoration, Burrough approached King Charles II to fund protection and relief of Quakers in New England, who were then being prosecuted by the Puritans. To edit this heavily, in 1661 a writ was delivered to stop the capital punishment of Quakers in Massachusetts, commanding authorities to instead send them for trial—however, they chose instead to release them. Hangings ceased, but imprisonment and flogging prevailed. A year later, Burrough was arrested for holding a meeting, which was illegal under the terms of the Quaker Act. Charles II signed an order for his release, but it was still ignored by the local authorities and he eventually died in Newgate on the 14th February, 1663, aged just 29.

Burrough was clearly a man unafraid to fight for what he believed in. This is a theme which colours "Thunder and Consolation,"—the album includes the bands biggest hit, "Vagabonds," with its rallying chorus, "we are old, we are young, we are in this together." over a marching beat which sounds almost militant, and folky strings which are consistent with the rest of the album, marking a slight change in direction. These strings draw on the past in a way the lyrical themes do—perhaps it was drawing inspiration from that that could have truly taught us about fighting against the authority of Thatcherism.

THE STONE ROSES—THE STONE ROSES

The battle between workers and authority would never reach the level that it had during the miners strike, but people were still seizing power—on 5th April, 500 workers on the Channel Tunnel went on strike in a protest against pay and working conditions. The Channel tunnel may have provided people with an easy escape, but it was clearly not so for those who were actively involved—once again, the workers had been neglected. The next day, there was a sharp blow to part of the nations workforce as the government announced an end to legislation which had effectively guaranteed secure work for more than 9,000 dockers for the reminder of their working lives. Who could drag some colour and positivity from the working-class world? Was it possible?

The debut album by The Stone Roses frequently tops polls as one of the greatest debut albums ever—sometimes, actually the greatest album. The band comprised four outspoken Manchester based musicians—vocalist Ian Brown, drummer "Reni," bass player Gary "Mani" Mounfield and the excellent, often experimental guitarist John Squire. To this day, Mani is fully aware of the bands impact of the bands impact as individuals as he said in 2009 "well, we had the best trousers, the best haircuts and were cheeky little monkeys." Whilst the first part of this statement is debatable, the characters of the band showed how easy it was to self-promote—power with the band, in the same way workers were exerting their own power. The band had already gained critical acclaim prior to the release of the album—they had formed five years earlier. It was this album which bought them a wider audience, enabling them to make their gigs truly special occasions, such as their one-off performance at the Empress Ballroom in Blackpool. These gigs had become something of a Mecca for indie fans, an escape from a dreary world in which Thatcher had now reached ten years as Prime Minister (she was the first British Prime Minister of the twentieth century to do so.) Clearly, the Stone Roses had come along at the perfect time and truly struck a chord with the working-class, but were they actually a political band? To a point, yes. The track "Elizabeth, my Dear," with its delivery of "its curtains for you Elizabeth my dear," is in the fine tradition of classic anti-monarchy songs, and whilst the famous artwork (actually created by the multi-talented Squire) may appear oblique, it has its roots in socialist dissent—it makes reference to the 1968 Paris riots which spawned the Situationist movement which had had such a powerful influence on music. Squire told Q "Ian (Brown) had met this French man when he was hitching round Europe, this bloke had been in the riots, and he told Ian how lemons had been used as an antidote to tear gas. Then there was the documentary—a great shot at the start of a guy throwing stones at the police. I really liked his attitude." The Parisian riots had also been linked with a series of strikes, something which was also occurring in 1989 Britian as worker protest and dissatisfaction continued its ascent—on 8th May, more than 3,000 British Rail employees launched an official overtime, walking out in protest at the end of their eighet hour shifts. At the end of the previous month, the London Underground had been at a standstill for a day as most of the workers went on strike in protest against plans for driver-operated trains. The eighties seemed to have been an ongoing battle between "worker" and "government,"—small wonder that support for the Conservatives was weakening, as they now stood equal. As Ian Brown sang, "I Wanna be Adored," on the opening track of "The Stone Roses," most of the workforce would have been happy to just not be ignored, never mind adored. But clearly, here was a man with higher ideas—closer "I Am The Resurrection," has him proclaiming his own divinity. The key part of this song, however, is not the lyrics but the instrumental, epic climax which would turn their gigs into giant raves—clearly, this was a band that were about bringing good times to the bad. Ian Brown is even credited with getting teenaged boys to dance after years of standing against walls.

With the Smiths no longer, and nearly a decade passed since the death of Ian Curtis, Manchester needed a new City-defining band. The Hillsborough disaster in neighbouring Liverpool was the major news story and it was still partly an industrial wasteland—the roots of its new scene would give it the kiss of life.

THE CURE—DISINTEGRATION-

The European elections on 19th June, 1989 yielded the beginning of the end for the Conservatives as Labour won 45% of Britains 78 seats, with the Conservatives winning 32. Could it have been a time for hope? If it was, then nobody told The Cure, as their eighth album "Disintegration," was as bleak and introspective as their earlier works. Their record label, Fiction, feared the album would be "commercial suicide," (they were proved wrong) as tensions within the band had peaked, resulting in the firing of founder member Loz Tolhurst, and Robert Smiths vast depression, worsened by a fear of turning thirty and dealt with the copious use of hallucinogenic drugs. The album can be seen as a perfect reflection of Smiths mind as he wrote all the songs single-handedly and said that if his bandmates had not liked them, he was prepared to record them as a solo album. They did like them and set about recording, but this itself was a difficult process. Tolhursts alcohol abuse had escalated and Smith was behaving awkwardly—he confesses "I was in one of my non-talking modes . . . I would be monk like and not talk to anybody." He also says of Tolhurst, "I didn't know who he was anymore and he didn't know either." He was fired and replaced with their live touring guitarist.

The unhappy vibes which fuel "Disintegration," reflect a wider misery in society. The nation still brimmed with dissatisfaction—on 22nd June, London Underground workers staged their second one-day strike of the year. With this album, Smith had actively sought to make a depressing record as a reflection of his won despondency. The American record label Elektra sent Smith a letter wanting the release to be delayed. Smith says, "they thought I was being 'wilfully obscure', which was an actual quote from the letter." Ever since then I realised that record companies don't have a fucking clue what The Cure does and what The Cure means." Conflict and ignorance were clearly a part of the labels world, as it was everywhere—the pinnacle of ignorance, the British National Party, staged a protest against the Islamic Community on the 24th June.

The listener is aware of what to expect from "Disintegration," from very early on—the opener "Plainsong," was described by journalist Jeff Apter as "unravelling ever so slowly in a shower of synths and guitars, before Smith steps up to the mic, uttering snatches of lyrics ('I'm so cold) as if he were reading from something as sacred as the dead sea scroll." However, it is not a completely bleak record. The darkness is broken up somewhat by "Lovesong," simply an honest love song that Smith wrote as a wedding present to his fiancée Mary, who he had been with since he was sixteen as is still with to do this day. The lyric, "whenever I'm alone with you/ you make me feel like I am young again," is given extra poignancy and weight by the knowledge of Smiths intense fears over his vanishing youth—it could be seen as one of the most honest love songs ever written. Smith, always unable to show emotion until now, says "it is a very open show of emotion. Its not trying to be clever. Its taken me ten years to reach the point were I feel comfortable singing a very straightforward love song."

Honesty was not exactly something in abundance at the time—the West Midlands Police Serious Crime Squad disbanded when thirty CID detectives were transferred or suspended after repeated allegations that the force had fabricated confessions. The politicians were no more trustworthy—the BBC programme Panorama accused Shirley Porter, Conservative leader of Westminster City Council, of gerrymandering. Clearly, in this world in which no-one could be trusted, The Cure were right to be making such dark music. It was an age in which people were quick to be positive (such as over the housing boom) but quickly had this optimism dashed (homeowners had to cut there asking prices by up to 20% to speed up the sales of their properties.) There was no longer any such thing as reassurance. A song which captures this perfectly on "Disintegration," is "Lullaby," which takes the supposedly reassuring lullaby form and uses it to recount a horrific acid trip about being devoured by a giant spider. The premise was inspired by the macabre lullabies Smiths own father sued to sing to him, as he recalls, "there was always a horrible ending. They would be something like, sleep now, pretty baby, or you won't wake up at all."

So yes, "Disintegration" was bleak. But the again, we need our masters of misery—this is simply the sound of The Cure fulfilling this.

"GENERATION CREATION AT THE END OF THE 80'S"
FELT—ME AND A MONKEY ON THE MOON
AND
THE JESUS AND MARY CHAIN—AUTOMATIC

Throughout the eighties, the distaste for Thatcherism called for a solid counterculture, which is why independent record labels were so important. One of the most important ones was Alan McGee's Creation label, which formed in 1983, its first ever release being the Jesus and Mary Chain's "Upside Down." But, by the end of the eighties, were the first wave of Creation acts still capable of making relevant, exciting music? The newer acts, after all, were not living up to expectations—Primal Scream's eponymous second album was released this year to a poor critical reception. Could the label rely more on its staples, The Jesus and Mary Chain and Felt, who both released new albums at this time? The Mary Chain's debut "Psychocandy," was regarded as an all-time great, whilst Felt were so important in the alternative community that Primal Scream's Bobby Gillespie said of frontman Lawrence, "There's old wave, there's new wave, and then there's Lawrence."

Their final album more than lived up to this; reviews of the Jesus and Mary Chains "Automatic," were less favourable—but as time has passed, reviews have become more positive. Was it just released at the wrong time?

There is something almost private about "Automatic," as the Reid brothers are not just the core, but practically the whole album as the drum machine becomes multi-purpose as a substitute for all other instruments. This seems to almost deny a role to other people in a world which yearned to give power to people.—on 19th September,

19,000 ambulance workers went on strike. The fears of a recession caused everyone to be in a position to worry; everyone in this together. Thatcherism had failed, but were there really any legible alternatives? On 15th September, SLDP leader Paddy Ashdown addressed his party's annual conference in Brighton with a vow to end Thatcherism and achieve the long term aim of getting the SLDP into power. But Ashdown himself lacked the potential to be a viable alternative. The Social Democratic Party could also not be seen as an alternative to Thatcherism—on 27th September, their leader, David Owen, admitted the party was no longer a national force. They had rejected a merger with the SLDP and in the process taken themselves out of the race.

Bands like Felt, the Jesus and Mary Chain and others of their ilk had captured the feeling of the eighties; as the decade drew to a close it seemed that little would change, and thus there music would endure. Something that both bands had toyed with was also religiosity—on Felt's earlier record "All The People I Like Are Those That Are Dead,", Lawrence sings, "When I'm around this town and I see what God has done/ and when I'm around him its so fun/ and I am a two-time tearaway God has told me so/ but I don't believe in him you know." Religion was a tricky theme—on 2nd October, three clergy claiming to be from the British council of Protestants, including Ian Paisley, caused a disturbance at a church service in Rome in which the Archbishop of Canterbury was preaching in protest at the suggestion that the Pope could become spiritual leader of a united Church.

So, very little was changing. There were some alterations in government—Nigel Lawson resigned as Chancellor of the Exchequer, replaced by John Major, whilst Douglas Hurd became Foreign Secretary. But fundamentally, things were still the same, which is why the first wave of Creation bands where still relevant at the end of the decade.

KATE BUSH—THE SENSUAL WORLD

As recession fears deepened and the ambulance strike caused chaos, the world was forced to be realistic and practical. Intellectualism and sexuality could have easily taken a back seat. Luckily, the ever-reliable Kate Bush proved otherwise.

The biggest influence on Bush's 1989 album "The Sensual World," is the heroine of James Joyce "Ulysses", the sexually liberated Molly Bloom. Her monologue at the end of the novel takes her to the climax of her self-induced orgasm in a piece of writing that sparked great controversy, but this was groundbreaking not just because of the taboo this broke in 1922, but because Molly is a woman, not a sexualised girl. The world of 1989 denied women the right to age, particularly in the media, but Bush had turned thirty when "The Sensual World," came out and seemed keener to exploit and embrace her sexuality than ever before—always aesthetically appealing, she has never looked more beautiful than on the Molly Bloom—referencing cover photograph of this album. Women as a whole were making progress—on 7th November, the General Assembly of the Church of England voted to allow the ordination of women. Bush was the daughter of a vicar and will have seen the full significance of this; it also makes her use of a character as controversial as Molly Bloom also seem like a kind of late onset rebellion. Unfortunately for Bush, she could not use the text as fully as she had hoped as the Joyce estate refused to release it. As an alternative, she wrote original lyrics which echoed the original passage, as Molly stepped from the pages of the book and revelled in the real world. But would Molly really have found much to revel in—at the end of the year, David Owen predicted another ten years of Conservative rule, with its continued privatisation (the regional water utility companies were privatised at this time) and capitalism (the developers of the Merry Hill Shopping Centre announced plans to build the worlds tallest building, a 2,000 tower including a hotel and a nightclub.) Not only were we apparently stuck with Conservatism, but Conservatism itself was not changing—Anthony Meyer challenged Thatcher for leadership, but she defeated him on 5th December.

Bush retreats into a fantasy world away from all of this to give Molly some hope. She also alludes to that hymn of positivity, William Blake's "Jerusalem," in a reference to how she had used Bloom's monologue ("and my arrows of desire rewrite the speech.") "Jerusalem" is about a world of joy and justice—at least we were seeing fragments of this as the Guildford Four were finally released, a move which made Bush's use of Joyce's text (as well as other elements of her Irish heritage such as Ulliean pipes, fiddle and whistle) all the more timely.

Whilst this is perhaps Bush's "Irish" album, it also shows acute use of the wider world, with the songs "Deeper Understanding," "Never Be Mine," and "Rockets Tail," all featuring backing vocals by the Bulgarian vocal ensemble Trio Bulgarka. It was an easy time to be aware of the wider world as we witnessed a key moment in global history—the fall of the Berlin Wall, which brought about the reunification of Germany forward after German's were allowed to travel between East and West Berlin for the first time since the Wall was built, in 1961, and between East and west Germany for the first time since the partition of the country after the War. Nearly a month later, Thatcher, George Bush and Mikhail Gobachev declared the end of the Cold War after forty years.

Clearly, it was a period of beginnings, largely positive. What better time to appropriate the words of Molly Bloom and all learn how to give birth to the self?

THE KLF—CHILL OUT   Jan1990

The end of the previous decade had seen the roots of positive change on the international stage, but Britain was still stuck in Thatcherite drudgery. It was the role of the arts in all their forms to provide excitement—for the past four years, one act fulfilling this was the KLF, a house band who were more than musicians but a wider conceptual art project. (They were also behind the book "The Manual" and the film, "The White Room.") Bill Drummond had made waves on the music scene already as a co-founder of Zoo records, manager of Echo and the Bunnymen and Teardrop Explodes, and guitarist with Big in Japan. The other half of KLF, Jimmy Cauty, had a less significant background, having been the guitarist with their commercially unsuccessful Brilliant. As a united force, the two of them would grab attention first as the Justified Ancients of Mu Mu, then as the Timelords, before the first release under the KLF name, March 1988's "Burn the Bastards/ Burn the Beat." If anything had truly endeared them to the public, however, it was the public, however, it was their 1989 performance at the Helter Skelter rave in Oxfordshire, were they had pelted the crowd with £1,000 of Scottish pound notes, each of them bearing the message, "children, we love you." By the time of "Chill Out's" release, this type of love and unity was practically mainstream, as some 50,000 people demonstrated on the streets of London to pledge their support of Britains ambulance workers—the ongoing ambulance strike had yet to end after four months.

Released on the KLF's own label, "Chill Out" is a single continuous piece, recorded in a "live" take at their studio Trancental (located in Cauty's squat in Stockwell.) Cauty says that "there's no edits in it. Quite a few times we'd get near the end and make a mistake so we'd have to go all the way back to the beginning and start again." The sound is inspired by the American Deep South—Drummond says that "I've never been to those places, but I can imagine those sounds coming from those places, just looking at the map." This is aided by a string of samples—a detailed news report of a fatal road accident, an evangelists sermon, and most significantly in the Thatcherite age of aggressive marketing, a particularly intense salesman. In spite of the American influence, the album has multi-ethnic tangents—Tuvan throat singers, Russian broadcasts, exotic birds and African vocal—along with a very British artwork of some sheep (which also appear on the record.) Drummond explains the artwork by saying, "That's a very English thing and it has a vibe of the rave scene over here. When you're having these big raves out in the country, and you're dancing all night and then the sun would come up in the morning, and then you'd be surrounded by this English rural countryside."

Sheep would go on to be further associated with the KLF, as they dumped a dead one with the message "I died for you," emblazoned on it over the entrance to a Brit Awards Party. Their own part in the awards had been to fire blanks from an automatic weapon into the crowd during a collaboration with Extreme Noise Terror, before their promoter announced that they had left the music business. The music business was just another part of capitalist authority, something the British public had had enough of at the time of "Chill Outs" release as the Conservatives suffered in the latest MORI poll.

The KLF may have retired in spectacular fashion, but it is "Chill Out,"s capturing of an escape from the final months of Thatcherism which remains their finest hour.

THE FALL—EXTRICATE   Feb1990

Some of the news which dominated in February 1990 showed not changes, but renewals of previous news. On the 9th, Ayatollah Khomenei renewed his fatwah against Salman Rushdie over "The Satanic Verses." However, there were other, more positive progressions on the news world, as we shall come to see—and, as ever, The Fall were there to soundtrack it, there role was a kind of omnipresent force also being something that was renewed in the nineties. However, the band themselves had seen some of the most major changes to their line-up, as Mark. E. Smith had divorced Brix—thus making this their first album without her. The divorce defined the themes and subject matter of the album, but also affected the sound; her background vocals and distinctive guitar notably absent. As a reflection of a world which just seemed to renew things, Brix's replacement was former member Martin Bramh, who had left in 1979 to form his own group, The Blue Orchids.

This restoration of diplomacy was a part of the wider world at the time, as the UK and Argentina finally restored diplomatic links after eighet years (the ties had previously been broken off in response to Argentina's invasion of the Falkland Islands in 1982.) In hindsight, the Falklands barely seemed worth fighting for; restoring relations with Argentina seemed like a new found awareness of the value (or lack of it) of parts of the physical world.

Such an awareness is reflected in the Fall on "Extricate," as they appear to give an aural nod to the scene which had emerged in their own city, Manchester. The track "Telephone Thing," is fairly similar to that of the dance-associated indie which had emerged from Manchester in the previous year. However, its origins actually lay in Smith's previous collaboration with Coldcut ("I'm In Deep") leading them to producing both this track and the album track "Black Monk

Theme Part II." The albums most noted and famous song, however, is "Bill Is Dead," a beautiful and tender piece of writing in which Smith reflects on the endings he had recently experienced—his divorce from Brix and the death of his father. (It was the only Fall song to top John Peel's Festive Fifty, although you get the feeling that they would have topped it every year if it had been based on Peel's own opinion, rather than listener votes.)

Endings were a theme at the time. People wondered if Thatcher's rule was coming to end, as the lastest MORI poll put Labour 17 points over the Conservatives. Another "ending," was the ambulance crew dispute coming to a close on the 13th March, when workers agreed to a 17.6% pay rise. This chain of endings peaked on 21st March, when Allan Roberts, Labour MP for Bootle, died of cancer, leaving the position open. "Bill Is Dead," may capture the moment of all this, but it cannot be called a typical Fall song—however, these are to be found elsewhere on the album. The edge Bramah brings to the band is one of distinct rawness, even verging on the rockabilly. The Fall's speciality, after all, was to soundtrack the more riotous parts of life—and there were certainly plenty of riots to soundtrack. On 9th March, there had been riots in Brixton against the new community charge (a fixed tax per adult resident, charging each person for the services provided in their community.) In a continuation of this, 200,000 protested in the Poll Tax Riots of 31st March. In a different field, 1st April saw the start of the Strangeways Prison Riots, which lasted for 25 days. The prison riots were not just limited to The Falls home city as they would go on to break out at prisons in Cardiff and Bristol.

The raw edginess of The Fall captures this perfectly. In an era which also saw the introduction of the Official Secrets Act 1989, which repealed and replaced section 2 of the Official Secrets Act 1911 (supposed to remove the public interest defence) the continuing relevance of The Fall's was something which was never going to be a secret.

THE INTERNATIONALE—BILLY BRAGG April 1990

There are no benefits to apathy. Sometimes, protest can really pay off. In the wake of the uproar over Community Charge, on the 3rd April the government forced twenty local councils to cut their proposed community charge levels.

Nobody knew about the value of protest more than the perpetual activist Billy Bragg, and his 1990 release "The Internationale" retained all the political passion and poetic integrity of his 80's albums. He had always thrived in environments of dissatisfaction, and thus it was a perfect time for him to release a new album. Inflation stood at 9.4%, the housing boom was over and unemployment had risen again. Typically, Bragg saw moving to the Left as the answer to the nations problems; one track on "The Internationale," "The People's Flag is Deepest Red," is as upfront as ever. The chorus runs "Then raise the scarlet standard high/ Beneath its folds we'll live and die/ Though cowards flinch and traitors sneer/ we'll keep the red flag flying here."

The spirit of unity and positivity which always marks him out as he looks at the potential in rising up against regimes is still present; "For you have nothing, you have no rights/ Let racist ignorance be ended/ For respect makes the empires fall/ Freedom is merely a privelige extended/ Unless enjoyed by one and all." Bragg has always been a very "British," songwriter, but with this album (you only have to look at the title) he is using lyrics which could be applied to people almost anywhere in the world. This resonated in an uncomfortable Britain-based story involving the international community which came to light on 4th April, when the doctor Raymond Crockett was struck off the medical register for using kidneys from Turkish immigrants that he had paid to donate them. Other news was dominated by conflict and violence—on 11th April, Customs and

Excise Officers seized parts of an Iraqi supergun in Middlesborough, whilst two days earlier four Ulster Defence Regiment soldiers had been killed by an IRA bomb in County Down. Such an environment meant that Bragg's inspirational lyrical style was called for more than ever. The title track of "The Internationale," was his most lyrically inspirational to date, as the chorus runs "so come brothers and sisters/ for the struggle carries on/ The Internationale/ Unites the world in song/ so comrades come and rally/ For this is the time and place/ The international ideal/ unites the human race." Unity was needed, but were could offer the option? Thatcherism evoked a turn away from society and altruism and towards promoting the individual. Thatcherism had also yet to win over any converts—in the Bootle by-election of 25th May, Labour managed to retain power as people but their faith in new MP Micheal Clark. The real losers, here, however, were the "rump" Social Democratic Party, who finished behind the Monster Raving Loony Party (on 3rd June, they wound up after just nine years in existence) Bragg's message on "The Internationale," makes the listener feel like we don't really need to turn to anybody; we can just unite with each other. The verses run as follows: "let no-one build walls to divide us/ Walls of hatred nor walls of stone/ come greet the down and stand besides us/ We'll lie together/ or die alone/ In our world poisoned by exploitation/ Those who have taken, now they must give/ and end the vanity of nations/ now we've but one on Earth on which to live/ And so begins the final drama/ in the streets and in the fields/ We stand unbowed before their armour/ we defy their guns and shields/ when we fight/ provoked by aggression/ Let us inspired by life and love."

I should not need to say any more about Bragg as a laureate of political hope. This should say it all.

MANIC STREET PREACHERS—THE NEW ART RIOT EP   June 1990

Without the decade that she defined, Thatcher's grip on power was weakening. The May 4th local council elections saw Labour win more council seats—plus, Labour were ahead in the opinion polls. But her time was not over yet; there was still need for voices of dissent—young, angry, new ones, who made exciting music not just the old staples. The most visceral rock music of the past few years had come from bands like Guns'n'Roses—who were American and whose singer Axl Rose was gaining a reputation for homophobia and misogyny. Luckily, there was a British band out there who combined the sound of Guns'n'Roses with politics which were not only more left-wing, but more informed, comprising political history students.

This band was the four-piece the Manic Street Preachers, hailing from the grim town of Blackwood in South Wales, the kind of working class mining town whose soul and liveliness had been laid to waste by Thatcherism. Sleazy, outspoken and glamorous, (they had the slogan Sex, Style and Subversion) they were a sharp jolt to an oft-bland musical landscape. Even the name of their first record "New Art Riot," implies all that is full-throttle and exciting. "We've just got pissed off with seeing so much ugliness about. Everybody knows life is ugly, but it seems to me all bands around today want to do is reflect it," said rhythm guitarist Richey 'James' Edwards at the time. "Bands like Northside (forgotten late 80's indie-rock band) the way they look is useless. They say they reflect their own culture and background, but that's boring. Were we come from, people come home from work in their dirty, filthy overalls and they just wanna dress up. Also, Northside and the rest are so traditionally male. You know, ''Ere I am, I am a man, ey up lad, drink Boddingtons' . . . its so boring, so degrading. How are we supposed to look up to that kind of thing?"

As Britain seemed to regress back to Thatcherism's darkest moments of unemployment and economic blight, people needed *something* to look up to—was Edwards right? It was this kind of soundbite that saw him act as a kind of band spokesperson ("Once he starts talking, he doesn't stop for about four and a half hours," wrote the journalist Sylvia Ince.) He also oversaw the artwork and wrote the lyrics, but was actually not such an impressive guitarist, only earning a place in the band because of friendship and his aesthetic beauty.

Being from a working-class background was no guarantee that an individual would be as politically exciting as Edwards and his bandmates. Michael Carr, the new MP for Bootle at the time, replacing Alan Roberts, was a former dockworker who later became a trade union official, but his political rise was actually due to the help he gave the Labour Party leadership in removing the influence of the Militant Tendency. On 14th June, 1990, Carr made his maiden speech in an Estimates Day debate on training. Within this speech, he criticised the governments Youth Training Scheme which had employed his own children as "providing cheap labour to employers who are more interested in job substitution than the provision of decent training."

This speech also tackled induction methods for MP's, and Thatcher's responsibility for the worsening economy, but it was not his politics which drew attention for the speech but his "extreme pallor," (Dr. Thomas Stuttaford, a Conservative MP and doctor watching him at the time.) Three days later, he died of a heart attack, just 57 days into his role. It was starting to look like the role of MP for Bootle was cursed with Carr's death being so soon after the death of Allen Roberts. This kind of atmosphere and circumstance is particularly captured by one track on "New Art Riot," "Last Exit On Yesterday": *"You're screaming so much/ That I feel sorry to breathe/ I wanna feel cold/ I wanna bleed you disease."* For all their fun, glamour and escapism, this band clearly had a darker side. A darker side which was ideal for an age still overflowing with problems—unemployment remaining one of the biggest issues in the UK. On July 11th, Labour MP's accused the Conservative government of fraud, in the midst of allegations that the 1,600,000 fall in unemployment since 1986 included a million leaving the list without finding work. It was so hard to know who to trust that everyone was expected to prove their integrity—the Manic Street Preachers would do so in spectacular fashion the following year, as shall come to see (in *Generation Terrorists)* in a stunt which showed a keenness for shameless self-promotion. However, relentless self-promotion also often results in not knowing when to stop talking, and Edwards once claimed to hate the shoegaze band Slowdive more than Adolf Hitler. He was not alone in making such sweeping, Hitler-related remarks—in a far more controversial moment, Trade and Industry Secretary Nicholas Ridely told the Spectator that the EU was like Hitler's Germany, a remark that resulted in his resignation. Edwards was young, new to the public eye and in spite of his blistering intelligence often lacked common sense—Ridley should have known better and his comments were inexcusable.

Elsewhere in politics, Ian Gow, a British MP fiercely in favour of the Britain/Ireland union told the IRA that the British government would never surrender and was thus killed by an IRA car bomb—another lesson in speaking at the wrong time. Capitalism also continued to rage with the opening of the Meadowhall shopping centre and Britain's first Aldi, but this seemed illogical considering Britain's lack of spending (high street sales were at their lowest for ten years.) Dissent in Britain, however, was not dead (20% of taxpayers in England and Wales had not paid their community charge), and nobody symbolised dissent better than the Manic Street Preachers. Socialist in the Thatcherite age, musically loud and brash in the era of the subdued, and dressed in skintight white denim and doused in Anais Anais in a time of baggy clothes and down to earth machismo—very few may have been aware of the "New Art Riot" but those that were had truly found something new and different to belong to . . .

"THE FALL OF THATCHER AND THE RISE OF MAJOR"—
THE HAPPY MONDAYS—PILLS 'N' THRILLS AND BELLYACHES AND
THE LA'S—THE LA'S

By Autumn 1990, things were bleak in Britain, especially considering the economy. On 22nd September, the leading British industrial minister John Banham warned that most of Britain was now affected by recession—and there was worse to come. Chancellor John Major firmly denied that their was any truth in this, however, rushing forward to make this claim almost as soon as Banham made his. Four days later, Thatcher also denied any possibility of a recession—the government seemed deluded as manufacturers reported enormous drops in output and the number of bankruptcies ascended, and sure enough, they were proved wrong when, on 14th November, the CBI announced that the whole of Britain was officially in recession. As she had done so many times since 1979, Thatcher had taken her people for fools. It was clearly time for her to go, for a range of reasons. Predictably, she was attacked by the opposition—as well as the economy, Kinnock saw the lack of standards in training and education as a problem, as he told his partys conference in Blackpool—but she was also attacked by her own crumbling, failing cabinet. On the 13th November, Geoffrey Howe made a dramatic resignation speech in which he attacked Thatchers hostility towards the EC. He had had issues with her European Policy for some time and it was directly this issue which led him to leave his role as Deputy Prime Minister, but there were far more issues for the public to disagree with her over. Clearly sensing this, the day after Howe's resignation Micheal Heseltine announced he would challenge her leadership. On 20th November, Thatcher failed to win an outright victory in a leadership contest, thus resigning two days later. However, it was not Heseltine that won the leadership but John Major.

So, how appropriate was the music of November 1990 for this transitional political period? Two classics usually seen on greatest albums lists were release in this month. One was the Happy Mondays "Pills' n' Thrills 'n' Bellyaches." Produced by Paul Oakenfold and released on Factory, the band once again capture the Hacienda's escapist vibe with anthems like "Step On," and "Kinky Afro," as if inviting the listener to celebrate the end of Thatcherism and join the party. Shaun Ryder also continued to be a great everyman-style frontman symbolic of ordinary Britain.

A more complex character was Lee Mavers, frontman of the La's, who made the other big classic album of the month. Mavers was a perfectionist who went through numerous changes of band and line-up before managing to release their sublime debut album—which he then decided he hated. "It's a piece of shit, there's not a single thing I like about it," he said. Thatcherism may have been on the way out, but would Major be any better? The nation suffered restlessness, dissatisfaction and a lack of self-worth; Lee Mavers seems to epitomize that. He is in the minority of hating his album; critics adored it then and adore it now, but the only song the public are generally familiar with is "There She Goes," a hymn to the escapism of drugs ("*Racing through my brain/ pulsing through my vein*"). This, coupled with the Happy Mondays party anthems, suggested that retreating into the joys of escape mde for the best listening material in times of political transition when nobody could fully know what to expect.

PART ONE/ CHAPTER TWO
THE JOHN MAJOR YEARS

MORRISSEY—BONA DRAG/ KILL UNCLE

As the frontman of The Smiths and then with his debut solo album "Bona Drag," Morrissey had been one of musics key voices under Thatcher, but this did not mean that a change of leadership made his music any less relevant, as Major was still very much a traditional Conservative. However, he was also noted for being a vastly different personality type to Thatcher, having a softly, softly approach which often had him derided as dull and uninteresting. One of his first acts as Prime Minister was to introduce Tax Exempt Special Savings Accounts as a way of producing personal savings, perhaps a wise move in the deepening recession but one that was hardly likely to grab headlines. The outspoken and the exciting was once again to be left in the hands of Britains musicians—little wonder, then, that Morrissey released two albums in the first few months of Majors rule, Bona Drag (in November 1990, as soon as he took over) and Kill Uncle (in March 1991.)

The months in between these releases brought little joy in the political world. On 19th January, 1991, it was announced that 1, 844, 000 people were unemployed in the United Kingdom and experts warned that that figure would exceed 2,000,000 before the end of the year. Just because Major had a "softer" approach it did not mean that he could not make controversial decisions, as in spite of the recession hurting many he still resisted the calls for interest rates to be cut as a way of combating this. Unemployment hit many companies hard—Barclays axed 13,000 workers, the Peugeot factory in Coventry 355, and Ford 10,000 (to name but a few) in just one month. This left life in the UK feeling dreary, mundane, hopeless. Could Morrissey's solo work capture the brilliant wit he had displayed with the Smiths which had both captured the moment and provided escape from it the last time the UK was hit so badly by these issues? It would appear that yes, it would, whilst remaining as gloriously controversial as ever—witness in particular Bona Drag's key track, "Last Of The Famous International Playboys." One particularly inspired line runs, "I never wanted to kill/ I am not naturally evil/ such things I do/ just to make myself more attractive to you/ Have I failed?" The angle of controversy here is that the song is narrated by someone enamoured with the Kray's—and Morrissey reinforced this by sending a wreath to Reggie Kray's funeral. But then again, Morrissey was no stranger to controversy. His comments on the Brighton bombings (see The Smiths LP) would have seemed just as distasteful as they did at the time as a whole new wave of IRA stories hit the headlines. Firstly, on 7th February, the Provisional Irish Republican Army launched a mortar attack against 10 Downing Street, blowing in all the windows of the cabinet room, during a session of the War Cabinet. Then, eleven days later, the IRA exploded bombs in the early morning at both Paddington and Victoria Station in London. But those comments were in the past. He would instead court a new type of controversy, one exposed on "Kill Uncle."

The song "Asian Rut," was the story of the murder of an Asian by three English boys, almost a sequel to "Viva Hate,"'s "Bengali in Platforms." Sung in a minimal, sombre tone, with strings and bass the only instruments, is this an important examination of English racism—or something more uncomfortable? When supporting Madness at Finsbury Park, Morrissey performed these songs whilst waving a Union Jack, potentially fanning the repulsive feelings of many of the far-right people who made up the audience. It is awkward territory; Morrissey was on very thin ice.

"Kill Uncle," is his "difficult" album, with or without "Asian Rut"—a difficult album for difficult times. Lyrically, it has its moments of brilliance which continue in much the same way as The Smiths. Perhaps wisely, the political is largely forsaken in favour of the personal. The most honest and personal songs are "Harsh Truth of The Camera Eye" and "(I'm) At The End of The Family Line." The first looks at the differences between public and private image, talking about "the pain because of the drain of smiling." The latter is his lament that by never having children, "an insult to fifteen generations before," who were "all honouring nature,'til I arrive."

This bought up the usual debates on Morrissey's sexuality; it feels poignant and timely given John Major's stress on traditional family values.

Not only did it Britain have the fastest rate of rising unemployment in Britain, but it had something else to put it on the map. The RAF joined Allied Aircraft in bombing raids on the UK. The Gulf War had begun.

The days of Thatcher may have been over, but war and unemployment all seemed uncomfortably familiar. And with the likes of Morrissey also raising eyebrows at Finsbury Park, it seemed hard to know were to turn for true, intelligent dissent.

THE FALL—SHIFT WORK April 1991

The Fall's first album during John Major's rule is "Shift Work," a title which captures the mundane world he perpetuated, but not without a wry irony considering how little work there actually was about. With a gentler Prime Minister, the band recorded amore introspective album, but they still managed to capture the unhappiness of the nation. On the track "Edinburgh Man," (which Smith himself notes as his favourite Fall song) he yearns to be in Edinburgh, capturing the way so many people wished they were somewhere else, in a grass-is-greener fashion. The song was described by reviewers at the time as being "surprisingly malice-free." Perhaps this made it more fitting for its release date—Community Charge had been scrapped, and justice had finally prevailed as the Birmingham Six were freed. But the bigger picture was still dark; in a way, The Fall releasing an album of hope in the midst of a back catalogue of tension was ideal in this particular month of Conservative rule.

MASSIVE ATTACK—BLUE LINES April 1991

By 1991, it appeared that the Conservatives were suffering somewhat—on the 17th, they suffered in another by-election which saw Labour gain their Monmouth seat in Wales. And small wonder, really—British unemployment stood far above the European average at 2, 175, 000. Labour also topped a MORI poll for the first time that year when they stood six points ahead of the Conservatives at 43%. Labour were suffering more personal types of defeat, such as the death of their Liverpool Walton MP Eric Heffer, than actively personal defeats as the Conservatives losses were there gains. If the world was to change (or specifically Britain) then maybe it was time for new, interesting forms of music to emerge and reflect this. This certainly happened in April 1991, with the release of Massive Attacks "Blue Lines." At the time, it was issued under the band name "Massive," the word "attack" dropped to avoid causing any Gulf War related upset, proof of the level of sensitivity it is deemed music and the media must show towards emotive political issues.

"Blue Lines" is an important album because it is the first of its kind—the very first "trip-hop" album. The band were Bristol based and this would become something of the unofficial home of the short-lived but inventive drama.

"Trip-hop," may be a narrow label which would only apply to a small selection of acts, but it needed to exist as such acts would have remained completely genre-free otherwise, not fitting in anywhere. It is almost a rebellion against set musical ideas. This "quiet" form of rebellion was also to be found in the wider world as at the end of May, the poll tax saga resulted in Martin Baltchford, a disabled father of three from Dudley, being arrested for being the latest in a series of objectors. The fact that people were prepared to face hail for their dissent shows what an emotive issue this was, but then again anything monetary was. On 6th June, Neil Kinnock once again condemned John Major for high interest rates, as banks were charging as much as 17% on small businesses.

So, were does "Blue Lines" as an album fit into all this? It is not the sound of working class poverty—the one criticism often made of Massive Attack is that they make "dinner party" music. But this is a great disservice. In fact, the songs here are sparse and haunting in a style which reflects the desolation of early nineties Britain. "Safe From Harm" and "KarmaComa," are absolute classics, both with a ripple of urban darkness running through them, but the defining song on this album is the modern classic "Unfinished Symphony," a beautiful but painful account of unrequited love. *"I'm a soul without a mind/ I'm a body without a heart/ I'm missing every part/ You're the book that I have opened/ And now I've got to know much more,"* sings vocalist Shana Nelson, before uttering the heartbreaking line *"the curiousness of your potential kiss/ that's what my mind and body is."* Whilst very much a love song, the themes of want and wonder could have applied to many Britons, in relation to many situations. Its classic, oft-copied video of Nelson wandering round a desolate looking UK backdrop looking anguished simply reinforced the state of the nation. So, more than "dinner party music," then.

On 28th June, Thatcher announced that she would stand down as an MP, seven months after her resignation as Prime Minister. Things were certainly changing; the new sounds of the early 90's capture that moment ideally—if not literally.

BLUR—LEISURE

Another month, another by-election, another Labour victory as a consequence. On 4th July, Labour retained the Walton seat in a by-election as new MP Peter Kilfoyle gained more than half the vote. Clearly, experience was not necessary for the nation to trust you—if anything, the nation were probably ready for the new, the fresh, the exciting. If this is to be reflected in the musical world, then it would be a good time to be releasing a debut album. Ideally, new bands breaking through at this time would have many of the qualities lacking elsewhere, both in music and in the wider world—for example, intelligence and unity. This is why Blur were an ideal band for the age—lead singer Damon Albarn and guitarist Graham Coxon had been childhood friends, and both their intelligence and their unity were reinforced when they attended London's Goldsmiths College together. It was there, in 1988, were they met bassist Alex James. Together with drummer Dave Rowntree, James and Albran made up the band Circus, who would later also take on the Coxon's services as a guitarist before renaming themselves Seymour after JD Salinger's work "Seymour: An Introduction." Salinger had always been something of a laureate for the misfits and misunderstood in America; the Great Britain on 1991, however, did not really need such a writer. The misunderstood was now the mainstream. Even our MP's were battling against authority as on 11th July, Labour Party MP Terry Fields was jailed for refusing to pay the poll tax. Even though many people had been imprisoned for this, he was the first MP to be so, receiving a 60 day sentence.

It was an age of uncertainty—when Seymour's label Food decided that they did not like the name Seymour, the alternative suggestion of "Blur," seemed perfect for an era in which nothing was clear.

Blur's first single "She's So High," was a moderate success (no. 48 in the charts) but they struggled to write a follow up which could have the same impact. What managed to change this was pairing them with the brilliant producer Stephen Street, who had previously been an important part of The Smiths sound. The resulting follow-up was "There's No Other Way," which turned out to be a bigger hit than "She's So High," helping Blur to fully cross over. The title implied a world of no alternatives; as every job vacancy was chased by 22 applicants at a time, this certainly tapped into something, particularly with Albarn's droll delivery of "chasing the fun/ out of everything."

The album which includes "She's So High," and "There's No Other Way," is "Leisure," released in April 1991. The title shows the bands knack for wry topical intelligence early on; "Leisure," was something associated with free time from work, but in the age of mass unemployment everyone had "leisure time,"—but no money or aspirations with which to use it. "Leisure," as a concept was dying, being replaced by boredom.

The age was difficult, and people wanted reflections. (Even children—in this year, the dark world of Roald Dahl officially overtook the saccharine world of Enid Blyton as children's favourite author for the first time ever.) "Leisure," would not completely fulfil Blur's potential for this, but we knew it was there. Their best was yet to come.

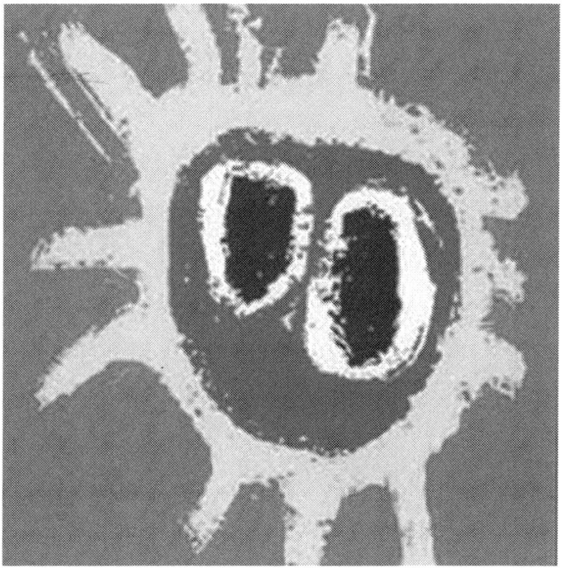

PRIMAL SCREAM—SCREAMADELICA

Sometimes, albums are more than just sounds. They can be fallen in love with. The very first album I ever had this relationship with was Primal Scream's "Screamadelica," in about 1998, so I did not even have the privilege of it in its October 1991 context, which shows how timeless it is.

"Screamadelica" was released in an age of riots. Cardiff and Leeds were the cities that sparked the chain. These were then followed by the third Handsworth riots (see "Coming of Age In The Riots": "Hounds of Love"/ "This Nations Saving Grace" and then riots in Kates Hill (in Dudley) and Blackbird Leys (in Oxford.) The riots in the latter ran for three nights following a crackdown on the persistent problem of joyriding. The core activity of the riots was the stoning of police officers by around 150 youths. The riots in the former were, predictably, race riots—Dudley had been the scene of Britain's first race riots in 1962, with black Caribbean immigrants being the target—the 1991 Kates Hill riots, however, were a clash between white and Asian youths. The most acclaimed album at this time was not, however, the sounds of riots but an escape through unity, multiculturalism and experimentation which contradicted the kind of narrow-mindedness which spawned such riots. Today, joy riding is still a problem in Blackbird Leys and racism is still a problem in Kates Hill (the English Defence League demonstrated there in 2010)—clearly, many negative things never change; maybe the environment today is not so different from the one which spawned "Screamadelica" was released in, contributing towards its timelessness.

Press had become difficult for Primal Scream prior to the release of this album. Their second album had been a weak effort which cast doubts over there potential as a whole. However, Creation

Records label boss Alan McGee refused to give in to the negative press, determined that the band could do well eventually. This kind of resistance was also occurring in British party politics—it was widely believed that the Labour Party were losing out because people disliked the personality of leader Neil Kinnock, but he stood firm as leader. After all, he did have some support—as did Primal Scream, mainly from producer Andrew Weatherall who remixed their song, "I'm Losing More Than I'll Ever Have." Elements of this mix would go on to become the core song of "Screamadelica," "Loaded" a classic song that went on to become a huge hit, something Alan McGee describes as "the biggest shock of my life." At the time, guitarist Rob Young hated dance so much that he threatened to leave the band—then the idea of fusing dance and rock emerged.

At the time of recording the album, heavy use of ecstasy had begun to move into the band. Songs like "Come Together," and the drug hymn "Higher Than The Sun," are perfect for the ecstasy sound, whilst "Don't Fight It, Feel It," is a soul song that fits with acid house. Singer Denise Johnson had to be recruited for this song—Bobby Gillespie had written something he could not sing. She also became an important part of the live show, even though she had initially been unsure about whether to tour with them. The gigs for this album were more like a rave than a traditional rock show—raves spat in the face of authority, like the riots of the time, but unlike riots celebrated love and unity, something fuelled by ecstasy.

The part of drugs on this album is undeniable—at times, the band were so high that they could barely make it to the studio, but this informs the sound—completely modern and forward looking, but with the spirit of psychedelia (something reinforced by Paul Cannell's classic artwork and the title, which took a full four days to come up with—Andrew Weatherall wanted the word "Scream" in the title, and was then inspired after playing a Funkadelic record.)

It was in this year that the first ever Mercury Music Prize came into being (now a key part of the musical calendar.) "Screamadelica" won, completely shocking the band. All these years later, it still seems like the right decision.

Bobby Gillespie described the album as "the sound of rushing on ecstasy." Thus, it is the sound of escapism in a bleak world. The sample from "The Wild One" which opens "Loaded"—"we wanna be free, to do what we wanna do!"—captured the feelings of the public and probably always will . . .

MY BLOODY VALENTINE—LOVELESS   Nov 1991

And so, from "Screamadelica", we move onto "Loveless", another Creation records classic. A good time for Creation, you might think. But things were not that simple . . .

The political landscape was not completely predictable or straightforward, at least not according to recent by-elections which brought about a wealth of changes—whilst Labour managed to retain its control of Hemsworth with new MP Derek Enwright, Kincardine and Deeside switched from Conservative to Liberal Democrat and Langbourgh from Conservative to Labour with the Indian born Ashok Kumar. The pattern here seems to just be a general dissatisfaction with the Conservatives as a whole—an album entitled "Loveless" certainly seems to tap into how Britain as a whole felt about its government. There is a restlessness to this record; it was recorded over two years, in nineteen different studios, with an ever changing list of engineers.

All this paid off, with an album critics cite as one of the best of the 1990's, but Creation had been as hopelessly optimistic (believing it could be recorded in five days) as Britain had initially been about the government. The costly recording process of "Loveless" also seemed to hark back to the Thatcherite selfishness her exit should have left behind, as Creation were short on money and Kevin Shields seemed to not consider this as he worked his way through staff and studios. At one point, Shields was complaining unexplainably about the Eastcoate studio Britannia Row, causing a relocation—but Creation was unable to pay for the move, and the studio refused to return the bands equipment. Temporary bandmate Anjali Dutt says, "I don't know what excuse Kevin gave them for leaving. He had to raise the money himself to get the gear out." The recording led to tensions (including a nervous breakdown for Dick Green at Creation) and the worst financial strain Creation had ever known. There were further delays when two members of My Bloody Valentine, including Kevin Shields, were diagnosed with tinnitus. Although Shields denied it, this was surely due to extremely loud volumes in their live shows, going so far as to dismiss these claims as "ill-informed hysteria." Maybe these claims allow us to be fairer to Shield's behaviour over "Loveless"—perhaps he was simply a deluded character, rather than blatantly selfish. But would deluded characters manage to produce an album as sublime as this? The process had been Hell for so many at Creation—second in command Dick Green said he would be "shaking with fear" opening the post because of the studio bills it would reveal. He also recalls, "It was two years into the album, and I phoned Shields up in tears, saying "you have to deliver me this record.""

And deliver they did—"Loveless" is the high point of shoegaze, and none of the things the genre's critics loathe.

But reaching this had been turmoil. Clearly, the way to get some greatness out of Britain is to go through a little strife first—but with the Conservatives still topping the MORI polls, it seemed we would never get to that dividend.

BILLY BRAGG—DON'T TRY THIS AT HOME

The big news story of the day in November 1991 was that, after four and a half years being held captive in Lebanon, British envoy Terry Waite was finally being released. One mans release could be spun into a positive story; but this does not mean that the political landscape of Britain as a whole by the end of 1991 was a happy one—on 19th December, unemployment stood above 2, 500, 000 for the first time since early 1988. In what is a consistent theme in this book, then, thank goodness there was Billy Bragg album released to give the nation a voice.

The title of this album, "Don't Try This At Home," is a popular warning—was it a time to be warned, warned that even though Thatcher was gone traditional Conservatism would still rage through John Major? Also, due to unemployment, more people were at home. If anything was to be "tried", it would be at home, most likely as a distraction from boredom.

Once again on this album, as with previous albums, Bragg mixes the political with the kitchen-sink personal. It is the latter which describes the song on "Don't Try This At Home," which would become one of his best known songs, "Sexuality," opening with "I've had relations with girls from many nations/ I've made passes at women from all classes/And just because your gay I wont turn you away/ I'm sure we can find some common ground." Whilst this is obviously tongue in cheek, its core message of embracing diversity is heartfelt. After all, not everyone out there was so happy to embrace it, as the likes of The National Front were still going strong. Bragg is all to aware of this, aiming a lyrical attack at them squarely on this album: *"While my countrymen piss in the fountain/ To express our national pride/ And to prove to the world that England/ is just as rotten as she looks,"* he sings. Always something of a consummate Englishman himself, here he reflects the shame felt by so many upon witnessing our nationalist, particularly when it comes to the matter of how they represent us in the wider world. He goes on to sing, "they repeat the lies that caught their eye/ at school and in the history books/ But the wars there fighting were all over long ago/ what do they know of England who only England now," exposing the miseducated excuses that nationalists make for their behaviour as the fragments of ignorance that they are.

"And the society that spawned them/ Just cries out whose to blame?/ And then wraps itself up in the Union Jack/ and carries on just the same/ oh, look my country patriots are hunting down below/ what do they know of England only England know," he rounds the song off with. This is typical Bragg; brimming with socio-political awareness, but putting it forward in a far more accessible way than many of his contemporaries. His everyman persona may not have been what the nation was looking for as it mourned the death of full-on showman Freddie Mercury from AIDS on 24th November, 1991, and sent "Bohemian Rhapsody," back to the top of the charts, but it certainly had its place. The working man was to often forgotten; Bragg was his laureate.

On 27th December, the last MORI poll of the year put Labour six points ahead of the Conservative's with 44% of the vote. Two days later, a quarterly opinion poll kept Labour ahead.

Dissatisfaction with the Conservatives was high enough to spark hope for Labour that they would win the next election. In the meantime, the voice of Billy Bragg was there to provide suitable dissent.

MANIC STREET PREACHERS—
GENERATION TERRORISTS   Feb 1992

1992 did not look as if was going to be an improvement on previous years. The first full week of the year saw 4, 000 jobs lost across the country in the continuing recession. The hardest hit company was Great Britain's leading telecommunications manufacturers GEC, accounting for 20% of these jobs cuts (in announced 750 redundancies on the 10th January.) The backdrop of Thatcherism which had spawned the Manic Street Preachers had left enough of a legacy for them to still be relevant, and their first full—length album, following on from1990's EP "New Art Riot," was released in this time. "Generation Terrorists" was everything that they had promised it would be—inflammatory, epic in scope, and exciting. The title alone was controversial enough, as IRA activity continued to dominate the news. On 17th January, a bomb attack near Omagh left seven dead and seven injured. This had been the highest number of casualties in an IRA attack since 1988—was giving an album a title with a terrorism reference at this time insensitive, or just provocative? Maybe it was just topical; this was, after all, a new generation of terrorism. It was, in fact, a new generation of everything from the recent past as problems became simply renewed and repeated, such a recession. It did not defer people from Conservative support, as the first MORI poll of the year showed that they were three points ahead of Labour with 42% of the vote.

The recession did, however, produce some "accidental Marxism"—for example, the Bank of Credit and commerce went into liquidation. These sorts of corporations were the kind loathed by left-wingers like the Manics, and "Generation Terrorists," searing attack, "Natwest-Barclays-Midlands-Lloyds" certainly felt timely. However, the bands Situationist sloganeering and appropriating of the rock history books did not convince everyone, and they were frequently written off as a louder, more superficial, knock-off version of The Clash, all style and no substance. The year before the release of "Generation Terrorists," after a gig at Norwich Arts Centre, Richey Edwards asked to "have a word" with NME journalist Steve Lamacq, who had questioned their authenticity. Edwards response to this was to take a razorblade out of his pocket and carve the words "4REAL," into his forearm, to an extent which resulted in seventeen stitches. Whilst he felt guilty about wasting hospital time, Edwards extreme act of self-publicity had fulfilled his aim and began to put a little attention on this previously unknown band.

However, if they were to really prove their point they would have to do so by producing a debut album as worthwhile and intelligent as they had promised. Luckily, they lived up to this, right down to the albums sleeve notes, a series of eighteen quotations from the likes of Camus, Kafka, Plath, Nietzsche, and the radical feminist Valerie Symonds. But, more importantly, they lived up to it musically. Whilst on the whole it is a Guns'n'Roses-esque orgy of noise which would not have been likely to win over those who were not already fans, the song "Motorcycle Emptiness," helped to bring them to a wider audience. "From feudal serf to spender/ this wonderful world of purchase power," runs one of the verses, an attack on the consumer culture which may have been set to reignite, as, on 9th February, John Major spoke of his hopes that the recession would soon be over now that the economy was showing signs of recovery. However, this seemed an empty promise considering how little the Conservatives had done about the problem up until now—six days after Major's claim, Neil Kinnock said that he believed that the Conservative governments failure to halt the recession would win the Labour Party the forthcoming election. The recession was certainly the biggest problem for the UK—the head of community relations, David Stevens, blamed it for the recent rise in crime across Britain, particularly in deprived areas. But no government can focus on one issue alone, and there were other concerns—at the end of January, Major had agreed a weapons deal with the new Russian premier, Boris Yeltsin, a man set to drag Russia into the realms of the right-wing. When even nations famous for their history of socialism were going down this path, a blatantly left-wing voice like the one found on "Generation Terrorists" was bold and refreshing. Gender politics also comes into the equation—former porn actress Traci Lords contributes a vocal to "Little Baby Nothing," a rant against the exploitation of women ("you're beauty and virginity used like toys") whilst, in another form of gender politics, they lay their own androgynous aesthetic bare on "Stay Beautiful" ("were a mess of eyeliner and spraypaint/ DIY destruction to chanel chic"), a song which truly signals their arrival. On 29th January, the Department of Health revealed that AIDS cases amongst heterosexuals had increased by 50% between 1990 and 1991—homosexuality was no longer the demon. The Manics (although all heterosexual themselves) capitalised on this with the slogan "all rock'n'roll is homosexual," and an electrifyingly homoerotic relationship between Nicky Wire and Richey Edwards (particularly dominant in their first NME cover shoot and the video for "You Love Us.") The press dubbed them "The Glamour Twins"—and with this album, the union of glamour and socialism was everything the grey Conservative world was not.

THE FALL—CODE:SELFISH

As John Major announced that the election would be held on the 9th April, the opposition needed to make their own position and policies clear. The Shadow Chancellor, John Smith, had condemned the recent Budget as "missed opportunity," claiming that they had done "nothing," for jobs, training, skills and economic recovery. Labour's own policy concerning the economy was that there would be no tax reductions that year.

It was difficult to say how likely a Labour victory was, but the Conservative government continued to let the public down, soundtracked by the current Fall album, "Code Selfish." The track "Gentleman's Agreement," with its vicious chant of "I thought we had an agreement," seems to distil how the public felt about a government that was cheating them. The nastiness of The Fall's music is also suitable for what was a particularly nasty election campaign, dominated by "The War of Jennifer's Ear." For their party election broadcast, Labour wanted to show the difference between those who could afford private treatment, who had been granted tax breaks, and those on the NHS—in this case, a five year old girl with glue ear who had had to wait a year for the simple operation to insert vents. Capitalising on the mismanagement and underfunding of the NHS by the Conservatives, the campaign slogan was, "if you want to vote Conservative, don't fall ill." Julie Hall, Kinnock's press secretary, described the girl's story as based on an actual case. In fact, a particular case had been the starting point for the team, working from a letter from her parents to shadow health secretary Robin Cook, they denied that it was supposed to be a recounting of her case. The little girl in question turned out to be the granddaughter of a Conservative Party MP, keen to bring down the case. The Sun leapt on the story with a support for The Conservatives so fierce and unshakable that it is often actually thought to have won the

Conservative government the election, as they resorted to a deluge of inflammatory headlines such as "If Kinnock will tell lies about a sick little girl, will he ever tell the truth about anything?" Nobody was even sure what the truth within the case was at this point, as many conflicting details had emerged, but were there are many "lies" as the heavily biased Sun made out?

So, a campaign full of nastiness, a bleak political landscape and a new Fall album—was this the time for The Fall to hit their peak of nastiness? Actually, no—whilst it certainly has its moments, like the aforementioned, it is often extremely mellow, with the cheerful "Time Enough At Last," and "Just Waiting." But this does not mean that "Code:Selfish," is out of step with the news. On songs like "Two Face!" and "The Birmingham School of Business School," there is a running theme of dense repetition which matches the way the news itself was constantly repeating itself in which Britain seemed stuck in a kind of never-ending cycle. However, at times even this repetition is mellow, for example in "Immortality."

The Fall had calmed down—at least, temporarily. It seemed the same maturity could not be applied to the sniping and backbiting of party politics.

THE CURE—WISH

April, 1992, and the latest opinion polls were showing a narrow lead for Labour, which would force a hung parliament in the next election. In his pre-election speech, Neil Kinnock promised a strong economic recovery if he led his party to victory.

It was a closely run thing—the final MORI before the election showed Labour one point ahead with 39% of the vote. The Liberal Democrats also had a continued surge in popularity with 20% of the vote. So, what was the great album of this election month? As the Cure released their latest album, "Wish," at this time, it would have to be that. "Wish," is neither The Cure's best known album nor their most critically acclaimed, but it did include probably their best known song, "Friday I'm In Love." It had taken Robert Smith ten years to write a straightforward love song (1989's "Love Song," see "Disintegration.") but now he seemed seasoned at it, as "Friday I'm In Love," captures the nuances of love perfectly, with its lyrics about feeling "as sick as a sheep spinning round and round." If this sensation was felt by the nation at the time, it was probably about more than love. The opportunity for change had been completely missed as the Conservative Party were re-elected for a fourth term in their first election under John Major's leadership. Their majority was reduced to 21 seats but they had attracted more than 14,000,000 votes, the highest number of votes ever at a general election. It was almost as if people were scared of change; the willingness of a band like The Cure to deviate by writing a song like "Friday I'm In Love," seems like a gamble, but it resulted in their biggest hit—could the public have gained similar dividends if they had been a little bolder with their vote? Of course, a general election always brings some degree of change—there were notable retirements from Margaret Thatcher and Micheal Foot, and most significantly, the resignation of Neil Kinnock. The competition for Labour Party Leader was open.

With his victory confirmed, John Major assured the public that he would lead the country out of recession, but this was a difficult promise to live up to. A week after the election, it was confirmed that unemployment had risen 23 months in succession.

The other flaw in the Conservative victory is how influenced people had allowed themselves to be the press, in particular The Sun newspaper, who after the election claimed that it won it for the Conservatives, accompanied by the famous headline, "It's the Sun Wot Won It." The first election, then, under a new leader—strange how, given the significance of this, the April 1992 election feels something of a non-event.

"NEW VOICES IN AN UNCHANGING WORLD:"
PJ HARVEY—DRY
AND
SPIRITUALIZED—LAZER GUIDED MELODIES

On 6th May, 1992, John Major promised voters improved services and more money to spend. But could he really be trusted? The past years in politics had been full of empty promises and the political world seemed as if it would never change. Perhaps the best thing that music could do was put forward some exciting new voices to break up the monotony of the wider world. Key albums released in that year so far were the The Fall's "Code: Selfish," and The Cure's "Wish,"—good albums, but from bands who had been around for years. Luckily, May saw the release of two exciting debuts by acts who would go on to become staples of the music scene, Spiritualized and PJ Harvey.

The lead singer of Spiritualized, Jason Pierce, is an important figure in 1990's music, but it would be misleading to describe him as a "new voice," in 1992, as he had previously come to the misleading to describe him as a "new voice," in 1992, as he had previously come to the attention of the public under the name Jay Spaceman with the band Spaceman 5. "Lazer Guided Melodies," continues in that vein, a drug-inspired trip of escapism from a world both bleak and uninteresting. PJ Harvey, however, was a complete newcomer, and what she was doing with the bold and exciting album "Dry," was like a jolt to the musical landscape. Harvey had been born in Bridport in Dorset and brought up on a small sheep farm—her parents were a stonemason and a sculptor who were also keen music enthusiasts—three years after the release of "Dry," she would say, "I was brought up listening to John Lee Hooker, to Howlin Wolf, to all these very compassionate musicians at a very young age, and that's what always remained in me and seemed to surface more as I've got older. I think that the way we are as we get older is the result of what we knew as children." These early influences were then extended in her teenage years as she developed a love for American alternative music by bands like Pixies, Television and Slint. This mix of influences creates something fresh and inventive. Spritualized's "Lazer Guided Melodies," is equally inventive, but with an extra angle of escapism that could have been designed especially for the bleak lack of changes in the world. The recession and unemployment meant that Britain looked to be never-changing. There was even a new inter-government conflict, just like in the days of the Westland affair. However, this one was more like a large scale extension of Geoffrey Howe's resignation as twenty-two "Maastricht Rebels," voted against the government on the second reading of the European Communities (Amendment) Bill. The Treaty of Maastricht had been signed on 7th February 1992 by members of the EC, leading to the creation of the Euro and the "pillar structure," of the European Union, dividing it into the EC pillar, the CFSP (Common Foreign and Security Policy) and the Justice and Home Affairs (JHA) pillar. They were all extensions of pre-existing policy structures, but this did not mean that the signing of the Treaty was welcomed by all of the government. The MP's who rebelled had the support of Tebbitt and Thatcher—Thatcher declared the Treaty "a recipe for national suicide." For all her unpopularity, her voice still seemed to count for something. In fact, female voices were gaining ground on the whole as on 27th April, Betty Boothroyd, the 62 year old Labour MP for West Bromwich West was elected speaker of the House of Commons, becoming the first ever woman to hold the position.

Few female voices were as upfront and raw as that of PJ Harvey, who had certainly emerged with perfect timing. Female voices as a whole may have been widely accepted, but her handling of raw, unfettered sex on "Dry," still managed to make many uncomfortable. The mix of primitive sexuality (Sheela-Na-Gig) and noveau feminism (Dress) was all to much for some, but it has ensured that she earned a place in the rock history book as one of the greatest debuts of the nineties.

So, then PJ Harvey and Spiritualized were the two new, brilliant voices showing that even if politics seemed hopeless, there was still hope to be found in modern music.

MORRISSEY—YOUR ARSENAL

The resignation of Neil Kinnock had spread like a ripple throughout parliament, but not as not as much as who his successor as leader of the Labour Party ended up being—it was John Smith, who had made some unpopular choices as chancellor, often blamed for Labour's defeat. However, could he have been more capable as leader of the opposition than he was as Chancellor? This wave of political change was an interesting climate for the release of a new Morrissey album, and not just because of John Smith's new role—Margaret Thatcher took her place in the House of Lords as Baroness Thatcher. She was now a true part of the elite establishment. Morrissey's role throughout the eighties as an outspoken critic of hers, then, was still relevant.

In spite of being elected as Leader of the Labour Party in July, it was not until September that Smith made his maiden speech. In this, he attacked John Major by calling him "the devalued Prime Minister of a devalued government." His track record for attacking the opposition was high, but he had a tendency to resort to throwaway pop culture references in order to win over the public with humour. When he was still chancellor, he once joked at a Labour Party rally in Sheffield that the Conservatives would have a box office hit with "Honey, I shrunk the economy," (in reference to the film "Honey, I Shrunk The Kids"). This tactic continued in his role as opposition leader when, at a Labour Party conference, he referred to John Major and Norman Lamont as "the Laurel and Hardy of British politics." But the press seemed alarmingly unconcerned with Smith's own policies and more interested in his admittedly impressive weight loss. The media obsession with the ideal body and the concept of one, set way to be is neatly subverted by Morrissey on "Your Arsenal" with the song, "You're the One For Me, Fatty."

But the same mark is on "Your Arsenal," as on previous albums; overshadowing the other songs is the song, "National Front Disco," his most controversial moment yet. "England for the English, England for the English," runs the controversial lyric. Regarding the controversy surrounding this song, Morrissey said, "The reason why 'National Front Disco' was pounded upon was really because—if I may say so—it was actually a very good song. And if the song had been utter crap, no-one would have cared. I was stopped by many journalists who obviously raised the topic in an accusatory way, and I would say to them, 'Please, now, list the lines in the song which you feel are racist and dangerous and hateful. And they couldn't. Nobody ever could, and that irked me. Even though, simply in the voice in those songs, on "Asian Rut," or "Bengali in Platforms," "The National Front Disco," one can plainly hear that there is no hate at all." To claim journalists could not locate potentially racist lyrics seems odd considering "England for the English, England for the English . . ." this is clearly a weak defence from Morrissey.

On 29th November, it was confirmed that ethnic minorities now accounted for over 5% of the British population. Racism should have seemed outmoded, but it seemed to continually hit the headlines as, on 23rd July, there were the race riots in Blackburn, Burnley, and Huddersfield. On 8th November, three Hindu temples were destroyed by arsonists (in Birmingham, West Bromwich and Coventry.) Morrissey's lyricism seemed horribly distasteful.

The saddest thing about this album is the other news stories we could be twinning. As songwriter of "The Queen is Dead," he had potential to write a perfect soundtrack for the queen's "Annus Horribillus." As a bemused nation sniggered and shrugged their shoulders over David Mellor's affair with actress Antonia De Sacha, his wry humour could have been perfect. But the inclusion of yet another racially sensitive song turns all of these into missed opportunities—making it instead the soundtrack to another era of racial tension.

RADIOHEAD—PABLO HONEY   Feb 1993

1993 brought with it some glimmers of hope as the economy had grown in the final quarter of the previous year (but not enough for the end of the recession to be declared) but this seemed insignificant in the wider picture. Unemployment increased for the 31st month running, and the terrible conflict in Bosnia had its first British fatality in 26 year old corporal Wayne Edwards. There was also an ecological disaster when MV Braer ran aground on the Shetland Islands, spilling 64, 700 tonnes of crude oil into the sea. These things were major worries, but they seemed to be more on the fringes of what was deemed newsworthy as the press put all its attention on Princess Diana's wish for a divorce from Prince Charles. The monarchy was increasingly irrelevant—bookmakers had even cut their odds on them being abolished by the year 2000 from 100 to 1 to 50 to 1—so did the mainstream press care at all about what people truly wanted to hear? What people cold have really empathised with instead is something which tapped into the feelings created by unemployment, which is what made Radiohead's debut album "Pablo Honey," so timely and relevant, even though it now sounds musically underdeveloped compared to their later albums.

However, in spite of this it does include what is still one of their most popular songs, "Creep," a dark piece of writing which was even excluded from Radio One's playlist for being "too depressing." But was the act of banning things on the grounds of their bleakness ignorance of the wider world? By the time of "Pablo Honey"'s release, the aforementioned unemployment problem had reached 3, 000, 000, at a rate of 10.6%, for the first time in six years. This was reflected in individuals societies as the number of unfit homes was reported to have increased from 900,000 to more than 1, 300,000 between 1986 and 1991. Dealing with this was always going to be difficult for the government, and thus something the opposition could capitalise on when it came to grasping for votes—on 17th February, shadow Chancellor Gordon Brown claimed that a Labour government would reduce taxation. This was a dramatic turn for a party which had always been known for high taxation—in an age of simply saying what people wanted to hear, it was a bold move of Radiohead's to release a song "too depressing" for mainstream radio. But "Creep" isn't depressing, not typically. Its verses are edgy, but tackle the same themes as any straightforward unrequited love song ("You're just like an angel/ you're skin makes me cry . . . I want you to notice when I'm not around.") It is only when the chorus kicks in that we get a full view of the narrators twisted psyche, running, "You're so very special/ I wish I was special/ but I'm a creep/ I'm a weirdo/ what the hell am I doing here?/ I don't belong here." The latter lines here capture the feelings of confusion and isolation experienced by so many in the wave of unemployment, but the former are putting focus on human flaws, something the British public found themselves thinking about on an uncomfortable level when two ten year old boys were arrested for the murder of toddler James Bulger in Bootle. Such incidents made the world seem bleak enough—happy, throwaway pop was favoured over bands like Radiohead.

Even the critics were unconvinced, but the NME's 7/10 review was prophetic, saying that it was "one of those flawed but satisfying debuts which suggests Radiohead's talents will really blossom later on."

But "Pablo Honey," also gained many favourable reviews—"promising," (Record Collector) "is best bits rival the mighty Sugar" (Q), but it is widely dismissed today. It is perhaps all a matter of relevance. As Thom Yorke sings such lines of want and dissatisfaction as "I want a perfect body/ I want a perfect soul," (on "Creep") he and Radiohead tapped into public dissatisfaction.

Unsurprisingly, given that unemployment rose in more Conservative constituencies than Labour, a MORI poll on the 25th February showed that 80% of Britons were dissatisfied with the way John Major was running the country—thus "Pablo Honey," is the sound of a future great voice, and reflection of dissent finding its feet.

THE FALL—THE INFOTAINMENT SCAN April 1993

April, 1993 saw the release of The Fall's sixteenth album, "The Infotainment Scan." By the time most bands are on their sixteenth album (though few ever make it this far), both press and public have begun to turn away. But this is not "most bands." This is The Fall, and this album saw them achieve perhaps more recognition than they ever had, charting in the UK album charts at number nine.

The time of the albums release was bleak, not because of specifically political issues but because of the overwhelming theme of death, in a series of unconnected incidents. Firstly, on the 3rd March, Tony Bland, who had been given the right to die by the High Court due to injuries suffered in the Hillsborough disaster, died after being in a coma for nearly four years, bringing the Hillsborough death total to 96. Then, at the end of March, IRA bomb attacks claimed the lives of two children. This was followed on the 22nd April by the murder of Stephen Lawrence, a black eighteen year old student. It was suspected that the crime was racially motivated—such despicable issues should have been dying out, but apparently they were finding even darker, more serious tangents. This was part of a wider crime wave in general—on 28th April, it was reported that 1992 saw a record 5, 600, 000 crimes reported in England and Wales. So why, in this time of relentless darkness, should The Fall be so successful? It could be seen as a question of light relief. Yes, the band can be inaccessible, but there is such a level of anarchic, quirky humour on "The Infotainment Scan," that it fulfils any duties of escapism. For example, it includes songs like "The League of Bald Headed Men," largely regarded as a "jokey conspiracy theory." There are tongue in cheek cover versions too, of Sister Sledge's "Lost in Music," and Steve Bent's "I'm Going To Spain," an obscure song performed by Bent on the talent show "New Faces" in 1974 and thus placed on a 1978 compilation entitled "The World's Worst Record," compiled by Kenny Everett. This is not the work of a band without a sense of humour.

One of the other major news stories to occur just before The Fall released "The Infotainment Scan," was the introduction of the child support agency on April 5th. This introduced child support—a contribution from a non-resident parent towards the financial cost of raising their child. Prior to its launch, child support disputes were handled by a court based system, which did not have the power to trace absent parents and was described as "arbitary and unfair," in a BBC news report. However, the transfer of what had previously been a judicial issue of family law to a government agency was, according to political historian Thomas Nutt, a "significant break with the past." If one positive, significant break with the past could be made, could more? Prior to this, the last spring budget had seen chancellor Norman Lamont unveil a plan which centred on economic recovery, together with the phased introduction of VAT on domestic fuel bills. With so many broken promises, the public had every right to be sceptical, even paranoid. Ever the masters of adaptation, for one song on "The Infotainment Scan," The Fall adapted the title of an episode of "The Twilight Zone," "Nervous Man in A Four Dollar Room," for the song title, "Paranoia Man in A Cheap Shit Room."

Considering public feeling, lack of money, and the decline in living conditions, once again The Fall understood perfectly how to appropriate the fantastical and make it relevant to the masses.

"ARTISTRY AND HONESTY":

PJ HARVEY—RID OF ME

AND

BLUR—MODERN LIFE IS RUBBISH

May, 1993—a month that bought a wave of art, a new chancellor, some dodgy dealings—and two great second albums. These were Blur's "Modern Life is Rubbish," and PJ Harvey's "Rid Of Me" Harvey, in particular, had a lot of expectations placed on her after her brilliant debut album, "Dry," and the last thing anybody wanted was disappointment. They clearly had enough of that with the government, as the latest MORI poll saw the Conservatives trailing Labour by 16 points. Luckily, neither Blur nor PJ Harvey disappointed with the follow ups to their debuts.

Harvey recorded "Rid Of Me," at a difficult time. During the summer, relentless touring had taken its toll on her—St Martins College refused to hold the place she had deferred any longer, she was exhausted and her relationship broke up. She left London (where she had relocated) and retreated back to rural Dorset, where she wrote the songs which would appear on Rid of Me. The resulting album is even more aggressive than its predecessor. The songwriting is fairly complicated, as he utilises "strangely skewed time signatures and twisty song structures," in "songs that tilt towards performance art," to use her own words. It was a good time to embrace artistry—Jay Jopling had opened the White Cube gallery, which would see Tracey Emin's first major exhibition that year, and the Tate and St. Ive's Gallery opened in Cornwall. Harvey was also experimenting with what her voice could do, pushing its limits in a way which fits the lyrical themes. Blur, also, were developing their songwriting. "Modern Life is Rubbish," is a leap forward in its refusal to be commercial—their record label feared that it was commercial suicide. Both albums were recorded with iconic, talented producers—Harvey's "Rid Of Me," was produced by Steve Albini, who was something of a maverick. Harvey said of him, "The way some people think of producing, is to sort of help you arrange or contributing or playing instruments, he does none of that. He just sets up his microphones in a completely different way from which I've ever seen anybody set up mics before, and that was astonishing. He'd have them on the floor, on the walls, on the windows, on the ceiling, twenty feet away from where you were sitting . . . he's very good at getting the right atmosphere to get the best take."

Blur had started out with XTC's Andy Partridge as the "Modern Life is Rubbish," producer, but the pairing did not work. So, instead, they reunited with Stephen Street.)

Both albums are also overflowing with excellent, relevant themes. The lyrics on "Rid Of Me," are frequently described as feminist. Feminism had hit its peak as an actual movement many years before, but the rise of women in artistry was ongoing(such as in the Tracey Emin exhibition.) However, Harvey says that, "I don't even think of myself as female half the time. When I'm writing songs I never write with gender in mind. I write about people's relationships to each other." But these relationships could be seen as relevant to the wider world, even though it is painfully personal, the title track about the end of a relationship. When an interviewer told her that it sounded almost psychotic, she said that she had written it "at her illest," and was "almost psychotic."

The lyrics on "Modern Life is Rubbish," are less unsettling, but just as brilliant. Often compared to Ray Davies, Albarn's lyrics here are a sharp social commentary and satire on modern English British life. It is cynical on the middle classes, but outright biting on American popular culture engulfing Britain—the immense Englishness of this album is a direct reaction against this. Bassist Alex James explains, "it was fucking scary how American everythings becoming . . . so the whole thing is a fucking big two fingers up to America." The NME called "Modern Life is Rubbish," a "thinly veiled concept album . . . a London odyssey crammed full of strange commuters, peeping Thomases and lost dreams, of opening the windows and breathing in petrol . . . it's the Village Green Preservation Society come home to find a car park in its place." It appeared, then, that Albarn had fulfilled his lyrical aims. He himself said that "it was me attempting to write in a classic English vein using a kind of imagery, and words which were much more modern. So it was a weird combination of quiet nostalgic-sounding melodies and chord progressions (with) these weird caustic lyrics about England as it was at that moment, and the way it was getting this mass Americanised refit."

As well as great music and lyrics, both albums have iconic artwork. That for "Rid Of Me," is a topless Harvey with drenched hair, taken in her friends bathroom, a room so small that the camera's viewfinders could not be looked into. When her record label asked the said friend (Maria Monchanez, who also took the photo) to remove the flaws in the picture she protested, saying that they were a part of it. "Modern Life Is Rubbish"'s artwork is a painting of a steam train, looking back to a forgotten Britain.

The month of both albums release saw Kenneth Clarke succeed Norman Lamont as Chancellor. Clarke had served first as junior transport minister, then Minister of State for Health. He had been a controversial health secretary, and then as Education Secretary he was one of the first MP's to advise Thatcher to resign—in her memoirs she refers to him as a "candid friend." After his time as Education secretary, he became Home Secretary, and then Chancellor when "Black Wednesday," damaged Lamont's credibility. He was a firm defendant of John Major's having always worked closely with him—later in the year, he would go on to say "any enemy of John Major's is an enemy of mine." The opinion polls would show that this meant he had a lot of enemies . . .

What the "second albums," of May 1993 show us is that change (personal in Harvey's case, national in Blur's) is not always positive. The appointment of a new chancellor in this time of economic strife did not necessarily promise improvement. Could anything the government said even be trusted anymore? In an era of lying and distrust, "Rid Of Me," and "Modern Life Is Rubbish," can stake their claim also as two truly honest pieces of work.

"FRAUD, CORRUPTION . . . AND GLAMOUR":

MANIC STREET PREACHERS—GOLD AGAINST THE SOUL AND

SUEDE—SUEDE

By June, 1993, although not selling the vast amount of records that they would go on to in the second part of the decade, the Manic Street Preachers had established a comfortable counter-culture following, a good basis for their second album, "Gold Against The Soul." This was partly due to the enormous level of uniqueness that they had in contrast with the rest of the almost dully masculine music scene. However, they appeared to be being rapidly transcended by the new kings of provocative glamour, Suede. Earlier in the year, their eponymous debut had become the fastest selling debut in history.

Both bands have an edge of sleaze, but Suede's was at an even wider extent than that of the Manics. Whilst the year of the albums release did not exactly brim with political sleaze per se—that would come the following year—June, 1993 did see an awful lot of dodgy dealings in the political sphere. On 24th June, Northern Ireland Minister Micheal Mates resigned over his links with the fugitive Asil Nadir. Nadir had been chief executive of Polly Peck, a company he took over as a small textile company, growing it throughout the 1980's to make it of the UK's top FTSE-listed companies. However, there was a great deal of fraud behind this—an investigation by the Serious Fraud Office unveiled 70 counts of false accounting and theft. In response, he fled to the Turkish republic of Northern Cyprus in order to avoid a trial in the UK. The idea of senior MP's having relations with such untrustworthy figures obviously made them themselves harder to trust. Such dodgy dealings also continued in the public sphere—Micheal Hunt, the former deputy chairman of Nissan UK, was jailed for eight years for his involvement in Britain's worst case of tax fraud.

The edgy sleaziness of Suede's music seemed to fit perfectly with all this; songs like "Animal Nitrate," (a play on amyl nitrate) are so raw and so oddly taboo that sex is out of the hands of the mainstream and back to being a shock-horror activity. The Manic Street Preachers fans still comprised the Cult of Richey, a largely-female fanbase prone to sending Edwards strange obsessive letters, but Suede's frontman Brett Anderson was now the androgynous sex symbol du jour.

This takeover of what had previously been the Manics unique selling point could have hit them hard, but instead they declared their admiration for Suede, Edwards naming "Animal Nitrate," as his song of the year. Whilst they were not selling records on the level that Suede were, the Manics were becoming increasingly relevant as their left-wing politics struck a chord—Conservative popularity dropped as they trailed 18 points behind Labour, whereas the unions were stronger than ever, particularly with the formation of public sector union UNISON. Their music was also developing new angles—with Suede now reigning in the world of trashy glamour, the Manics showed signs of becoming deeper and more reflective. Edwards was a troubled figure, blighted by an extensive range of issues—depression, alcoholism and anorexia—and the signs of his fragility are set out on "Gold Against The Soul." "Roses In The Hospital" is particularly heartbreaking, with its lyric of *"I want to tear my fingernails out/ I want to cling to something soft."* Hospitals were a timely, emotive subject anyway—on 11th August, the Department of Health revealed that the number of people on hospital waiting lists had reached 1,000,000 for the first time. However, if one issue defines the second half of 1993, it is racism. In August, a wave of vandalism in Southampton saw anti-Semitic slogans daubed on 150 Jewish graves. Then, in September, the British National Party was its first council seat in Tower Hamlets. This sparked rioting between anti-fascist campaigners and neo-Nazis. Fascism was not a thing of the past; it was if elements of World War II and other battles against fascism had failed. Bu, then again, the modern world seemed all a bit to unconcerned with history, as the respect for our war veterans decreased. One song on "Gold Against The Soul," "La Tristesse Durera," (meaning "the agony goes on", words lifted from Van Gogh's suicide note) laments this—*"I am a relic/ I am a cenotaph souvenir . . . one minutes silence in a century of screams."* On, the 30th September, the Queen approved in honorary knighthood for General Colin Powell, the former chief of the American armed forces—but he had retired just the day before, his achievements not on the same plateau as the heroic, forgotten veterans. In spite of some signs of positivity, there was still plenty out there to keep the Left complaining. As a vote of "no confidence," from the Maastricht rebels did not succeed, the UK Independence Party was formed. Whilst many left-wingers also supported a break away from the EU, UKIP was yet another right-wing force in British politics. National identity was an enormous theme for everywhere at the time—on 21st October, the Welsh Language Act placed Welsh on an equal footing within the public sector in Wales (no doubt to the bemusement of Richey Edwards, who considered it an outmoded language.) National identity also continued to cause active problems—on 23rd October, the Shankill Road bombing killed ten, including the bomber. Two days later, the retaliation "Greysteel Massacre," killed another eight.

National identity in England was les problematic, encompassing our pop culture as "Britpop" began. Suede were seen as a key part of this; the editors of Select superimposed Anderson's image over a Union Jack, arousing his complete disgust, having never wanted to be associated with such an image. After all, was being British really such a matter of pride? Northern Ireland was vowing to fight against us, militant racism was also becoming militant homophobia (with the murder of five gay men) and we were welcoming Yasser Arafat on a state visit. The world Suede created allowed a thrilling escape from this (even though their debut is not without its realism, for example, "So Young," a song about a friends death from an overdose.)

Whilst Suede and the Manic Street Preachers sound quite different, the two tend to share a fanbase; the intimacy and homoeroticism combined with the aesthetic to twin their demographics. However, the homoerotic relationship between Wire and Edwards seemed increasingly sweet—in an interview from this time, Wire tells Edwards he loves him "more than anything else in the world"—Brett Anderson and Bernard Sumner seemed far more thrilling, with their tension and jealousy. Even though he had just been in a relationship with former bandmate Justine Frischmann, Anderson was open about being sexually confused. It was at this time also that John Major launched his Back to Basics campaign, a vague campaign designed to keep politics free of sleaze and scandal—at least there were two albums out there showing how thrilling these things could be.

PRIMAL SCREAM—GIVE OUT, DON'T GIVE UP   March 1994

In 1991, on the brilliant album "Screamadelica," Primal Scream had told us, "Don't Fight It, Feel It." Now they were telling us "Give Out, Don't Give Up." But could the recycling of semantic structures really promise a continuation of "Screamadelica"?

Perhaps, in all fairness, the worst thing the band could do would be try and make another "Screamadelica." Instead, they flaunted their ability for versatility in order to make this truly entertaining album.

The beginning of 1994 provided something a mixed backdrop for the band to release the album into. Privatisation continued its ugly ascent as on the 19th January, the privatisation of London buses began with the first sale of a bus-operating subsidiary, Westlink, in a management buyout. There was also an almighty game of international tit-for-tat raging as on 4th January, the Foreign Office ordered the Sudanese ambassador to leave Britain in response the expulsion of the British ambassador from Sudan. Another negative news story was the closure of four more coal mines, a love costing 3,000 jobs. The tradition of the workers being let down under Conservative governments was truly being upheld. Primal Scream would go onto become a truly articulate voice of dissent, their socialism colouring their music (see "XTMNTR.") So, why, in the midst of all this, why did an album including such light-hearted songs of rebellion as "Rocks," and "Jailbird," seem so strangely right, so timely? Perhaps this just has a lot to do with the chain of controversy which added such life to the beginning of 1994?

On the 10th January, two government ministers resigned. One was Lord Caithness following the suicide of his wife, a sad story which should be left alone, unpoliticised. But the other was Tim Yeo in far more scandalous circumstances—the revelation emerged that he fathered a child with Conservative councillor Julia Stern . . . and the scandal of this was nothing compared to an event on the 7th January. The Conservative MP for Eastleigh, Stephen Milligan, was found dead at his home in Chiswick. Police described the death as "suspicious." This was revealed as something of a euphemism; on 11th February forensic tests revealed that he had died of asphyxiation resulting from an auto-erotic sex practice. These events show a time in which traditional morality was dying out, thus making the unashamed sex-and-drug anthems of "Give Out, Don't Give Up," so appropriate. "Rocks," is almost an drug anthem, outlining a dissolute lifestyle with its opening verse *"Dealers keep dealin'/ Thieves keep thievin'/ Whores keep whoring/ Junkies keep scoring/ Trade is on the meat rack/ Strip joints full of hunchbacks/ Bitches keep bitchin/ Clap keeps itchin'."* There's certainly a double meaning to be found in the line "*always got a line for the ladies*," while lines about "*cops keep bustin,*" show a defiance to continue such a lifestyle in the face of authority. The great, straightforward rock song "Jailbird," follows a similar theme, opening with the lines "scratching like a tomcat/ got a monkey on my back," a reference to addiction. Lyrical references to cadillacs, sex with "bad girls," ("*gimme more of that jailbird pie*") "strutting your funky stuff," "funky jammin free" and yet more drugs *("I've got medication honey/ I've got ways to fly")* ensure that every cliché possible is thrown in—the effect is great, immoral fun. If everybody was going to be rock'n'roll, then surely rock'n'roll needed to go the extra mile?

Other sparks of controversy at this time flew when The Duchess of Kent joined the Roman Catholic Church, being the first member of the Royal family to convert to Catholicism for nearly 300 years. But to create controversy out of religiosity seems odd—in an age of scandal perfectly soundtracked by Primal Scream, the notion of anything advocating traditional morality seemed almost quaint.

MORRISSEY—VAUXHALL AND I March 1994

The dangerous lyrical territory that Morrissey had been treading in recent years could have seriously damaged him. The world of indie may be prepared to tolerate a lot, but suggestion of racial intolerance is a complete "no." But he was such an enormous indie icon that people wanted to forgive and forget—all he had to do was make an album which was both brilliant and avoided the uncomfortable theme of race. With "Vauxhall and I," an album he himself regarded as his finest, he managed it. Something people often note about this album is its "funereal," feel. This is probably because Morrissey suffered three bereavements in close succession before recording "Vauxhall and I," a fact which makes it a deeply poignant album.

The month of the albums release saw some horrific news stories; on 28th March, Hall Garth School in Middlesborough was the scene of a masked former pupil breaking in, stabbing one pupil to death and wounded two others. The news was also dominated by the arrest of Fred West over the murders of eight women whose remains had been found buried in his garden (one believed to be his own daughter). The problem with such stories being splashed all over the news is the sensationalising of death that it creates; horror overtakes sadness. Of course, this relates to circumstance, but with some of the beautiful music on "Vauxhall and I," Morrissey is reminding us how true grief really feels. Furthermore, the bereavements that Morrissey suffered at this time were all of a professional nature—his video director Tim Broad, his manager Nigel Thomas, and his producer Mick Ronson. The heavy feeling of loss on "Vauxhall and I," conveys the way that the professional can also become so very personal. This kind of intimacy is reflected in the albums pared-down, acoustic style—producer Steve Lillywhite's influence on the sound is key as he drives Morrissey to let the listener. It was released in an age of inclusion—on 12th March, the Church of England ordained its first women priests, the first being Angela Berners-Wilson—but Conservative rule also meant that that era saw many individuals suffer at the hands of laissez-faire policy, feeling ignored and invisible. Recent history had shown how this tended to spark a kind of revenge, as with the miners strike. This adds an edge and relevance to to the best-known song from "Vauxhall and I," "The More You Ignore Me, The Closer I Get." This is not a political song (it is an unrequited love song) but anything on the theme of being ignored would have struck a chord with many. "I am a central part of your minds landscape/ whether you care or not/ I've made up my mind," runs the first verse, putting the power in the hands of the ignored. "Beware I bear my grudges than lonely high court judges," it continues, "when you sleep, I will creep into your thoughts like a bad debt/ That you can't pay, take the easy way and give in." This kind of lyrical anthem for the ignored puts Morrissey's songwriting back in the same vein that he used with The Smiths. There is also a return to great British literary influences on "Vauxhall and I," such as quotations and use of characters from Graham Greene's classic 1939 novel "Brighton Rock" on "Why Don't You Find Out For Yourself?"

After the unpleasant aftertaste of some of his other earlier solo albums, this return to what he does best means "Vauxhall and I," would be his musical recovery—the world was ready to forgive some of his dubious lyrics and actions. After all, he's Morrissey . . .

"VERY BRITISH VOICES: WHO ARE THE BRITISH?":

BLUR—PARKLIFE

AND

PULP—HIS N HERS

In 1994, two albums were released by bands who were already acclaimed for their oh-so-British music. April saw the release of Pulp's crossover album, "His 'n' Hers" whereas July saw the release of Blur's "Parklife." Neither band had had huge commercial successes with previous albums, but pitch-perfect timing ensured that these were the albums that bought them to wider attention. Coincidentally, "His 'n Hers" was released at a time, when, in one field at least, the two were no longer separated—on the 1st April, the Womens Royal Air Force fully merged into the Royal Air Force. Even though four months separates the release dates of these albums (and I shall go on to write about albums whose release date falls in between these two) they are worth writing about as one. Both are early examples of what would go on to become the "Britpop," genre, which would enjoy huge popularity, but at this stage was really still in its infancy. "Britpop" really just meant any British guitar-based music, usually (but not always) with a heavy does of commercial appeal, but "Parklife" and "His 'n' Hers" seem more deserving of that label than many other albums released in this period, with their perfect capturings of the nuances of Englishness—Pulp representing the North (Sheffield) and Blur the South (Essex).

The Englishness of Blur's previous album, "Modern Life is Rubbish," is continued here—its cover art depicts racing dogs, a typically British activity. The original idea for the artwork, accelerating this theme even further, was going to be a fruit and vegetable cart. Frontman Damon Albarn told the NME at the time, "for me, "Parklife," is a loosely linked concept album, involving all these different stories. It is the travels of the mystical lager-eater, seeing what's going on in the world and commenting on it." The biggest influence on the album was Martin Amis' novel "London Fields," an extremely seedy and voyeuristic piece of writing.

Pulp, also, were making music inspired by the seedier side of life. One of the standout songs on "His 'n' Hers" is "Babies" but rather than being inspired by the dark, murderous sexuality of "London Fields," it is inspired by the natural perversities of adolescence, opening with the lines *"well it happened years ago/ when you lived in Stanhope Road/ We listened to your sister when she came home from school/ cos she was two years older and she had boys in her room/ We listened outside and heard her/ well that was alright for a while but soon I wanted more/ I wanted to see as well as hear so I hid inside her wardrobe."* The sex on "Parklife," has not matured that much more from this, as opener "Boys and Girls," was inspired by the hedonism witnessed by Albarn on an 18-30 holiday, as he felt torn between repulsion and wanting to be a part of it. Its not all sleaze and smut, though—"End of A Century," and "This is A Low," are beautiful songs which rank amongst the bands finest moments, whereas the title track is simply a reflection on day-to-day life, with a guest vocal by Quadrophenia star Phil Daniels.

Both these albums document normal life, be it coming—of-age rituals or getting up to go to work. Answering the question "what is Britishness?" is difficult, but under a Conservative government beset by problems boredom and the mundane are probably factors—it is to Pulp and Blur's credit that they used this to make these hugely entertaining albums.

THE FALL—MIDDLE CLASS REVOLT   May 1994

By May 1994, Conservative support had fallen to 26%, their worst showing in any major opinion poll since they had come to power 15 years previously. Local council elections on may 5th saw them lose 429 seats and control of 18 councils—this was a reflection on the British public being increasingly dissatisfied and bored with their government. And is it any wonder? Politics from this time has little to define it in history, John Major remembered for being largely, well, boring. The leader of the opposition John Smith is also scarcely remembered, perhaps due to the brevity of his time in the position—on 12th May, he died suddenly and unexpectedly of a heart attack. Music had a duty to be exciting at this time in order to fulfil its role as an escape route. Sadly, it largely was not. It was in this era that Wet Wet Wet's cover of "Love Is All Around," spent 15 consecutive weeks at number one, the longest spell ever attained by a British act. Luckily, there was also a new album by the ever reliable Fall, who were proving themselves as relevant as ever on "Middle Class Revolt." The title track, in particular, is brilliantly satirical swipe at the middle classes and the class system in general. The old, simple class system had been replaced by the complicated numbers and letters system (D1, C2 etc) these classes obliquely but intelligently referenced in this extremely clever piece of writing. It also reflects on something of a mundane lifestyle, which many people in Britain knew of all to well. When, on 25th May, the Camelot Group consortium won the contract to run the UK's first National Lottery, the public rushed to play it. They did not care that it was straight out of "1984"—for them it was an escape, a glimmer of hope to cling on to in an unexciting world. Gambling had always been the preserve of a few—now, it had been sanitised and was ready to go mainstream in the form of the lottery. At least, with The Fall in action, we were shown somewhere along the line that the dullness of realism could still be turned into the something exciting.

MANIC STREET PREACHERS—THE HOLY BIBLE   June 1994

Its not every album which uses what is widely regarded to be the most taboo word in the English language in its very first line, but then again the Manic Street Preachers finest hour, "The Holy Bible," is far, far from everyday. It is instead a portal into a rapidly disintegrating mindset which was, reasonably enough, named as the Darkest of All Time in a 2011 NME list.

Were times really so bleak in June 1994 to warrant such a demanding, uncomfortable album? In short, for Richey Edwards, yes—for the world, probably not. At the end of the previous month, Tony Blair and Gordon Brown had had dinner at the Granita restaurant in Islington, were they allegedly made a deal on who would become the next leader of the Labour Party. This may seem like democracy and rationality, but there was actually something faintly Machiavellian about it all; both determined to ensure that they would get what they wanted in the end. Whichever it was would probably, after all, become Prime Minister, considering the disastrous time to Conservatives were having. There were signs of their decreasing popularity on 9th June when David Chidgey won the Eastleigh seat for the Liberal Democrats in the by-election sparked by Stephen Milligan's death, as this left the Conservative majority with 15 seats compared to 21 two years ago. This was a sign of things to come—on the 13th June, they suffered their worst election results of the century, winning just 18 out of 97 of the nations seats in the European Parliament elections.

Even though they were still leaderless, the Labour Party won 62 seats. Unsurprisingly, in the wake of all this, Sir Norman Fowler resigned as chairman of the Conservative Party.

This rapid slide in Conservative popularity should have been cause for left-wing popularity should have been cause for left-wing musicians to make positive music, but things were not that simple. History had taught us not be to be optimistic to soon—and "The Holy Bible," is an album defined by references to political history. The key moments on this album for this are "Of Walking Abortion," and "The Intense Humming of Evil." The former is a song which raises questions in the listeners own mind as it looks at dictatorships, and the flaw in human flaw in nature which causes them to get voted in in the first place. Within the space of a few lines, it has referenced Mussolini, Hitler, Horthy and Tiso, hardly conventional names to hear in contemporary music, before closing with the repeated lines "whose responsible?/ you fucking are." Whilst obviously not on the same level, people in Britain had voted for a government they now appeared to hate, making this hugely relevant. "The Intense Humming of Evil," does not raise as many questions, but is one of the most disturbing songs ever written, reflecting on the Holocaust. The band had visited Auschwitz and Dauchau and Edwards had found himself unable to sleep afterwards for dwelling on the Holocaust; the resulting song presses heavily on the listener with its lines of "six million screaming souls," twinned with the controversial "Churchill no different/ wished the workers bled to a machine." Of course, any good political songwriter will focus on the contemporary, not just history. "Ifwhiteamericatoldthetruthforonedayitsworldwouldfallapart," is a biting critique of modern American politics, particularly with its closing lines "fuck the Brady Bill,"—the Brady Bill being the laws introduced by Bill Clinton to control the ownership of guns by black people, even though it was shown that it was the white "redneck" population responsible for most gun crime.

Other contemporary issues are tackled on "PCP", a rant against excessive censorship and EU-imposed health and safety and political correctness, opening with the lines "Teacher starve your child PC approved as long as the right words are used/ system of atrocity acknowledged as long as bilingual signs on view." Lyrics such as "beware Shakespeare bring fresh air," and closing lines, "this land bows down yours/ unconditional love and hate/ pass the prozac/ designer amnesiac," cover the spectrum of issues and problems posed by the censorship and the EU, highly topical considering the recent Maastricht Treaty.

For all the politics here, "The Holy Bible," is famously personal, to the point of uncomfortable. Edwards was hospitalised after the albums recording as his depression had clearly accelerated. Drinking over a bottle of vodka a day down to six stone in weight as a consequence of anorexia nervosa (something documented on the almost voyeuristically honest "4st 7lb" running "self worth scatters self-esteems a bore/ I long since moved to a higher plateau/ this disciplines so rare so please applaud") he was far removed from the brightly funny and sexually appealing figure of the "Generation Terrorist" years. The song "Yes" includes one of the most honest reflections of this, with its lyric of "can't shout/ can't scream/ I hurt myself to get pain out."

This was the bands last album with Edwards. He was last seen on February 1st, 1995 at the London Embassy. Two weeks later, his car was found by the Severn Bridge, a popular suicide spot, with signs that it had been lived in. His whereabouts ever since have proved a mystery—there have been various sightings, all unconfirmed. He once said of suicide, "in terms of the "s" word, that does not cross my mind. I am so much stronger than that," but nonetheless he declared legally dead in 2009. Edwards disappearance has turned him into a rock 'n' roll mystery, whose fame has accelerated since he went missing, but he should be remembered for the power of his lyricism, not this. "The Holy Bible," may be bleak, but it is one of the greatest albums of the 90's, not just lyrically but musically also. Wherever Edwards is, or whatever happened, the creation of a piece like this in age of political vagueness means that his place in music history hastily been earnt.

OASIS—DEFINETLY MAYBE   June 1994

On 21st July 1994, Tony Blair won the Labour Party leadership election. This was a new age for the Party as its working class roots were edited out with the introduction of "New Labour," a major spin-based rebranding of the party. The Conservatives would remain in power until 1997, so it is strange how much the "Britpop" movement in music is associated with New Labour. In fact, the genre's major albums, such as Blur's "Parklife," and Oasis "Definetly Maybe," were largely released during John Major's time as Prime Minister. The dissatisfaction of the working classes under Conservative rule left them yearning for a voice they could relate to; when Oasis appeared on the scene, it was in something of a blaze of glory.

"Definetly, Maybe," is a classic debut. The band had been signed by Creation in May 1993 and had been playing local gigs under the name The Rain for years; by the time the album came out, there was a lot of expectation placed on it. Of the environment which gave birth to the album, Noel Gallagher said in a 2011 interview with Q that "it was a time for heroes. There was a vast amount of people who didn't believe in anything, just not getting off on music any more." As Gallagher told the nation that Oasis were going to define the generation, it was obvious that they were going to be the "heroes"—heroes with ambition and self-belief who, whats more, were genuinely representative of the Northern working class—as Paul "Bonehead" Arthurs, the rhythm guitarist at the time puts it, "we were five kids, straight off the street." The process of recording the album was fun and riotous, taking place in Monmouthshire under Kinks and Skids producer Dave Batchelor, with The Stone Roses recording their second album under a mile away. The two bands bonded, resulting in alcohol and narcotics-fuelled nights which the album seems to capture perfectly. Opener "Rock'n'Roll Star" is a perfect reflection of popular dreams coming true—*"look at you now you're all my hand,"* sings Liam Gallagher, probably the greatest frontman of the nineties, spinning the class system on its head as the neglected working-class seize power by making all their dreams real—their *rock'n' roll* dreams.

This album brims with sentiments for the masses to cling on to—on one of the standouts, "Cigarettes and Alcohol," Liam sings *"it's a crazy situation/ to find yourself a job when theres nothing worth looking for."* As the recent recession left hoardes unemployed, Liam's delivery of this is inspirational. The band certainly believed in their own brilliance, even though Noel Gallagher considered "Live Forever," such a good song that he did not believe he could possibly have written it, thinking it must be an obscure song he had subconsciously ripped off.

Oasis could not have appeared at a better time—the working class needed a voice somewhere along the line, having lost out on having one in mainstream politics as "New Labour," was now the alternative to Conservatism—but the two were practically the same. New Labour's first leader, Tony Blair, had been a boarder at the prestigious Fettes College Independent School—during this time, he met Charlie Falconer, a pupil at the rival Edinburgh Academy, who he would go on to appoint as Lord Chancellor—were these really people the British working-class could identify with? The term "New Labour," gained clearer definitions the following year, as we shall go on to see, but in the meantime, it simply implied a change from working-class tradition. With nothing to hold on to, all the masses could do was escape. Noel Gallagher summed up "Definitely Maybe," by saying, "'Lets have it' was the main ethos. All the songs were about leaving were you came from and ending up in the sunshine, taking drugs and drinking for the rest of your life. Its all about escapism—a pint in one hand, your best mate in the other, and just having a good time."

It really could not have come along at a better time. The new heroes of the age had been borne.

SUEDE—DOG MAN STAR   Oct 1994

The success of Suede's eponymous debut album, both critically and commercially, had been enormous as they provided a darkly thrilling escape from a mundane, often bleak Britian. By the time their second album "Dog Man Star" was released, the nation had more reasons for happiness—the economic recovery was continuing at a strong rate; by 16th October unemployment had fallen to under 2,500,000 for the first time since the end of 1991. However, politics remained blighted by scandal, with the 20th October unmasking the cash-for-questions affair. The Guardian newspaper reported that two Conservative MP's, Neil Hamilton and Tim Smith, took bribes from Harrods owner Mohamed Al-Fayed to ask questions in the House of Commons. A wave of these kinds of underhand dealings had been one of the factors in the sleaze of Suede's exciting debut seeming so relevant; the ideal context for this was still in place, but sales for "Dog Man Star," were poor compared with "Suede." This is simply because it is a far less commercial album, with no obvious hits. Critical acclaim was still very much present. Perhaps Suede had done the best thing they could do in terms of keeping critical acclaim high—made a "difficult" album for a difficult age. In spite of the positivity in the worlds of employment and economy, there were complications in law. The Criminal Justice and Public Order Act received Royal Assent. This changed the right to silence of an accused person, allowing inferences to be drawn from their silence, increased police powers of "stop and search" and gave them greater rights to take and retain intimate body samples—it was as if the modern world decreased human rights, rather than increased them. The act also criminalised some previously civil offences, and tightened the law on obscenity and pornography—the raw sexuality of Suede's music had become more taboo, not less.

However, the act did have some positive dividends. The age of consent was lowered from twenty-one to eighteen for homosexuals, bringing them one step closer to equality, whilst the age for female acts was set at sixteen, which was the first time English law recognised the existence of lesbianism. It would be all to easy to say that the homoeroticism present in Suede was more relevant than ever, but this element had vanished from the band with the departure of guitarist and co-writer Bernard Butler.

Replacement Richard Oakes was, however, a capable guitarist—and with "Dog Man Star," the band had shown that their could be life after Butler.

PORTISHEAD—DUMMY   Oct 1994

On the 19th November, the first UK National Lottery took place. People all over Britain crossed their fingers and dreamed big—gambling had found its "acceptable," form in order to be instantly popularised.

Something else which had once had a small, specific demographic and was now ready to be popularised was the musical genre of "trip hop,"—Portishead's "Dummy," is one of the most popular albums of the genre, something aided by its victory in the Mercury music prize. The band were Bristol based, which confirmed the cities reputation as the capital of trip-hop. It was a city which was acknowledged for very little else—most attention at the time was looking over to Ireland as, on the 9th December, there was the first meeting between the British government and Sinn Fein in over 70 years. This was in the wake of events of the 31st August, in which the Provisional IRA had declared a ceasefire. This level of peace reflects the calm subtleties of "Dummy," but to label it a "chill out" album is to overlook its haunting darkness. "Sour Times," is the key track for this, with its haunting instrumentals and gentle crack in singer Beth Gibbon's voice as she pines, *"nobody loves me its true/ not like you do."* And could a song with a title like "Sour Times," really be more appropriate? Under John Major's government, 40% of the workforce had been unemployed at some point since he came to power. No wonder disillusionment with the Conservatives was growing—the latest MORI poll put Labour support at 61%—39 points ahead of the Conservatives. A Dudley West by-election resulted in a seat for Labour's Ian Pearson—taking over a role left vacant by the death of the Conservative MP, John Blackburn, two years ago. This left the Conservative majority at under thirteen seats. Disillusionment, like that clearly felt by the British public, tends to breed a sense of loneliness—with "Dummy" Portishead had managed to distil that into sound.

LEFTFIELD—LEFTISM   Jan 1995

After a series of MORI polls suggesting that sixteen years of Conservative rule had nearly come to an end, the first MORI poll of 1995, on January 20th showed that the Conservatives had actually cut Labours lead from 39 points to 29. It really did look as if things would never change—at least the beginning of this new year implied that music could be exciting, innovative and completely new-sounding. The band Leftfield had formed five years earlier in London. Its two members, Neil Barnes and Paul Daley, were both respected producers, something reflected in the flawless production of their timeless debut.

"Leftism," is instantly brilliant. Its artwork of a sharks jawbone and a speaker combining to make an image of a human eye summarises it perfectly—unusual elements making something that you would never usually associate with them. It may be a dance album, but rock contributions are what make its standout tracks. Toni Halliday, the singer was goth act Curve, is the vocalist on "Original," a song about the joys of being, well, original. As people returned back to the Conservatives, singing on the joys of being original was refreshing, especially when done so in Halliday's haunting manner.

The standout on this album for me, however, is "Open Up," to which John Lydon contribute one of his finest ever vocal performances. *"You lie! You hate! You cheated!"* he yells, summarising some feeling towards the government. *"Tragedy or comedy/ probably publicity*,*"* he continues, a lyric which would remain relevant as the spin based New Labour continued to make themselves known. Lydon had shown with PiL that he was not scared of experimentation—here, that is showcased along with all the original spite of the Sex Pistols, particularly in the sneered line, "Burn, Hollywood, burn" showing that this was a band keener on the counterculture than mainstream celebrity. From the minute the powerfully minimal reggae-tinged opener "Release The Pressure," kicks in, it is clear that this is much more than the average dance album. Its follow-up, "Rhythm and Stealth," had moments of brilliance (particularly "Dusted", a collaboration with Roots Manuva) and saw them cross into the mainstream as the song "Phat Planet," was used on a hugely popular Guinness advertisement, but cam nowhere near to matching the glories of their Mercury-nominated debut.

A band called Leftfield when everyone strived for the mainstream, an album called Leftism when we had a Conservative government—this is music out of step with all around it, and all the better for it.

PJ HARVEY—TO BRING YOU MY LOVE

AND

THE FALL—CEREBRAL CAUSTIC

By February, 1995, the opposition was full of changes. Not only had Labour's new leader Tony Blair removed the party from its origins with the advent of "New Labour," but their former leader Neil Kinnock resigned from Parliament after 25 years in order to take up his new role as European Commissioner. In the musical world, this month saw changes and progressions, but in the releases of albums by already-established acts rather than new bands. Firstly, as there seemed to constantly be, there was a new album by The Fall, "Cerebral Caustic." This was also the month which saw PJ Harvey release her third album, the critically acclaimed "To Bring You My Love."

Both albums mark a return to the spotlight for formidable women. The Fall's "Cerebral Caustic," sees Brix Smith return to the line-up after initially leaving in 1989. Her impact was immediate, with her co-writing five of the albums tracks.

PJ Harvey had also spent some time out of the spotlight, being absent from the music scene throughout 1994. She had spent this time living in virtual isolation, describing her rural home as being "completely in the countryside. I have no neighbours. When I look out the window, all I see are fields." It was here that she would write songs which would appear on "To Bring You My Love."

Whereas her writing process was solitary and isolated, a reflection of an age still recovering from Thatcher's dismantling of society, songwriting within The Fall was often a group effort. However, the problems in Conservative society were now creeping into the band as their own relations grew fractious. The line-up had not changed for five years, but immediately after the release of "Cerebral Caustic" Mark. E. Smith dismissed both Dave Bush and Craig Scanlon. But why Scanlon? He had been with the band for 16 years and co-written over 120 of their songs. We shall return to this shortly.

Whilst changes within The Fall were material, "To Bring You My Love," marks a transitional period in Harvey's music. Whereas the songs on "Rid of Me" had been aggressive, vengeful attacks, "To Bring You My Love," brims with loss and longing, and employ a great deal of Biblical imagery, for example on the yearning title track which runs, *"I've lain with the devil/ cursed god above/forsaken Heaven/ to bring you my love."* Harvey is not a religious person and never has been, having never been baptised or attended church as a child. On her use of such imagery, however, she says, "I look towards religion as possibly one means to finding an answer, to making sense why were here. That's what drives the creative force, to make sense of ones life. A very natural place to look is that divine area, because its so strong and has been here long before us." In an age of vagueness and uncertainty, then, especially in the political world, Harvey gains some sense in turning to the past—in particular religion, a common source for answers.

There is a lot of archaic artistry here; the cover image of Harvey floating in the water, with the slight frame and stark pallor of a nineteenth-century artists model evokes paintings such as Millais "Ophelia" or Watts "Found Drowned," images of death. The Fall also employed death imagery for "Cerebral Caustic," artwork, which depicts a skull. This is not the only sign of darkness on the album—it is the record which marks the period in which Mark. E. Smith developed a drink problem, hence the illogical sacking of Craig Scanlon. In 2008, Smith publicly admitted in a heartfelt fashion that his drinking had impacted upon the group, and that he hugely regretted dismissing Scanlon from the line-up. The album also marked a decline in sales for the band after a period of relative commercial success. Harvey, on the other hand, was beginning to cross over, as the hauntingly disturbing song "Down by The Water" received a surprising amount of airplay and MTV coverage—quite something considering its murderous subject matter. It is also surprising given the lack of convention on the musical compositions—for example, using two guitar parts but with hardly any bass, bass being generally substituted by a deep organ. (The track "Long Snake Moan" is the only one to feature an actual bass.)

The strength of writing on the music of February 1995 is reflected in the fact that this was a time in which a good writing ability could be an advantage in any field. Neil Kinnock's replacement for the Islywn seat was Dan Touhig, who had been a journalist from 1968-76. From 1976-1990 he had been the editor of the free press of Monmouthshire, and then from 1988-1992 general manager and Edito-in-Chief of the Free Press group of newspapers. The only question this throws up is how do you go from creating the news to *being* the news?

There were, however, far more dominant stories in the news than local politics—headlines that year had brimmed with death (Fred West was found hanged in his cell) and casual violence (Eric Cantona's kung fu kick on a Crystal Palace supporter). As a consequence, these two deathly, unsociable albums were perfectly timed.

RADIOHEAD—THE BENDS   March 1995

Considering the background of Conservative rule and mass dissatisfaction which provided its background, Radiohead's debut album "Pablo Honey," was remarkably personal and small scale. There globally significant, truly brilliant follow-up "The Bends" would mark a turn away from this to show the world here was a band of true importance.

All the omens for "The Bends" were good. Firstly, they had managed to obtain their producer of choice, the legendary John Leckie, something which genuinely encouraged them in the songwriting process. Sessions were due to start in January 1994, but then their fellow Oxford band Ride asked Leckie to do some last minute emergency work on their forthcoming album. In order to accommodate Leckie, Radiohead postponed the albums sessions, using the time to practice their new songs. This is a lesson in patience, even though this practice time was not as constructive as one might expect, as Yorke said "we had all these songs and we really liked them, but we knew them almost to well . . . so we sort of had to learn to like them again before we could record them, which is odd." In a way, the British public were in a similar situation politically; they liked Blair's Labour, but without a general election due they could do little about it. But whilst, once in power, Blair would go onto disappoint, "The Bends" does everything but. The themes tackled on the record are broad, and often interesting—"Fake Plastic Trees" is about the development of Canary Wharf, whereas "Sulk" was written as a response to the horrific Hungerford massacre of 1987. There are issues and stories which would have reached a lot of people, and thus would have been recognised by so many, but there are moments of high-culture intellectualism also, fore example the haunting closer "Street Spirit (Fade Out)" was inspired by Ben Okri's book "The Famished Road." Both musically and lyrically, this song captures the feeling of twentieth century alienation, its opening line of *"rows of houses/ all bearing down on me,"* making the everyday feel imposing.

"The Bends" was also released at a time when the Conservatives were beginning to fall out of favour. On the 4th May, the local elections saw them gain a mere eight councils (Labour controlled 155 and the Liberal Democrats 45.) They held no seats whatsoever in Scotland and Wales—a 25th May Perth by-election sparked by the death of Conservative MP Nicholas Fairbank saw the SNP's Roseanna Cunningham take over the seat, taking the Conservative majority from 21 to 11 seats in just three years. On the 27th July, this was reduced even further to nine seats as the Liberal Democrats won the Littleborough and Saddleworth seat in Lancashire. The Conservatives were also 22 points behind Labour in opinion polls.

In the midst of all this, in a bid to re-assert his authority, John Major resigned as leader of the Conservative party, triggering a leadership election. He won the election (gaining 218 votes to John Redwoods 89) but it seemed a petty way to assert his authority—and what if he had lost? He would have only had himself to blame. One "The Bends" singles "Just" now seemed prophetic with its chorus of "you do it to yourself you do . . . you do it to yourself/ just you, you and no-one else."

Dissatisfaction ran through the UK; as a consequence, it began to look backwards, not forwards. The racism which was often thought to be fading showed itself to be horribly alive when there were race riots in Bradford. Lurching from brutal (the title track, "My Iron Lung", "Just") to detached and lonely ("Fake Plastic Trees", "Street Spirit") "The Bends" captures all the emotions of those alienated by the exclusion which is linked to such riots. And people seemed lacking in anywhere to turn to turn to—the government was to unpopular for that.

On the 24th May, former Prime Minister Harold Wilson died of cancer aged 79. He was not without his flaws, but in the current climate we would certainly have been grateful of another like him.

ELASTICA—ELASTICA   May 1995

What a victorious year for women 1995 was turning out to be. On the 13th May, mountain climber Alison Hargreaves became the first woman to climb Mount Everest without oxygen or sherpas. Then, a month later, Pauline Clare was appointed as the first female Chief Constable, with the Lancashire Constabulary. On top of all this, it was largely women who were behind the biggest-selling debut album that year, Elastica's eponymous, post-punk inspired classic debut.

Elastica were formed by two former members of Suede—Justin Welch and Justine Frischmann—who were then joined by Annie Holland and Donna Matthews, two fantastically nonplussed-looking female musicians in the Kim Deal (Pixies, Breeders) tradition. The band are often ranked alongside other "Britpop" bands from the time, but they were post punk in all but era; The Fall and Wire being obvious influences.

Regardless of the talents of her bandmates, Justine Frischmann was undeniably the heart of the band as well as the face, writing all the songs, being the key musician (vocals and lead guitar), and was always an entertaining and interesting interview. Her relationship with Blur frontman Damon Albarn turned the pair of them into a kind of indie-royalty (the label King and Queen of Britpop was given to them) but her own background was far from regal, instead being much darker and more complex. Her parents were Judeo-German holocaust survivors, and the theme of international relations and fascism which had defined the holocaust were relevant all over again—it was during this year that Britain became involved in the Siege of Sarajevo, the "high point" of the ongoing conflict between Bosnia and Yugoslavia. Within Sarajevo, major military positions and the supply of arms were all Serb-controlled, particularly dangerous streets becoming known as "sniper alleys." An average of approximately 329 shell impacts per day was reported. By September 1993, 35,000 of Sarajevo's buildings had been completely destroyed. The single biggest loss of life, however, had been the first Markale marketplace massacre, which saw the deaths of 68 civilians and the wounding of 200. The following year would see a second Markale massacre which killed 37 and wounded 90. As Serb forces raided a UN monitored weapons collection site, NATO jets attacked Bosnian Serb ammunition depots, alongside other strategic military targets. Fighting also escalated on the ground as joint Bosnian and Croation troops went on the offensive. This enormous and frantic conflict was in some ways perfectly soundtracked by Frischmann's riotous songwriting, her background surely having had some kind of impact on her, but the conflicts on "Elastica" are somewhat more personal. For example, "Waking Up," a song about being an underachiever, has been described by Frischmann as "exorcising her personal malaise," with its lyrics of *"I'd work very hard/but I'm very lazy/ I've got a lot of songs but there all in my head/ I'll get a guitar/ and a lover who pays me/ if I can't be a star I won't get out of bed."* Laziness may be a character flaw, but in the hands of someone whose family had fallen victim to "Arbeit Macht Frei," sloganeering, it becomes almost a liberation.

Female sexual liberation is the other kind which is dominant here; the song "Line Up," is a knowing account of eager, oral-sex dispensing groupies. Frischmann also once boldly claimed "I really like the thought of a sixteen year old boy looking at a picture of me and having a wank." Even more interestingly, their flaunting of their sexuality was accompanied by an aesthetic of scruffy, androgynous clothing and no make-up, turning conventions of female sex appeal on its head—and making them appear miles away from the groomed, glossy "products" of the mainstream pop world.

But this was not a band immune to sexism; a startlingly backward-looking press tried to suggest that surely Damon Albarn wrote "Elastica," as if in 1995 a woman needed her boyfriend to do everything for her. The evils of the such as sexism and nationalism were very much present (to heavily simplify the roots of The Siege of Sarajevo, the formation of a multiparty democracy in the wake of the death of Tito spawned a wave of nationalism—an example of so-called democracy failure.) So, a victim of on, and due to her parents no doubt all to aware of the dangers of the other, Elastica's Justine Frischmann seemed perfectly qualified to write the songs which soundtracked the age.

MORRISSEY—SOUTHPAW GRAMMAR   Aug 1995

It is not unheard of for the timing of an album in relation to its themes to feel prophetic to the point of downright strange—one such album is Morrissey's vaguely conceptual album, "Southpaw Grammar." The concept of this record is boxing—the original cover photo is a wonderful image of boxer Kenny Lane taken from the April 1963 issue of boxing magazine The Ring. The title is also a reference to the subject—"Southpaw," is boxing slang fro a left-handed punch. The "grammar" part is a reference to grammar schools, casting boxing as a sort of school itself.

The eerie prophecy of all this is that, two months after the albums release, boxing would become a hugely controversial subject. The boxer James Murray was pronounced brain dead after a fight. He died two days later, prompting for calls for boxing to be banned. A message conveyed on "Southpaw Grammar" is that violence is everywhere in society; banning boxing would be nonsensical. This was also prophetic as the final months of 1995 saw a string of violent events take place—on 8th December, for example, three drug dealers, part of the notorious "Essex Boys," gang, were found shot dead in the back of a Range Rover on an isolated country road.

One key track on "Southpaw Grammar," looking at violence in wider society is the analysis on violent schoolchildren "The Teachers of Afraid of The Pupils." Some see this as turnaround of Morrissey's stance on the Smiths song "The Headmaster Ritual," as he goes from berating discipline in schools berating a lack of it. Many saw this as sheer hypocrisy. But maybe it is just a case of looking at what was right at particular times—and, in another alarming coincidence, headteacher Philip Lawrence was stabbed to death outside his school, St. George's Roman Catholic Secondary School.

In spite of the loose concept of the album, there are moments of vaguely personal reflection which continue directly from previous album "Vauxhall and I", for example the lyric "no-one ever sees me cry," on "Reader Meets Author." But on the whole this is Morrissey's most experimental album, opening with a two and half minute drum solo from Spencer Cobrin, featuring songs epic in length and sampling a Shostakovich symphony. Maybe this is simply due to Morrissey's confidence in his band accelerating—after all, he had now been with Alain Whyte and Boz Boorer for as long as he had been with Johnny Marr.

This experimental record, tehn, shows that Morrissey was never predictable . . . but strangely, his lyricism could certainly be weirdly *predictive*.

"THE BATTLE OF BRITPOP":
BLUR—THE GREAT ESCAPE
AND
OASIS—(WHAT'S THE STORY) MORNING GLORY

It seems faintly ridiculous, considering how much was happening in the world, that the story of a chart battle between two of the keys acts of "Britpop" should have been turned into a newsworthy item, but it was. The genre had certainly captured the public imagination—but do the enormously successful albums which spawned this battle, Blur's "The Great Escape" and Oasis "(Whats the Story) Morning Glory" warrant this level of attention? Both acts had a lot to live up to considering the successes of their previous albums (Blur's "Parklife" and Oasis "Definitely Maybe"). Oasis had befriended fellow Mancunians The Stone Roses whilst recording "Definitely Maybe,"—would they go down the same path, following up a classic debut with a famously awful follow-up?

Thankfully, no. Whilst not matching the dizzy heights of their debut, there is enough anthemic joy behind "(Whats the story) Morning Glory" to make it a classic in its own right. It was, at this point, however, when cracks began to show in the band. Even though drummer Tony McCarroll says that "the idea that Liam and Noel punched each other all the time was a media creation, I never once saw them do that," he and Noel Gallagher did have issues between the two of them, as McCarroll goes on to say, "I couldn't deal with Noel's attitude. Once you've crossed Noel, your card is marked."

Gallagher still speaks scathingly of McCarroll to this day, but producer Owen Morris still speaks highly of him, claiming it was difficult to replicate his sound.

Difficult in the recording studio, then, but instantly accessible for the listener, this album spawned hit after hit: "Some Might Say," "Wonderwall," "Don't Look Back In Anger," etc. However, this was not enough to prevent one track from the album, "Roll With It," being beaten by Blur's "Country House" (from "The Great Escape") in the much-hyped chart battle. Perhaps Blur just knew how to capture the moment better—the video for "Country House," was directed by Damien Hirst, who was very much a man of the moment as British contemporary art went global. The "YBA"'s (Young British Artists) had already had their fair share of attention this year with the British Art Show, and on 22nd October they exhibited their "*Brilliant!*" exhibition at the Walker Art Centre in Minneapolis, USA. References in "Country House," to escaping the rat race would also have resonated with the masses; the basic level of income tax may have been cut, but the dreary world of work, tax and Conservative drudgery was still life for most people.

Both "Whats the Story," and "The Great Escape" also have moments of reflection. The former ends with the epic "Champagne Supernova" opening with the rhetorical questions "*how many special people change?/ how many lives are living strange?*" whereas "The Great Escape," includes the stunning slice of existentialism, "The Universal." And to a point, both albums really were universal, but in spite of a prevalent realism escape is an obvious theme on both albums, something manifest in their titles (the title track of "What's the Story" is a hymn to escape through cocaine, running "*all your dreams are made/ when you're chained to the mirror and the razorblade.*")

For all these similarities, however, these really are two very different albums by two very different bands; the press simply pitted them against each other because they love a conflict. What's more, times had changed so little that they specifically love a *class* conflict. In the eyes of the media, this was not just about music—it was not about working class Northerners battling against educated Southerners. But does this class difference really show in their music? Yes, Blur have a tendency to use more high culture references (surely "Country House" is the only number one song to ever namecheck Honore

De Balzac?) but to drag class into what I cannot help but see as a purely musical battle is flawed and bizarre. Anyway, class was becoming far to complicated to be summarised so easily. The recent recession had created problems with big businesses, but the Old Left associated with the working classes also seemed set to disappear as the New Labour manifesto said they were about "ideas . . . not outdated ideologies," sweeping away the party's long-term key members in an unsavoury fashion.

So, had this apparent new political disdain for the working classes had a role to play in Oasis losing the chart battle? I do not think so; for a start Blur were hardly working-class representatives, having clearly socialist ideals and singing scathingly about somebody "*educated the expensive way*," on "Charmless Man."

I think that this over-hyped battle was about music and nothing else. But were *British*—how could we resist bringing class into something if it was remotely possible?

PULP—DIFFERENT CLASS   OCT 1995

By October, 1995, Britpop had well and truly swept the nation, having hits its peak with the "Blur vs Oasis" chart battle. Such a popular genre, however, surely had to produce a defining album in terms of the social and political context—it delivered all this and more with one of the genre's classic albums, Pulp's "Different Class."

Having released their debut in 1983, Pulp were seen as a post-punk tinged indie band for most of their career. Nobody could accuse them on jumping on the Britpop bandwagon; it simply came to them. They had also been signed to Rough Trade (although Different Class and other later releases were released on Island) which meant that the label had now made a contribution to every major musical movement in Britain in some way.

"Different Class" is full of successful chart songs, but when listened to as a whole it is not as accessible as one may expect. It opens accessibly enough, with the brilliant "Mis-Shapes," a song celebrating the joys of intelligence and individuality, whilst bemoaning the fact that these seemed to be negative things in society. *"You could end up with a smack in the mouth/ just for standing out,"* sings Jarvis Cocker in an exasperated fashion, a sentiment reflected on the statement printed on the albums inlay, "Please. We don't want any trouble. We just want the right to be different, that's all." However "Mis-Shapes," is not completely despondant as it imagines this collection of indivuals exacting their subtle revenge: *"Just put your hands up, it's a raid/ we want your homes, we want your lives, we want the things you won't allow us/ we won't use guns, we won't use bombs/ we'll use the one thing we've got more of/ that's our minds,"* runs the chorus. With lines about how *"we learned to much at school,"* the sentiment is straightforward: the geek shall inherit the Earth.

There were real life, more literal riots at the end of the year, as on 13th December, rioting broke out in Brixton following the death of Wayne Douglas, a 26 year old black man in police custody. The chaos lasted for five hours and ended with 22 arrests. Whilst this was a very real violence, as opposed to the more cerebral actions endorsed in "Mis-shapes," the sentiment was accurately reflected—maligned sections of society rioting in the case of what they thought was right in a part of the fight for their rights.

"Mis-shapes" was released as a double A-side with what would come to be one of the albums most controversial moments, rave-culture reflection "Sorted for E's & Wizz." The song is refreshingly open, neither condemning nor condoning drug use, looking at is highs and lows in the De Quincey tradition. Even though he openly endorsed drug use at the following years Glastonbury festival (implying that the arrests of those who simply wanted to enjoy themselves through drugs for the weekend was wrong) the horrors of the comedown are well-documented enough in this song for it to seem an almost cautionary tale, especially when placed in the vast context of illegal outdoor raves ("I lost my friends and danced alone/ its six o'clock, I wanna go home.")

However, drugs were to become a more controversial and difficult topic than ever before. On 16th November, the eighteen year old Essex student Leah Betts died in hospital three days after taking ecstasy. A hysterical press chose to ignore the fact that she had drank eighteen pints of water and drowned her body and ecstasy became the demon of the hour. Pictures of her dying in hospital were plastered across billboards everywhere as an anti-ecstasy warning.

Naturally, Pulp were swept in this hysteria as the press were horrified by "Sorted For E's and Wizz." "BAN THIS SICK STUNT," ran tabloid headlines, concerning the fact that the record contained instructions on how to make a speed wrap.

Drugs are not the only taboo broken on "Different Class." Sex is probably the most frequently recurring theme on this album, but it is a form of sex miles away from the romantic gloss music usually gives to the subject. Songs like "Underwear", "I Spy," (which continues the theme of sexual spying found on "His' n' Hers" song "Babies," to an even more voyeuristic level) and "Pencil Skirt," (on infidelity) into a seedy, perverse act. This hits its peak on the uncomfortable "F.E.E.L.I.N.G.C.A.L.L.E.D.L.O.V.E" which casts off all the romantic pretensions of sex in order to display it for what it is, "not red roses" but a "small animal that only comes out at night." It also places the actual act of intercourse in a very physical, real setting, talking about glimpses of the chest of drawers from the corner of the eye. But then, it is realism that makes this album what it is. One of the biggest hits on the album is "Disco 2000" a piece of realist storytelling, perhaps the song most responsible for the label of "music's Alan Bennett," given to Jarvis Cocker. It truly evokes a sense of time and place as it recounts a love which should have been, but never was, its descriptions of growing up in a working-class Northern England of the recent past particularly evocative, with its descriptions of "woodchip on the wall," and "Deborah," the female protoganist, ignoring the narrator even though he walks her home from school sometimes. Even though unrequited love is a universal theme, Cocker's take in it is particularly working class, an enormous theme of this album (as we shall go on to see.) "Disco 2000" is almost unabridged in its account of the relationship between "Deborah," and the yearning narrator who still wants her in his life *("What are you doing Sunday baby?/ Would you like to come and meet me maybe?/ You can even bring your baby")* It was an age for this kind of openness, in real life as well as in storytelling—on 20th November, Princess Diana had given a revealing interview to Martin Bashir on the Panorama show on BBC One, in which she openly discussed every aspect of her life in candid detail. A month later, the Queen wrote to her and Prince Charles, urging them to divorce as soon as possible. This subject may not have featured in Pulp's lyrics, but it was a basis for another subversive comment from Jarvis Cocker. During Pulp's heyday, there was a section in Smash Hits in which musicians were asked random, irrelevant questions to which they would give random, irrelevant answers. However, in response to the question "whats Princess Diana doing right now?" Jarvis gave the answer "probably shagging someone she shouldn't be." To Smash Hits credit, they printed this answer and passed no comment on it; the monarchy was so increasingly irrelevant that few would take genuine offence. Rather than aspiring to higher class statuses as they once would have done, the public now seemed keener to romantacise being working-class, which ahd been appropriated and made horrible trendy—as comedian Mark Steel put it, if they could have bottled rickets it would have sold.

This appropriation of working-class culture by the middle classes forms one of the most relevant songs on "Different Class," Pulps big crossover hit "Common People." This is the story of a girl who *"studied sculpture at St. Martins College/ that's were I/ caught her eye,"* who tells the protagonist that *"her dad is loaded."* But in spite of this privilege, she claims *"I wanna live like common people/ I wanna do whatever common people do/ I wanna sleep with common people."* Cocker's narration here goes on to be scathing of such people. In the full-length version of the song, rarely given mainstream airplay, Cocker tells this section of society "everybody hates a tourist/ especially when they think its all such a laugh." The message here is that for those that these middle-class people attempt to emulate, this is a consistent way of life that they would not want to be a part of *("Rent a flat above a shop/ cut your hair and get a job . . . when your lay in bed at night/ watching roaches climb the walls, if you called your dad he could stop it.")* Being working-class in not romanticised (*"with the dance and drink and screw, because theres nothing else to do")* but the people themselves certainly come across better than the middle-class "tourists" who are being viewed with a certain level of spite *("Laugh along with the common people/ laugh along cos there laughing at you/ and the stupid things that you do/ 'cos you thinks its always you.")*

This unpicking of social pretensions, particularly in the context of such a socially sharp album, makes this one of the most lyrically relevant albums of the time. Perverse, intelligent, and political in its own way, "Different Class," is the perfect snapshot of a Britain were the government was struggling and class was an increasingly complex subject.

"LIFE GOES ON":

MANIC STREET PREACHERS—EVERYTHING MUST GO

AND

THE FALL—THE LIGHT USER SYNDROME

The first few months of 1996 were musically dry, with few noteworthy albums. May, however, brought with it an explosion of significant releases. There were youthful, exciting debuts from bands such as Ash and the Super Furry Animals, but there were also "life-goes-on" efforts from bands continuing without their co-writers. The Fall released their first album without Craig Scanlon, "The Light User Syndrome," and the Manic Street Preachers released their first album without Richey Edwards, their crossover piece "Everything Must Go." Changes had raged throughout the political landscape in the months leading up these albums release, particularly in the left-wing world. On the 13th January, Arthur Scargill announced that he was defecting from the Labour Party to set up his own Socialist Labour Party. Scargill was acting the way any good socialist with Labour Party affiliations would have rightfully done as, under the leadership of Tony Blair, the party had effectively "sold out." By entitling their album "Everything Must Go," the Manics had tapped into this perfectly. The title is actually drawn from a play by Nicky Wire's brother Patrick Jones; the act of writing was clearly strong in the family as it is on this album that Wire asserts himself in the role of lyricist in the wake of Edwards' disappearance.

Scargill's departure from the Labour Party was an event that kept him in the news; he had been somewhat absent for a while. But his role battling against Margaret Thatcher in the miners strike would have him nailed to history; his relevance continued to be echoed as the coal industry continued its slow death in Britain. Miners were as much a fading, neglected part of society as they had ever been, in spite of their role in the nation and its history. This is a theme that runs through "Everything Must Go,"—the voice of the mining town is at its strongest here. The opening lines of "Design For Life," run "libraries gave us power/ then work came and made us free," an allusion to the Newport library funded and built by local miners, with the words above the entrance reading "KNOWLEDGE IS POWER."

Six days after Scargill announced his departure from the Labour Party, environmental news manifested itself as six major environmental organisations added their support to the campaign over the Newbury by-pass in Berkshire (the organisations were Friends of The Earth, The Council For British Archaeology, Greenpeace UK, the RSPB and the WWF.) A joint statement from all the organisations involved said that "a solution to the serious traffic problems was needed but that the proposed by-pass route was not the answer. Traffic on the A34 in Newbury will be back to the intolerable levels of today within five to ten years of the bypass opening." Such a concern for the environment over a situation which, when taken at face value may have made life easier, suggested that the nation may have been becoming more altrusistic, miles away from traditional laissez-faire Conservatism. And Conservatism continued its downward slide in popularity as the first MORI poll of 1996 showed the Conservatives with a showing of 55% and a lead of just 29 points. On the 22nd February, Conservative MP Peter Turnham announced his resignation from Parliament, reducing the partys majority to just two seats. Resignations and by-election defeats had cost the Conservatives 19 seats since the last general election just under four months ago. Basically, the Conservatives were undergoing the nations biggest line-up change, and it was having a major effect on the party.

The effects of the line-up changes in The Fall and the Manic Street Preachers are as personal as they are musical. Brix Smith continues her role in The Fall after rejoining on "Cerebral Caustic"; an unusual move for a divorced couple to be playing music together. The departure of Craig Scanlon was also a huge source of regret for Mark. E. Smith that it is widely believed that he attempted to reduce his drinking around this time, hence the albums title.

The Manics loss of Richey Edwards was also hugely affecting for them—the song "Australia," has the sound of an upbeat pop song but could be seen as a lyric about how life without your best friend means you would sooner be anywhere than were you are now. In the midst of a very political album, "Australia" reminds us of the very human situation behind this record. It is an album full of epics, but tinged with sadness due to its context. The change in sound was also significant, the early strident rock exchanged for a more sedate, commercial feel. (The Fall, however, were as typically brutal as ever, something enhanced by a new minimalism.)

The huge popularity of the musical voice of socialism on "Everything Must Go," was a reflection of the dissatisfaction clearly felt by the public towards the Conservative government as they made unpopular decision after unpopular decision, something which peaked with Home Secretary Michael Howard's plans to give courts power to give such heavy sentences as an absolute minimum of six years for all drug offences, which would increase the prisons population by more than 20%. Ina further blow, on the 15th February a report on the Arms-to-Iraq affair was highly critical of government ministers. The report took three years to produce and outlines mistakes made by ministers. Attorney General Sir Nicholas Lyell and Treasury Chief Secretary Williams Waldergave were singled out for criticism in the report, carried out by senior High Court Judge Sir. Richard Scott. One of the main problems highlighted in the report was the governments decision not to inform parliament of reforms to arms export laws for fear of public outcry, concluding that the policy on export of military goods was changed following the Iran-Iraq ceasefire of 1988 in a way which should have been reported to the Commons. The fact that this related to 1980's matters did not make it any less relevant; it often felt like we were going back to this time with continued privatisation (the privatisation of British Rail) and the return of the IRA after a 17 month ceasefire (the 9th February Docklands bomb).

"Physical" change, then, does not mean that everything changes. "Everything Must Go" still has some of Edwards marks on it due to him co-writing two of the songs ("Kevin Carter," about the iconic photographer, and "Small Black Flowers That Grow In The Sky," about the maltreatment of animals in captivity) whereas "The Light User Syndrome," is typical thrilling, slightly frightening stuff from The Fall—witness, in particular the fierce riff and false ending of "Chilinism.")

Whereas a lack of apparent political change was a source of despair for the public, "Everything Must Go," and "The Light User Syndrome," show that, after waves of negative change, life must go on.

SUPER FURRY ANIMALS—FUZZY LOGIC   May 1996

The first half of 1996 was not looking promising. BSE was one of the nations biggest ever food scares, the Dunblane massacre horrified the nation and three British soldiers were sentenced for the abduction, rape, and manslaughter of Danish woman Louise Jensen. The real world was so uncomfortable that it was perhaps for the best that one of the albums of the year was gloriously psychedelic. This album was the debut of Creation's Super Furry Animals, "Fuzzy Logic." The title comes from a mathematical term which describes terms in an approximate rather than precise way, highly appropriate considering what a vague government we had on policy. The bands psychedelia was obvious from the moment they appeared, considering their debut single had the title "Hometown Unicorn" which was chosen as NME's single of the week by guest reviewers Pulp. Its follow-up, the blistering "O God! Show Me Magic!" was also an NME single of the week.

The album is not just all colour and liveliness; for example "Gathering Moss" is a beautifully yearning ballad. But this is vastly outweighed by the wonderfully anti-authority attitude often found on the record—the cover art depicts Howard Marks, the international drug smuggler, who also receives a full tribute in the song "Hangin' with Howard Marks,." (They would later strike up a huge friendship.) Then, there is the decision to release "The Man Don't Give A Fuck," a song which features the word "fuck" over fifty times, thus resulting in a lack of airplay. This was a band truly doing things on their own, subtly rebellious, terms.

The British public were dissenting in a more legitimate, everyday way—at the polling station. In a 22-point swing, Labour won the Staffordshire South-East seat from the Conservatives in a by-election, cutting the government majority to three seats—four years ago, they had a 21-seat majority.

As the governments popularity dropped at this level, it is little wonder that "Fuzzy Logic" received much acclaim—not just for the colourful escapism it provided, but because a dissatisfied Britain recognised something of itself (or at least wished it did) in anti-authority—and well and truly not giving a fuck!

BELLE AND SEBASTIAN—TIGERMILK/ IF YOUR FEELING SINISTER

On the 15th June, 1996, a massive IRA bomb exploded in Manchester city centre, devastating its commercial district. This was one example of violence and brutality being a huge part of the modern world—making the emergence of Belle and Sebastian, with their famous whimsy, welcome respite. If the bands early works sound faintly "studenty," its because they are—Stow College music course produces and releases one record a year on the college's label Electric Honey. This particular year, however, the label was so impressed with Belle and Sebastian that it allowed them to produce a full-length album, the now-classic "Tigermilk," which was recorded in just three days. Frontman Stuart Murdoch once described the band as "the product of botched capitalism." But this cannot be described as true capitalism, particularly in the context of Conservative Britain and the wider music industry. If anything, the band were everything capitalist authority was not, shaking us out of the adult world and into something childishly special, with song titles like "Dog on Wheels," and a band name derived from a series of French children's books. The artwork for "Tigermilk" shows a woman "breast-feeding," a cuddly toy tiger, a mix of the childish and the mature.

In this year, playing with nature seemed a common theme—the first genetically modified foods had gone on sale, and on 5th July, Dolly the sheep, the first mammal to be cloned from an adult cell, was born at the Roslin Institute in Scotland. The amount of ethical questions cloning raises is enormous, one of the biggest grey areas in science. Individuals could even argue with themselves over the matter, so complex it is.

So, were do Belle and Sebastian fit into this? The prettiness and delight of their music is straightforward; the childhood allusions evoking a simpler time. These first two albums were timely, but also timeless, their cult status remaining ever since. In a world full of people playing God, here was a band happy to just *play*.

SUEDE—COMING UP   Sept 1996

If any album really, properly defines the second half of 1996 in terms of musical popularity, it is certainly the Spice Girls November debut "Spice", as the popularity of the group reached astounding levels. Take That may have split earlier in the year, but the enormous dominance of pop music seemed unshakable. What, then, for established guitar acts—where did this landscape leave them? Perhaps the wisest option was to embrace a more commercial sound themselves, which is what Suede did on their third album "Coming Up," a change in direction after the more "difficult" Dog Man Star. That album had been a commercial failure; now Brett Anderson was keen to bring the band back into the mainstream, saying that "I think that the next album will be quite simple, actually. I'd really like to write a straightforward pop album." The departure of Bernard Butler after the recording of "Dog Man Star" enabled the current guitarist Richard Oakes, who by now had toured extensively with the band, to be a part of the songwriting team. (However, two songs written in the bands early days, "Lazy" and "By the Sea" did make it on to the album.)

The band are very frank about the pop influence and ambition of the record. Anderson said that "I wanted it to be a complete turnover from the last album, which was very dark and dank. I wanted it to be communicative and understandable." This desire to communicate and connect with the public was a sharp move in a Conservative laissez-faire era were understandings between authority and public were at a low. The band also knew just the right person to help them achieve this, as they turned back to producer Ed Buller. He shared their vision of something more simple, as bassist Mat Osman clarifies, saying "he was really keen on using all those devices: the big repeated end, the handclaps, the straightforward chorus, making it big and obvious." Ins spite of all this, the lyrical themes on

"Coming Up," are not necessarily ones which everyone can relate to, tapping into a controversial part of the zeitgeist. "Heroin chic," models were currently courting controversy—"Coming Up," is a record that gives them their voice. "*High on diesel, gasoline,*" opens "Beautiful Ones" one of a clutch of songs which endorse, rather than condemn, the trend. The record still gives a voice to the indie perennial, the mocked misunderstood, but it is a more glamorous tangent of it—the song "Trash" opens "*maybe maybe it's the clothes we wear/ the tasteless bracelets and the dye in our hair.*" The album many have had a more commercial sound, but they were still clearly appealing to the counterculture, something that popular manufactured groups never could. The public were embracing such groups as an aspect of their seeming desire to buy into shiny, carefully cultivated images—hence the ascent of New Labour. An 8th November MORI poll put Labour ahead, but the Conservatives had cut their lead to seventeen points. This was one of the narrowest gaps seen between two leading parties in any opinion poll over the last three years, but the sad truth was neither of them had much to offer. All authority seemed irrelevant to the public—the government had disappointed and the monarchy was unpopular (as Charles and Diana completed their divorce, the public "sided" with Diana in an almost canonising fashion.) Obviously people wanted accessible music as an escape. But did sheer pop have to be purely manufactured? Whilst making "Coming Up," Suede immersed themselves in the work of T. Rex, a proper unadulterated pop band who were no the product of greedy moguls like contemporary acts were.

With this record, Suede got the commercial success they were aiming for—showing that sometimes, it can come from *you* in an era were success seemed largely down to spin and management.

BLUR—BLUR   Jan 1997

It may have been the start of a new year, but history was what was making the news—on 17th January, a jury at the Old Bailey ruled that 86 year old Szyman Serafinowicz was unfit to stand trial on charges of murdering Jews during the Holocaust. By rights, this twisted take on justice should have been the main headline of the day, but, on that same day, East 17 singer Brian Harvey publicly commented that use of ecstasy was safe. The press outrage over at this illogically far outweighed press reaction towards the Serafinowicz case. Horrific murders in general were all over the news in the first two months of 1997 (the murders of student Nicola Dixon, children Kayleigh Ward, Billie-Jo Jenkins and Zoe Evans, and the jurors at the inquest into the death of Stephen Lawrence ruling that he had been unlawfully killed in a completely unprovoked racist attack.)

Clearly, the capacity for human cruelty—a problem which usually takes the Holocaust Serafinowicz was involved in as its example—was as strong as ever, yet drugs were as controversial. This is what makes moments of Blur's lo-fi fourth album "Blur" so provocative—the lead track "Beetlebum," is a hymn to drug use, particularly the shared, hazy drug moments between Damon Albarn and his partner Justine Frischmann. The woozy, downtempo style of this song shows a band capable of moving on from their Britpop roots (the new sound was constructed largely by guitarist Graham Coxon, who also takes lead vocal duties for the first time on "You're So Great." The record also shows changes in less obvious ways, outside of the music—for example, it is the first one of their albums not to use cover art by design group Stylorogue.

Change in the musical world reflected change in the political world; a new, Labour government seemed increasingly likely. The death of Conservative MP Iain Mills left the party without a majority.

New Labour were full of promises as they prepared to take over, vowing not to raise income tax. But was this really a promise that they would be able to stick to? After all, the course of their policy must accommodate the potential for change.

The scientific world was also producing much of this. Dolly the sheep had been born at the Roslin Institute as a result of cloning the previous year, but it was not until February 22nd, 1997, that scientists at the institute announced this, leaving the public to consider the ethical dilemma. Another enormous ethical dilemma was raised in the case of Diane Blood, a widow challenging for the rights to use her late husband Stephen's sperm for her own insemination. On 6th February, the Court of Appeal warranted this right, but this does not necessarily mean everyone thought it was right.

There never seemed to have been so many ethical dilemmas and grey areas in the news—it was verging on being quite a headache. Little wonder, then, that one of the most popular songs on "Blur" became the refreshingly simple "Song 2"—just two minutes in length, it is a throwaway flash of loud guitars, droll delivery and straightforward chorus of *"woo-hoo!"*—welcome respite from an increasingly complicated world.

There was nobody who felt more "left behind" in this climate than the increasingly unpopular John Major, who on 25th February announced plans to privatise the London Underground (a typical, privatise-everything Conservative policy.) However, as a Labour victory in the Wirral South by-election was a further dent to the government, it seemed that it was a waste of time announcing any new policies. Change was well and truly on the way, something perfectly captured by the ever-evolving Blur.

ECHO AND THE BUNNYMEN—EVERGREEN

On the 17th March, John Major announced that the general election would be held on the 1st May. In spite of the opinion polls putting Labour far ahead, he said he was convinced that the successes of this government (unemployment was currently low and the economy currently strong) would give the Conservatives a fourth successive term. If this was to occur, then perhaps the most relevant voices in music would be found not in new bands, but in those who had effectively soundtracked the Thatcerite age, which is why the reunion of Echo and The Bunnymen was so well-timed. During the eighties, everything the band had produced had been brilliant and relevant, but they had lost their way after the departure of Ian McCulloch—the heart, soul, voice and face of the band. After the unwise decision to make the album "Reverberation" with a different singer, Noel Burke, in 1990, the acclaim of the band declined and they split in 1993.

However, early 1997 would see them reunite and return to their former glories, releasing the album "Evergreen" later in the year. The Conservatives may have been in power, but naturally a lot had changed since the bands heyday, particularly in the political world. Who supported who, for example, had changed as John Major fell out of favour—on 18th March, The Sun newspaper, always a traditional Conservative paper, described the party as "tired, divided and rudderless," declaring their support for Tony Blair. This was in stark contrast to five years previous, when they claimed it was their support which won the Conservatives the election.

So, how could a new album by Echo and the Bunnymen keep them as relevant as they once had been? Well, for a start it seems apt that, in the wave of change, the albums best known song was entitled

"Nothing Lasts Forever." It is a great song, but it feels more personal than political. The strength of this record owes something to the fact that the band clicked back into place naturally. McCulloch says—"right from the demo (of Evergreen) we realised that we'd still got that chemistry." But the poignancy comes from the fact that it is not the complete line-up; drummer Pete De Frietas having been killed in a motorcycle accident. The flow of the reunion had been very natural—McCulloch had been working with Smiths guitarist Johnny Marr on an album which satisfied them, but label boss Rob Dickins felt something was missing, so he recruited Bunnymen guitarist Will Sergeant. In the midst of all this, the McCulloch and Marr demo tapes got lost. However, McCulloch and Sergeant continued to work together under the name Elecrafixion, until the demand for Echo and the Bunnymen songs in their live set persuaded them to completely reform the group.

They were unafraid to return other original aspects of the band, as production was again overseen by McCulloch himself (alongside Paul Toogood). The albums dark and atmospheric cover photograph of the band against a backdrop of trees at night (shot in Marrakesh but looking like a mystical world) heavily evokes the sleeve of their debut, "Crocodiles." Adam Peters, who had provided the string arrangements on their 1984 album "Ocean Rain," was also recruited for the strings on "Evergreen."

However, they also embraced music's recent icons. "American alternative," such as The Smashing Pumpkins had become successful in the early 90's, and the death of Kurt Cobain in 1994 sealed his role as an icon for the age. Cliff Norrell, the producer for one such "American alternative" band, REM, oversaw the final mix of the album. Such bands on the whole had recently influence McCulloch, aiding a heavier sound. Over in the UK, Oasis were the dominant musical voice—they had been recording their underwhelming third album "Be Here Now" in the next studio whilst Echo and the Bunnymen were recording "Evergreen", which resulted in Liam Gallagher contributing backing vocals to "Nothing Lasts Forever."

McCulloch says, "We just hit it off right away, and after a few beers he ended up singing on the record."

Acknowledging the current, then, mixed it with knowing what made them great in the first place ensured that Echo and the Bunnymen could be just as relevant as they had been in their heyday.

PART TWO
NEW LABOUR

CHAPTER THREE
THE BLAIR YEARS

OK COMPUTER
RADIOHEAD

RADIOHEAD—OK COMPUTER   June 1997

On the 1st May, 1997, the results of the general election saw Tony Blair's Labour Party defeat John Major's Conservative Party to win the election in a landslide result, winning 418 seats. Several high-profile Conservative MP's lost their seats. The moment in which Michael Portillo, who many had tipped to be the next leader of the Conservative party, loses his seat is a moment of pure, classic televisual gold.

Tony Blair was promising to take Britain into a new age, keen to seem relevant. His arrival at 10 Downing Street was accompanied by a star-studded party dotted with music industry figures—it was hard not to feel cheated as Noel Gallagher, the heart of a band who had thrived on a working class image, sipped champagne and shared banter with the new Prime Minister (the famous exchange between the two ran—Gallagher: "How did you manage to stay awake through all the election results?" Blair: "Probably not the same way you did.") Unlike John Major's Conservatives, New Labour dived straight into policy and announcements—in his first week as Chancellor of the Exchequer, Gordon Brown announced that the Bank of England was to assume independent responsibility for UK monetary policy (does this show decision making ability, or is it a cop-out?) The day after Blair was appointed Prime Minister, the UK won the Eurovision Song Contest for the first time since 1981 with Katrina and the Waves "Love Shine A Light." A nation basked in victory; duped by Blair's carefully constructed image, the UK rode on the waves of "Cool Britannia."

A month later, an album was released which showed not everyone was ready to join the party, instead tapping into another feeling felt throughout the UK—pre-millennial angst. That album is frequent "Greatest Albums" list favourite "OK Computer." Right from the start, this is a paranoid, often frightening record—opener "Airbag," heavily influenced by touring partner DJ Shadow, was "designed to sound like a car accident" and documents a near death experience. This is followed by "Paranoid Android," one song constructed over four separate units, and whilst it draws its title from a character in "The Hitchikers Guide to the Galaxy," the theme of imperial collapse is inspired by the Philp. K. Dick novel "Valis."

Other books which influenced the record were Jonathan Coe's black comedy "What a Carve Up!" a satirical attack on Thatcerite greed, and Eric Hobsbawns "Age of Extremes: The Short Twentieth Century," a gloomy look at the past century which concludes with the "global fog" of the nineties. These politicised texts show that this was a band prepared to be the voice of dissent whilst all those around embraced the manufactured, spin-driven new government. But in spite of this, this left-wing band were open about struggling to put their politics into song. "There's been a lot of looking at headlines and feeling wildly impotent," said Yorke at the time, but they managed so sublimely on the song "Electioneering." "What can you say about the IMF or politicians?" asked Yorke, "you just write down 'cattle prods and the IMF' and people who know, know." Here, then is a band crediting people with some intelligence, under an image-based government that did not. The song drew on memories of the 1990 poll tax riots, a moment in recent history showing that the unpopularity of the Conservatives was not brand-new. All the same, the partys popularity was even lower than it had been back then; in a bid to keep up with New Labour, they swapped John Major's leadership for that of William Hague, their youngest leader in 200 years.

The lack of fear which comprises some of "OK Computers," boldest moments is particularly reflected on the song "Lucky." This was originally recorded for the War Child charity album "Help," in which every contributor has to record the song on the same day. Most of the bands involved chose cover versions, but Radiohead opted to write this brilliant, entirely new song. Contributing help to a charity like War Child, meanwhile, is not a matter of left or right, but right or wrong. The sense of reaction against global injustice colours "OK

Computer" as a whole, making it an ideal soundtrack for certain news stories at the time—in particular, the "McLibel Case," the longest trial in English legal history. The case was a lawsuit field by McDonalds against two environmental activists, Helen Steel and David Morris, for distributing a pamphlet critical of the corporation. The pamphlet—"Whats wrong with Macdonalds: Everything they don't want you to know," outlined legitimate points—the corporation banned unions, maltreated animals, sold unhealthy, addictive food, exploited children through advertising and practised economic imperialism. The pair were denied legal aid and forced to represent themselves; Macdonalds poured money into their defence. It was inevitable that Steel and Morris would lose, something confirmed on 19th June. Such huge global corporations were impossible to fight against—this was the world "OK Computer," soundtracked, not the wave of British optimism.

Whilst the album does have its commercial moments—"Karma Police" and "No Surprises"—it is the paranoia which distinguishes it. The chilling "Climbing Up The Walls," combines statistics on serial killers with Yorke's concern over the "care in the community" policy derived from his former part-time job at a mental hospital. "Fitter Happier," is also described by Yorke as "the most upsetting thing I've ever written . . . I was feeling incredible hysteria and panic." He also describes another song, "Let Down," as expressing both "an enormous fear of being trapped" and the suspicion that "every emotion is fake." Happy stuff? No. But those who write Radiohead off as simply miserable are missing the point—in an age were the global corporation raged and the new government was built on lies and image, Radiohead were the voice of the truth that apparently nobody else could see.

SPIRITUALIZED—

LADIES AND GENTLEMEN WE ARE FLOATING IN SPACE

June 1997 was certainly a vintage month for albums, seeing the release of both "OK Computer," and "Ladies and Gentlemen we Are Floating In Space." But whilst "OK Computer" provided a fantastically paranoid soundtrack to events of the previous month, "Ladies and Gentlemen . . ." seemed ideal for events in the following two months. It was another perfectly timed album.

At the very beginning of July, the UK transferred sovereignty of Hong Kong, the largest remaining British Colony, to the People's Republic of China as the 99 year lease on the territory formally ended. The ideology of "empire" is all to often glorified, being something which is unscrupulously gained, but the final death of the British Empire is still a key historical event. Britain was increasingly small-scale—by making such an epic, sweeping album, Spiritualized were showing that its music did not need to be. The next day, Chancellor Gordon Brown launched the first Labour budget for nearly twenty years. It included a £3.5 billion scheme to get single mothers, under 25's and long-term unemployed back into work, and £3billion for education and healthcare—the mantra of the Labour party was now "education, education, education." But not everyone was as convinced by the Party as it may have seemed—on 31st July, they lost the Uxbridge by-election to the Conservatives. No matter who was in power, there was now going to be a significant "us and them" gap. The working class were looked down on from such a schism of separation that they practically disappeared from view. It is worth noting that the title of "Ladies and Gentleman . . ." is drawn from the philosophical novel "Sophies World" by Jostein Gaarder, running "Only philosophers embark on this perilous expedition to the outermost reaches of language and existence. Some of them fall off, but others cling on desperately and yell at the people nestling deep down in the snug softness, stuffing themselves with delicious food and drink. 'Ladies and Gentlemen,' they yell, 'we are floating in space!' But none of the people down there care."

Whilst casting the Labour Party as "philosophers," would be a mistake, the idea of them being placed above the masses who did not care turns this into a contemporary allegory. The old British idea of "not being happy unless were miserable," was fading as the nation viewed positive news over negative. A July IRA ceasefire was momentous, but that was just one event. Political demons like privatisation still raged—on 27th August, an international survey showed the full consequences of this as it revealed that British rail fares had risen by 12% since privatisation, making them the most expensive in the world.

However, on the 31st August, it appeared that the nation as a whole were unconcerned with politics as they plunged into a mass wave of grief. The widely-adored Princess Diana had died as a result of her injuries in a car crash in Paris. Diana had been labelled the "queen of hearts," and "the peoples princess"; public grief verged on the hysterical.

The heartbreak of a whole nation somehow seemed on a par with the heartbreak of one man communicated on "Ladies and Gentlemen..." The wave of sadness had its soundtrack there, readymade. The bands frontman and songwriter Jason Pierce had recently broken up with the keyboardist, Kate Radley, after she had secretly married Verve frontman Richard Ashcroft. The title track is particularly heartfelt, running, *"I will love you till I die/ and I will love you all the time/ so please put your sweet hand in mine/ and float in space and drift in time."* This was true love and true grief, not the sometimes-fabricated emotions what were building around Diana.

There is something of a moral victory in this record—The Verve's "Urban Hymns," was also released this year, but it was "Ladies and Gentleman," which took NME's Album of The Year title—the loser of the love story becoming the winner of the musical story. It was widely hailed as a "masterpiece," and also sold well, reaching no. 4 in the charts. Clearly, as heartbreak swept the nation, we still had a taste for it in our music.

THE FALL—LEVITATE Sept 1997

Looking at the best-selling music at this point raises questions over whether it was really merit which sold records. Oasis third album "Be Here Now" had been released the previous month, and sold 350, 000 copies on its first day of release—but it was a disappointed, half-hearted album loathed by critics; still their very worst. In the meantime, Elton John's tribute to Princess Diana, "Candle In The Wind," was becoming the second biggest worldwide selling single of all time.

Perhaps the best place to turn to was the counterculture. The Fall had always been a dominant part of this—and their latest album "Levitate," showed them on typically fine form. However, it is also the sound of a band beginning to disintegrate. Brix Smith and longtime drummer Simon Wolstencroft had both quit. The album also spawned their most shambolic tour yet. One night, in Ireland, Mark. E. Smith sacked the entire band, only to reinstate them within a few days. Over the course of the US tour, however, the whole band fell apart and had to be "rebuilt," which we shall return to (see "The Marshall Suite.")

The sensation and trouble which seemed to follow The Fall about kept them interesting. Controversial art was being seen as something to strive for—the "Sensation" exhibition at the Royal Academy courted controversy when the artist Marcus Harvey displayed a powerful image of Myra Hindley created from children's handprints. Rather than seeing this image as excellent art giving humanity to Hindleys victims, people were so outraged at the mere use of her image that the piece fell prey to vandal attacks, forcing it to be removed from display.

There was general unrest in Britain; in varying degrees. One of our most major food scares truly gained ground when British scientists confirmed a link between BSE-infected meat and Creutzfeldt-Jakob disease. And the UK found itself questioning the issues of the wider world when, on 25th September, a Saudi court sentenced British nurse Lucille McLauchlan to eight years in prison and 500 lashes for being an accessory to the murder of Australian nurse Yvonne Gilford in December the previous year. Robin Cook, the foreign secretary, condemned the sentence of flogging against her as "wholly unacceptable in the modern world." As Britain condemned the disorder of the international world, The Fall's US tour for "Levitate," showed that the international world could also cause disorder within this most British of bands.

PRIMAL SCREAM—VANISHING POINT/ ECHO DEK

Primal Scream probably rank as one of the most inconsistent British bands of all time; always unpredictable, its hard to know whether their next album will ever be weak or genius. Luckily, their first album in Tony Blair—ruled Britain, "Vanishing Point," is a fine album, confirming that this is an act who benefit from experimentation. It was their first album with former Stone Roses member Mani, who had always cited "Velocity Girl,"—era Primal Scream as their main influences.

The album itself is informed by culture, being named after and inspired by the 1971 film "Vanishing Point," in particular the song "Kowalski," designed to be an alternative soundtrack to the film. Bobby Gillespie said that "the music in the film is hippy music, so we thought 'why not record some music that really reflects the mood of the film?' It's always been a favourite of the band, we love the air of paranoia and speedfreak righteousness. It's impossible to get hold of now, which is great! It's a pure underground film, rammed with claustrophobia."

Adoring something which had become so obscure showed that Primal Scream were not about to bow down to the mainstream world; the fact that it was the paranoia and claustrophobia that they loved kept them out of step with the fake smiles of Blair's Britain.

The whole album was written and recorded in two months, largely from live improvisation. Whilst they did not get everything they wanted for this record—the track "If They Move, Kill 'Em," was supposed to include a sample from "The Wild Bunch," but it could not get cleared in time—both the band and the critics seemed happy with this album. Gillespie labelled it "an anrcho-syndacilist speedfreak road-movie record!" In fact, the album was such a success that a dub-remix version, "Echo Dek," was released a few months later. The influence of speed that Gillespie is so frank about seemed even more relevant as months passed and drugs featured more highly in the news. In a particularly amusing story, the anti-drugs Foreign Secretary Jack Straw suffered the embarrassment of his own son Will being arrested on suspicion of supplying cannabis. This led to lots of questions and debates about drugs, largely on who was responsible for drug use of the young—clearly, the parents could not always be blamed. Being as pro-drugs as Gillespie was a controversial move.

Elsewhere, on 18th December the bill to establish a Scottish Parliament was unveiled by Secretary of State for Scotland Donald Dewer. By producing albums as bold and experimental as "Vanishing Point," and "Echo Dek," Primal Scream showed it was not just Scotland itself becoming more independent, but its brilliantly confident musicians.

PULP—THIS IS HARDCORE   March 1998

Pulp's previous album, "Different Class," had been a massive breakthrough for them—and an era-defining record of John Major's Great Britain, something which has given it classic status. The follow up, "This is Hardcore," does not have the same classic status, but is every inch as voyeuristic and complex.

On the 5th January, the UK took over the Presidency of the EC's council of minister until 30th June. Just under two months later, the construction of the Millenium Dome began. Britain seemed to be feeling a sense of momentous importance. But once again the working classes were being forgotten—the complete changes in the Labour Party had left them without a mainstream voice, and on 6th March, we saw the closure of South Crofty, the last tin mine in Cornwall. Pulp were still very much a working class voice, but on this album they broaden the "voice of the outsider" to other sections of society. "Help The Aged," is exactly what the title suggest: "Help the aged/ one day they were just like me and you," it opens, urging us to leave behind laissez-faire individualism to offer our altruism to this oft-neglected segment of society. Ageism was not the only prejudice to scar Britain—racism and sexism also prevailed. Britain's racism was, in one case, helping to fuel paranoid conspiracy theories—on 12th February, Mohamed Al Fayed said that he was "99.9%" certain that the car crash which killed the Princess of Wales was a conspiracy to kill rather than an accident, claiming that Dodi had also been preparing to propose to Diana. A lawyer in Al Fayed' native Egypt was planning to sue the Queen and Tony Blair on the grounds that they had conspired to kill Diana because her love for the Muslim would embarrass the state.

It was another deathly blonde that would add the controversy to "This Is Hardcore"—the waifish nude on the sleeve, directed by

Peter Saville and the American painter John Currin, known for his figurative photos of exaggerated female forms. Howard Wakefield digitally enhanced the image—the woman appears almost eerily perfect. This artwork was viewed by some at the time as misogynist, but it is representative of this album—blatant sexuality with a darker side. The title track is an x-rated, upfront account of making a pornographic film. It begins with a description of the appropriate lighting and backdrop for such a film, over the sort of seedy jazz beat that often soundtracks them. Jarvis Cocker's narration ("*I want to make a movie with you*") is vague enough to belong to either director of actor. The closing bars are as triumphant and breathless as orgasm ("*What a hell of a show/ But now, what do you do for an encore? Because this is hardcore*") The lack of subtlety (lyrics include "*Oh . . . that goes in there/ and that goes in there*") make this the most frank exploration of sex since My Bloody Valentine's "Soft as Snow (But Warm Inside)." It is the actual music that keeps this song dark; the low notes and lack of real chorus. Sexuality had reached its darkest points in the real world as well, as on 16th January, two ten year olds went on trial for rape, the youngest ever to be accused of this.

The following month, Anthony Gormley's landmark sculpture "Angel of The North," was erected at Gateshead. With Pulp continuing their relevance through experimentation, the voice of the north in the arts was clearly at its strongest.

MASSIVE ATTACK—MEZZANINE   April 1998

By April, 1998, Massive Attack had truly become a musical force to be reckoned with. Their first two albums, "Blue Lines" and "Protection," were great pieces of landmark ambience, but underpinned by a dark undercurrent. On this third album, they capitalised on their darker elements and allowed them to be a more central part of the sound. They had parted with band member Andrew Vowles by this point, due to "creative conflicts."

The end of conflict was an enormous part of British news at the time—on 10th April, the Good Friday Agreement, an agreement between the UK and Irish governments, and the main political parties in Ireland, was signed. It established the Northern Ireland Assembly with devolved legislative powers and marked a de-escalation in the Troubles. It included a list of principles to extensive to reprint, but its key elements included the acknowledgement by the government of the UK and Ireland that it is for the people of Ireland alone, without external impediment, the commitment by all parties to use "exclusively peaceful and democratic means," the establishment of a principle for any major decision taken by the Assembly; establishment of a "power-sharing," Northern Ireland Executive, using the d' Hondt method to allocate Ministries proportionally to the main parties, abolition of the Republics territorial claim to Northern Ireland via the modification of articles two and three of its constitution (as a result, the territorial claim which had subsisted since 29th December 1937 was dropped on 2nd December 1999) and the Repeal of the Government of Ireland Act 1920.

Using history and at times, logic, in order to build a fair agreement made this very progressive. On 23rd May, the Agreement was endorsed by the voters of Northern Ireland in a referendum. Blair may have been a disappointing Prime Minister, but his Northern

Ireland minister Mo Mowlam was clearly a shining jewel in the dull New Labour crown, having done more for the cause and with more diplomacy than anybody previously. Violence in the news this month was on personal individual cases—for example, the soldier Miles Evans was imprisoned for the murder of his nine year old daughter Zoe. Such news stories were highly uncomfortable for the public, showing that we were still living in potentially dark times. The hauntingly dark sounds of "Mezzanine," soundtracked this fittingly, with moments of sheer beauty. *"Love, love is a verb/ love is a doing word,"* runs the beautiful "Teardrop." In an age of action, but also brutality, reminders of the active part of love in just was perhaps just what we needed.

MANIC STREET PREACHERS—
THIS IS MY TRUTH TELL ME YOURS

With the UK is politically bland territory, and so much having changed over the years, what was to become of long-running bands who were defined by their political ire, such as those great autodidacts who had first broken through when Thatcher was still in power, the Manic Street Preachers? In short, they grew up, hence the hugely mature album "This Is My Truth, Tell Me Yours."

However, their politics were clearly still very much in place—the album title is a quote from Aneurin Bevan. And we certainly needed political voices as much as ever. On the 15th May, the 24th G8 summitt was held in Birmingham. Just six days previously, the city had played host to the Eurovision Song Contest. Still all very international, but quite a change all the same. Traditionally, the host country of the G8 summit sets the agenda for negotiations, which takes place primarily amongst multi-national civil servants in the weeks before the summit itself, leading to a joint declaration that all the countries can agree to sign on. At this summit, the leaders proclaimed an "Action Programme on Forests," with a pledge to report back on progress in 2000, but there has been no evidence of follow-up action. Contemporary politics was clearly lacklustre and disappointing. Young people also seemed to be losing an interest in the subject as the previous wave of activists were now all grown up—hence the mature sound on "This Is My Truth . . ." exemplified on songs like "You Stole The Sun From My Heart," and "Tsunami", two of the albums biggest hits.

This is also the album which produced the bands biggest hit, the historical protest of "If You Tolerate This Your Children Will Be Next." Taking its cue from George Orwell and The Clash's "Spanish

Bombs," this is a song on the theme of The Spanish Civil War, teaching us the lessons we can learn from history. *"The future teaches us to be alone/ the present to be afraid and cold/ so if I can shoot rabbits, then I can shhot fascists,"* it opens, a reference to Franco's ordered clampdown on rabbit hunters on the grounds they could be dangerous against the government. Firmly grounded in historicity, with specific fighting-ground references (*"I've walked Las Ramblas/ but not with real intent"*) and primary source influences (the title is drawn from a propaganda piece) this is the sound of a truly intelligent band. It might not be their most musically exciting moment, but the commercial success of this song is cause for happiness as it shows a willingness on the publics part to embrace political history. The Spanish Civil War is a hugely catastrophic tragedy in both its outcome and its events; the Manics were making sure we did not forget that.

A month before this albums release, the Crime and Disorder Act received Royal Assent. One of the things this introduced was the Anti-Social Behaviour Order, which has since been overused and abused. Anybody who thought they would be truly effective in tackling anti-social behaviour was most optimistic. It would also appear we had been to optimistic about Ireland following the Good Friday Agreement—on 15th August, a car bomb exploded in the Irish town of Omagh, killing 29 people.

Clearly, the Good Friday Agreement, Action on Forests and The Crime and Disorder Act made this an age of good beginnings faltering later on. *"In the beginning/ when we were winning,"* runs one track on "This is my Truth . . ." "The Everlasting. This may be the work of a very different band to the early nineties quartet, but they still showed signs of relevance.

"HUMAN RIGHTS AND MUSICAL FLIGHTS":

BELLE AND SEBASTIAN—THE BOY WITH THE ARAB STRAP AND

PJ HARVEY—IS THIS DESIRE?

The second half of 1998 overflowed with eventful news. On the 8th September, the Real IRA announced a ceasefire. Two days later, events in Ireland continued to be significant—David Trimble of the Ulster Unionist Party met Gerry Adams of Sinn Fein—the first such meeting between Republicans and Unionists since 1992. What, then, were the key album releases this month, and did they effectively soundtrack the rest of the year?

To answer the first question, the key releases could probably be seen as Belle and Sebastians "Boy With the Arab Strap," and PJ Harvey's "Is This Desire?" both of them albums which are the sounds of moving and progressing—very apt considering surrounding events.

"Is This Desire?" is the first PJ Harvey album to print its lyrics on the inner sleeve, reflecting a new-found confidence in its lyricism—and apparently her abilities in general, as she still says that it is her favourite of all her albums. Public and critical opinion would probably generally disagree with this and name "Dry," as her best album, but reviews if "Is This Desire?" were still favourable. Dazed and Confused said that it "would be a classic of the next 10 if not 20 years," whereas Q described it as "disturbing and excellent." It marked a move away from guitar-heavy rock and into a more subtle tone of atmospheric soundscapes.

It was the right time to be creating such disturbing music, as Britain was forced to think about the darker aspects of other nations when police placed General Augusto Pinochet, the 83-year old former dictator of Chile under house arrest during his medical treatment in Britain at the request of Spain. But whilst PJ Harvey continued the path of darkness she had been following for a long time, Belle and Sebastian were becoming known for their "tweeness," making them an antidote to the dark aspects of the world.

On 9th November, the Human Rights Act received Royal Assent. Its aim was to "give further effect," in UK law to the rights contained in the European Convention of Human Rights. The Act made available in the UK courts a remedy for breach of a convention right, without the need to go to the European Court of Human Rights in Strasbourg. In particular, the Act makes it unlawful for any public body to act in a way which is incompatible with the Convention, the judges are not allowed to override it. All they can do is issue a declaration of incompatibility. The Act is not the huge landmark it had potential to be though, merely officialising things that were already in place, like the abolishment of the death penalty. With both acts taking the tactic of adding layers of sound, PJ Harvey and Belle and Sebastian were showing they could really progress through doing, as opposed to just saying.

BLUR—13　　　　　　　　　　　　　　　　March 1999

On the 1st day of 1999, the Euro currency was launched, but Britain's Labour government had no plans to introduce the currency here, preferring to stick to the pound sterling. We were clearly not ready to completely abandon our identity yet, and the euro seemed to be an issue which united left and right. The change of currency would also have been temporarily confusing for the British public; for once, the establishment seemed to actually consider how they would feel about something. If any tangent of authority was coming across badly, it was the police force—on 24th February, the report into the murder of Stephen Lawrence condemned them as "institutionally racist," as well as condemning its officers for "fundamental errors." The public had every right to still feel disillusioned and let down. The release of Blur's latest album, the melancholy "13", ties into this. Often described as Blur's "break-up" album on the grounds of Damon Albarn's relationship with Justine Frischmann coming to an end it is actually more than that—it is the sound of quiet but brilliantly talented guitarist Graham Coxon coming into his own, gaining a more powerful voice of his own. He had sung on one song on their previous album, but on "13"'s "Coffee and TV," he is given the duty of fronting one the albums singles. "Coffee & TV," is a highly personal song documenting Coxon's recovery from alcoholism. *"I've seen so much I'm going blind and I'm braindead virtually,"* runs the chorus with upfront honesty. *"Take me away from this big bad world and agree to marry me/ so we can start over again,"* it continues, but you did not have to have similar problems to Coxon's in order to want to escape. The previous month had seen Britain's worst ever serial killer, Harold Shipman, charged with fifteen murders. On a different scale, scientists at the Rowett Research Institute in Aberdeen reinforced warnings that genetically modified foods, which by now had slipped into everyday life may be damaging to the human body. It seemed to be all bad news—to a point, we could all relate to Coxon. He also designed the cover art for "13", an abstract style human figure, void of features and thus void of emotion. To dwell on Coxon's achievements on this album is not to take anything away from the strength of Albarn's songwriting on this album. The opener and closer on this record are particularly effective. It opens with "Tender," an epic and inspirational (*"come on, come on . . . get through it"*) piece, and closes with "No Distance Left To Run," a beautiful and heartbreaking song in which we learn the full extent of Albarn's emotions in the wake of his break-up (*"Its over . . . you don't need to tell me/ I hope your with someone who makes you feel safe in your sleep."*) The mere concept of having "no distance left to run" could certainly be spun into something of wider relevance. But the UK government had only been in power for two years—they had long way left to run, and a lot of mistakes from previous governments to try and amend.

On the 26th March, some form of compensation was received when a total of £2billion in compensation was paid to 100,000 former miners who were suffering from lung disease after years of working in British coalfields. This was, however, not enough to make New Labour seem empathetic with the working classes—for example, Tony Blair sent his children to private school. When Damon Albarn publicly said that he did not see how he could justify this, he received a letter from the government asking him to keep his opinions to himself. We may have been living in a world were our musicians were silenced . . . thankfully, that did not seem to stop them.

SUPER FURRY ANIMALS—GUERRILLA   June 1999

There is a lot be critical of Tony Blair and his New Labour government for. But on 1st April, they made perhaps their greatest contribution to the socio-political landscape—the introduction of the minimum wage, set at £3.60 an hour for workers over 21, and £3 an hour for workers under 21. These days, it is hard to imagine a world without the minimum wage. Its introduction was certainly cause for celebration—the joyous, carefree sound of Super Furry Animals third album "Guerrilla," two months later certainly fits with this. Singer Gruff Rhys openly said that the lyrics on the album were "self-consciously disposable, happy."

On the whole, this kind of happiness could be seen as more escape than reflection. On the same day that the minimum wage was introduced, Anthony Sawanuik became the first person to be convicted of Second World War crimes in a British court when he was sentenced to life imprisonment for the murder of 18 Jews in his native Belarus (he had lived in Britain since 1947.) This forced us to consider the horrors of history, something which would have been a very different issue if we were in a position to say that at least the modern world played host to peace, but sadly it was not the case. On 14th April, Edgar Pearce ("the "Mardi Gras Bomber") was convicted for a series of bombings and sentenced to 21 years in prison. (The label "The Mardi Gras bomber" came about because he often left a calling card reading "welcome to the Mardi Gras experience.") The story behind Pearce is quite interesting in its relative normality—he grew up in Leyton, an intelligent child, who at the age of eleven went to the Nelson House school in Oxford as his parents hoped to give him a better life. But they were incapable of paying the fees, and thus he returned to school in Leyton three years later, before leaving aged sixteen to work in advertising.

Clearly, the turn in his life was unpredictable as waged a series of bombings targeting branches of Barclays Bank and Sainsbury's, in the hope of obtaining money from each of them. Lawyers acting for him claimed he had Binswangers disease, a rare form of dementia that effects the way people think. On August 14th 1999 he was convicted of 20 charges, leading to this imprisonment.

But this series of bombings were not actually the main bombings which rocked the nation in 1999. There were a series of bombs in London throughout April which horrified the UK. On the 17th, one in Brixton injured 15. On the 24th, one injured 13 on Brick Lane. This then all reached a head on the 30th when a bomb exploded in the Admiral Duncan pub in Soho, the centre of the London gay scene. It killed two people and injured over 30. These bombings were the work of the BNP's David Copeland, determined to start a wave of minority anger which in turn, would create a backlash so fierce that all the white people would vote BNP.

In a world full of ignorance and violence, the Super Furry Animals made use of some interesting antidotes. The bouncy pop song "Do or Die," is inspired by the Quit India speech made by Mahatma Gandhi on 8th August 1942 at the Gowalia Trust in Bombay, in which Gandhi called for his fellow Indians to use non-violent resistance to end British Imperial Rule. Gruff Rhys was pleased with the fact that he had written a song young children could jump up and down to singing "Gandhi lyrics." It was not just an era of violence, but of political sleaze and corruption. Anybody thinking that that age was over was truly mistaken. On the 8th June, Jonathan Aitken was sentenced to 18 months in prison for perjury. Four years earlier, The Guardian had carried a front-page report on his dealings with leading Saudi's, the result of a long investigation carried out by the papers journalists and the "World in Action," television programme. In spite of threats from a panic-stricken Aitken to sue, the programme went ahead, exposing an arms deal with Aitken's business partner, and evidence that Aitken had encouraged his teenaged daughter Victoria to lie in court. It also emerged that he was the chairman of a secretive right-wing think tank, "Le Cercle," who received CIA funding.

However, it is important to consider that Aitken was part of the previous government, not the current one—had the age of corrupt MP's ended? In short, no, but the era of such events being such a regular occurrence had most likely ended. One track on "Guerrilla" is "The Door To This House Remains Open," about starting a new chapter in life. Was this something the nation could align themselves with?

There are actually a range of recent and contemporary influences on the lyrics of "Guerrilla." "Wherever I lay my Phone (That's My Home)" is a comment on the effects of mobile phone radiation on people's health, whilst the unashamedly poppy "Northern Lites," was inspired by the 1998 El Nino climate pattern. The combination of accessible music with fresh-in-the-mind lyricism should have made this album far more commercially successful. However, it did not sell as well as hoped, causing the band to make a far less accessible album the following year—the lo-fi Welsh language album "Mwng." Maybe, given the creation of a Welsh assembly and the newsworthy status of the country at the time, they should have released that first, not "Guerrilla." But, all the same, "Guerrilla," stands as a fragment of joy in a depressing world.

DEATH IN VEGAS—THE CONTINO SESSIONS   Sept 1999

In the summer of 1999, there seemed to be far more names from the recent past appearing in the news than new names. On the 1st July, the press announced the death of Thatcher's deputy Prime Minister William Whitelaw. Three days later, rogue trader Nick Leeson returned home to England from Singapore, nearly four years after he was jailed there after his illegal dealings led to the collapse of Barings Bank with losses of £850million. Then, on the 9th July, former Labour leader Neil Kinnock was back in the news as he was appointed vice president of the European Commission.

Something similar was happening in music. A few years ago, the band Death in Vegas were being mentioned here and there, but their debut album "Dead Elvis," was disappointing. It was not a bad album, but people had expected something darker and dirtier—something they finally achieved on their second album "The Contino Sessions."

There are some wonderful instrumental pieces on this album, but it is on the use of guest vocalists that the bands full potential is unveiled. The crossover hit here is "Aisha", on which Iggy Pop darkly narrates, "*Aisha/ we've only just met/ and I think you ought to know/ I'm a murderer.*" The band were denied the right to play this song on Top Of The Pops in spite of its surprise-hit status, due to the recent sentencing of Harold Shipman.

The two greatest moments on the album, though, are "Broken Little Sister," a tense, crackling and dirty song with a vocal from the Jesus and Mary Chain's Jim Reid, and "Soul Auctioneer," a skin-crawling song sung by Bobby Gillespie. With references to violence, broken wings, demons and "Marxist priests," this could be the most rock'n'roll song ever recorded by a so-called dance band. "*Eggs bearing insects/ hatching in my mind,*" sings Gillespie uncomfortably, over a dizzying soundscape which evokes a broken and squalid room. These two songs use vocalists who don't actually have brilliant voices, but they make these songs brilliant.

In politics, there was another major Scottish figure determined to bring something above the "average" mark—on 9th August, Charles Kennedy was elected leader of the Liberal Democrats. People had always joked that "a liberal vote was next to apathy." With little difference between New Labour and the Conservatives, could Kennedy change this and make them a party worth voting for? Sadly not; his policies increased privatisation and still left the working-classes without a mainstream party to turn to. Labour were still faring better than anybody—a MORI poll showed support for them at 49%, giving them a 22 point lead over the Conservatives. However, it was the first time since the election two years previously that they had polled at under 50%.

Maybe people were starting to realise that they had been cheated.

The opening of "The Contino Sessions," "Dirge," has guest vocalist Dot Allison of One Dove repeating the line "la, la, la," over and over whilst the music gets louder, causing her voice to be lost. How terribly appropriate—this is just what was happening to the working-class in Britain.

"THE OLD, THE NEW, THE MISANTHROPY":
THE FALL—THE MARSHALL SUITE
AND
MUSE—SHOWBIZ

October 1999 saw the release of two noteworthy albums—"Showbiz," by the brand new, scarily young band Muse, and "The Marshall Suite," by the long—established The Fall. Both acts had a lot to live up to—The Fall had years of acclaim, and their was a fair amount of hype surrounding Muse.

"The Marshall Suite," manages to live up to expectations by using various elements of the bands previous works. The beats of their previous album "Levitate," are kept in place, blended with the rockabilly sound pioneered by earlier Fall line-ups. It was also recorded in the wake of trouble and altercations within the band after an onstage fight in New York, which had resulted in the majority of the band returning to England whilst Smith stayed in a New York prison. His girlfriend, the bands keyboardist Julia Nagle, chose to stand by him and help him put a new band together. The result could all to easily be the awkward sound of a new line-up trying to find their feet—instead it is a triumph. Inexperience and youth could also potentially have made Muse's "Showbiz" an awkward affair, but instead it brims with a strident confidence often lacking in even the most established of bands. However, they seem keen for the listener to be aware that this is not an overnight success, as vocalist Matt Bellamy sings on the lead track "Muscle Museum *"I have played in every toilet."*

Around the time of these albums release, a rumour circulated that "The Marshall Suite," was going to be a concept album about "The

Crying Marshall." Smith never fully denied this, saying "I thought it would be good to do the story of his life, a themed LP, with a thread running through it." In the same vein, "Showbiz," is certainly not a concept album, but does seem to have a thread running through as Bellamy plays the loser-in-love at the hands of cold women. (Later, as their sound got bigger and Bellamy became regarded as a guitar hero, their lyrical themes also grew, wrestling with huge sci-fi inspired themes.) Even with this small-scale theme, Muse exude seriousness—see for example the ballad "Unintended" running, *"I'll be there as soon as I can/ but I'm busy mending broken/ pieces of the life I had before."* This earnest sentiment caused the band to be labelled "The new Radiohead." Lyrics on "The Marshall Suite," by contrast, are frequently playful delights. The excellent, catchy "Touch Sensitive," runs *"and you're dying for a pee!/ so you go behind a tree!"* It was as if Mark. E. Smith had passed the baton of musical misanthropy onto newer bands, like Muse. "Touch Sensitive"'s lyrics also deal with social convention, an interesting theme in the post-Thatcherite years. We may no longer have been living in a world which preached "there's no such thing as society," bbut could society ever be rebuilt? And even if it was, was it to governed by rules and stained by history to ever fully click into place again?

The last few months of 1999 seemed strangely void of actively political news, as instead the nation dwelled on the celebrations of the upcoming millennium. And, with albums like "The Marshall Suite," and "Showbiz," bringing in critical acclaim, at least something that looked promising for the next millennium was confident relevant music from acts both old and new.

PRIMAL SCREAM—XTMNTR   Jan 2000

The new millennium had arrived. Celebrations had taken place all throughout the UK, and the much-anticipated Millennium Dome was opened (to a muted critical reception.) It was a new era in terms of the calendar, but a new political era was a long way off. Nearly three years into Blair's leadership, people were growing wise to the New Labour machine which had let so many of them down. And the first key album of the new century was a fierce voice of this, one of the most aggressiveand political albums of Blair's leadership, Primal Screams "XTMNTR."

"XTMNTR" marks the beginning of one era and the end of a musical one as it was the last album to be released on Creation records. The following month, the labels biggest selling act, Oasis, would release their fourth album, "Standing on the Shoulders Of Giants," on their own label, but it received mixed reviews. When it came to the former School of Creation, this was really Primal Screams year as head boys. The whole album is an attack on the government, the police, and multinational corporations. It was a key time to be attacking greed-based corporations. A month after "XTMNTR"s release, the Royal Bank of Scotland succeeded in its hostile takeover bid for Natwest, successfully defeating a rival offer by the Bank of Scotland. British Nuclear Fuels was another corporation which was causing controversy as, on 28th February, its chief John Taylor resigned over a scandal at the company's Sellafield reprocessing works in Cumbria. A damning report by the Nuclear Installations Inspectorate into the falsification of plutonium safety there had been disclosed by the Independent. Initially, Taylor refused to resign, something of a reflection on the general greed of corporations. But the government had serious concerns about the issue and eventually he had to give in. "It was a shambles and it was made worse by BNFL's refusal to recognise that it had a problem," said Stephen

Byers, the then-secretary of State for Trade and Industry, "I welcome John Taylor's decision to resign. In the circumstances, it was the appropriate course of action."

This opposition to Sellafield was not limited to the UK—it was also present in Germany, which had been fed by revelations that as long ago as 1996, safety data had been falsified on batches of product destined for them. It seemed that unscrupulousness was no barrier to corporations continuing—worse still, Taylor received a £300,000 pay off. Money was not just the root of all evil; it was almost a prize for the immoral. On "XTNMNTR"'s standout track, "Kill All Hippies," Bobby Gillespie sings *"you've got the money/ I've got the soul,"* as if the two are mutually exclusive. At the time, it probably seemed that way. It would take more than a new century to change what had been occurring for years. *"Into the future/ into the future!"* runs the albums most accessible moment, "Accelerator," summarising the mindset of the public. But the truth is, politics was going backwards, not forwards—on 11th February, the Northern Ireland Assembly was suspended. The Unionist Party had pulled its two ministers, Peter Robinson and Nigel Dodds. The party wanted devolved government to continue, but only if Sinn Fein were excluded from the power-sharing executive which ran the province. It was as if people could not see past their own needs. Were we sinking back into Thatcherism? If we were, then "XTMNTR" was an appropriate soundtrack. The title track, in particular, is unflinching in its political intensity.

"Everyones a prostitute/ everyone's a prostitute/ no civil disobedience/ no civil disobedience," run the lyrics. To a point, this was true. New Labour had sold out both themselves and the history of the party. In government, most people really were prostitutes, but it was their souls they had sold, not their bodies. As for the lack of civil disobedience, this was certainly true on the whole as people blindly accepted the New Labour government, but naturally there were always voices of dissent—that years May Day riots were amongst the most fierce of all time.

On 2nd March, the UK returned General Augusto Pinochet to Chile to face trial. Pinochet had been responsible for some of the worst atrocities of the age as his awful, brutal regime brought oppression and mass torture to Chile. The role that the UK now had in Pinochet's trial bought these atrocities closer to home. Where global politics was concerned, the UK often has the option of ignorance. This was something alerting the nation to open its eyes to wider issues, something also dominant on "XTMNTR," as it casts its view beyond the UK and looks at the wider world. But any album can cover issues in its lyrics—this goes further than this, involving the listener far more. Initial copies of the album came with a postcard championing the "free Satpal Ram," cause, inviting fans to fill it in and actively participate in the cause. This was more than political music—this was music adopting a political duty.

Primal Scream interviews at the time of "XTMNTR," were heavily political as Gillespie railed against the state, refusing to talk about personal matters. He was particularly thorny at any mention of the name of his former housemate Justine Frischmann, who had recently said of their time living together that "he couldn't function as a human being . . . he couldn't feed himself and was to paranoid to answer the door." But this tension, this paranoia, is a worryingly ideal mindset for creating the album which was the true reflection of Blair's Britain.

"HIDDEN DARKNESS":
THE DELGADOS—THE GREAT EASTERN
AND
BLACK BOX RECORDER—THE FACTS OF LIFE

May, 2000 saw the release of Black Box Recorder's "The Facts of Life," and The Dealgados "The Great Eastern"; pretty albums oozing with lightness and loveliness. Or are they? . . .

Black Box Recorder (a band comprising the Aueter's Luke Haines, the Jesus and Mary Chain's John Moore and vocalist Sarah Nixey) never had any pretensions that they were an innocent act. They once released a song called "Unsolved Child Murder," as a Christmas single and opened their live set to the strains of Elton John's Princess Diana tribute "Candle in The Wind." Their previous album "England Made Me," had led one critic to label them "Cruel Britannia," something developed even further on this record. In contrast to the cold, stiff upper-lip Englishness of Black Box Recorder, the Delgado's have a warm sound evoking the smaller, rural communities of their native Scotland. He twinned vocals of Emma Pollock and Alun Woodward, over a broad selection of instrumentation, gives them a rich and multi-layered sound.

The themes on both albums vary; "The Great Eastern," has a largely personal feel, whilst the themes of "The Facts of Life," take many aspects of the outside, usually at its most discomfiting. Driving, usually a straightforward, everyday theme gains disturbing new ground on two songs, the oddly hypnotic "The English Motorway System," and the opener "The Art of Driving," which turns the act of learning how to drive into a sex act, resulting in the death of a speeding participant. Other themes include childhood sexual awakenings, particularly on the track "May Queen," and the title track, on which Nixey sings, *"when boys are just eleven they begin to grow in height/ at a faster rate that they have done before/ they develop curiosities and start to fantasise about the things they've never thought of doing before."* This goes onto endorse these fantasies as *"no more harmful than the usual thoughts that boys have of becoming football stars or millionaires,"* which is of course true, but it still makes for a discomfiting listen, particularly when Nixey's cut-glass vocal lists a range of locations adolescents are likely to have intercourse, before breathing, *"experimentation/ familiarisation/ its just a nature walk."* Children were always going to be sensitive subjects when dealt with this way; something exacerbated by Myra Hindley's third High Court appeal against a Home Office ruling that her life sentences should mean life (she lost the appeal).

A track on the Delgado's "The Great Eastern," deals with similarly uncomfortable themes—"Knowing When to Run," features the lyrics *"a boy that's so scared lying under the stairs / begs for mercy from all his torturous days . . . bloody bundle picked up from the floor/ back from the country of business today/ a boy and a problem are buried away."* Meanwhile, on "Gift Horse," Black Box Recorder tackle out and out murder (*"their digging up human remains/in our back garden"*) and arson on the standout, the beautiful The Deverall Twins." (*"they started the fire/ they stifled their grins/no-one suspected/ the Deverall Twins."*)

The darkness on "The Great Eastern," is drawn more from personal strife. *"American Trilogy,"* is heartbreaking in its unflinching descriptions of depression—*it's the simple things that crush/ and I'm crying far to much/ so much so/ that I'm feeling/ my control of life is shrinking."* Elsewhere on the album, "No Danger," mixes the bleak with the inspirational as it finds joy in being an outsider. It was a timely piece of writing—on the 4th May, the would-be outsider Ken Livingstone was elected Mayor of London. An independent candidate who had been nicknamed "Red Ken," when he was with the Labour Party, Livingstone was an unlikely winner, defeating the Conservative's Steve North and Labour's Frank Dobson.

On the whole, this point of the year was defined by Acts and laws coming into force. Section 27 of the Access to Justice Act 1999 came into force (allowing recovery of fees from the losing party in civil actions, extending the availability of conditional fee arrangements) and the Immigration and Asylum act gave immigrants the right to food vouchers. Then, on 25th May, the National Waste Strategy was published. It would be seven years before its figures were reported back, showing just how much we wasted. This wasteful, disposable culture was a product of the modern mainstream. Something "The Great Eastern" and "The Facts of Life," share is their desire to embrace the counterculture. "Alternatives we'll find," sing the Dealgados (on "No Danger") whereas Black Box Recorder are sneering about a "straight life/ away from alternative culture," (on "Straight Life.") Given how little the mainstream has to offer, this was certainly a refreshing alternative.

"WIT AND WHIMSY IN THE AGE OF HOSTILITY":

BADLY DRAWN BOY—THE HOUR OF THE BEWILDERBEAST

AND

BELLE AND SEBASTIAN—

FOLD YOUR HANDS CHILD, YOU WALK LIKE A PEASANT

On the whole, Tony Blair had received a positive reception from the public, even if it was not always warranted. June 7th, however, would see him receive a hostile reception from a rather unlikely source—the Womens Institute. Here, he found himself heckled and slow hand-clapped as he gave a speech to them. Clearly, it was the supposed "gentler," sections of society who could provide the greatest voices of dissent. Fittingly, this was the month that saw the release of two wonderfully whimsical albums, Belle and Sebastian's album, "Fold Your Hands Child, You Walk Like A Peasant," and the Mercury music prize winning debut from singer-songwriter Damon Gough, AKA Badly Drawn Boy, "The Hour of The Bewilderbeast."

Being whimsical was not just a rebellion of sorts because of the Womens Insititute reaction to Blair, but because aggression was a part of the mainstream. On the 18th June, UEFA threatened to expel England from the Euro 2000 if there was any more trouble from England fans following a spate of hooliganism. Both the aforementioned albums have influences that some may consider uncouth—the title of "Fold Your Hands . . ." is drawn from some graffiti, whilst "The Hour of The Bewilderbeast," includes a song called "Pissing in the Wind," but this just adds to their versatility. It is not just the whimsical which marks out these albums, but their multi-layered eclectism. "The Hour of The Bewilderbeast," opens with a brass section and continues to take strange, quirky routes throughout. It is full of surprises. Meanwhile, on "Fold Your Hands, Child . . ." Belle and Seb introduce many stylistic changes—four different members of the band sing lead vocals at various points, and a strings section is added. The band were clearly keeping an open mind—as was there native Scotland, as it repealed Section 28 of the Local Government Act 1988 which prevented local authorities from "promoting homosexuality."

In spite of this, on the whole the gentle joys of both these albums seemed gloriously out of step with the hostile world.

On 30th June, David Copeland was found guilty of causing the three nail bomb attacks of the previous year. He was sentenced to life imprisonment and the judge recommended he should serve at least 30 years before being considered for parole, meaning he was likely to remain in prison until 2029. Was the turn of the new century to be marked out by hostility, hatred and disappointment? The government had attempted to create more out of it, but were failing. The Millennium Dome had been a disappointment and this month the much-hyped "Millenium Bridge" was opened in London—before having to be immediately temporarily closed again due to excess swaying.

If all this was to be expected of the age, at least the counter culture was offering some gentler alternatives that were the perfect refuge.

RADIOHEAD—KID A   Oct 2000

Nowadays, Radiohead's third album "OK Computer," is widely regarded as one of the greatest albums of all time. But it is worth remembering that when there record label heard it, they were hesitant to release it, fearing commercial suicide. So it was certainly worth persevering with their fourth album, the hugely experimental "Kid A," even though it greatly confused pretty much all those that heard it upon its release.

Yes, it is a change of direction. But, after being considered downright weird at the time, it now sounds so right—it was simply an album ahead of its time.

"Kid A," was released in an environment were anger and dissent swept the nation. Even people who may have formerly considered themselves apolitical were protesting in the 8th September UK fuel protests, in which protestors blocked the entrances to oil refineries in protests against high fuel prices. Panic buying by motorists had led to nationwide petrol shortages, with between 75-90% of all UK petrol stations closing due to low supplies the following week. The sounds of a furious, dissatisfied Britain are reflected in the series of noises that colour "Kid A." Highlights include "How To Disappear Completely," one of their greatest ever soundscapes, which draws its title from Doug Richmonds manual on how to go missing effectively, and "Idioteque," a relentless beat accompanied by looping repetitive lyrics. Whilst there were no singles released from "Kid A," "Idioteque," was the song most frequently played as the promotional song, presumably deemed the most commercial. If this was the most the commercial the album was going to get, then its general lack of accessibility was clear. Yes, the album confused many, but then again it was a confusing age. We had a Labour government who appeared more Conservative and there was political change everywhere (for example, on 18th July Alex Salmond had resigned as leader of the Scottish National Party.)

What we are actually hearing when we listen to "Kid A," is the sound of progress, something else which could be found in the UK in this year—on 28th July, the last 80 prisoners left the Maze prison in Northern Ireland as part of the Northern Ireland peace process. But things like this, which were a victory to a few, seemed less significant in the bigger picture of discontent, largely spawned by the fuel crisis. An angry Britain responded by putting the Conservatives two points ahead of Labour on 38% in a 14th September MORI poll. This is typical British behaviour—voting *against* what they are dissatisfied with, rather than *for* what they want. The masses may have benefited more daring to look beyond the narrow margins—like Radiohead were doing musically.

All those who felt confused by "Kid A," at the time would benefit from hearing it again now. It was not Radiohead that were strange. It was the rest of us that needed to catch up.

PJ HARVEY—

STORIES FROM THE CITY, STORIES FROM THE SEA   Oct 2000

Two hugely important albums were released in October 2000. One was Radiohead's "Kid A," which saw them become far less accessible, the other was PJ Harvey's "Stories From The City, Stories From The Sea," which saw her become far more accessible. In fact, when played alongside her earlier albums such as "Dry," "Stories from the City . . ." sounds almost like a glossy pop record. But she still managed to hold on to critical acclaim—reviewers loved the album, and it would go on to win the Mercury Music Prize—and remain adored by her longterm fans. How did she manage this?

Firstly, let us give the album the privilege of context. It was released in a month when the British seemed happy with their government—a 23rd October MORI poll put them 13% ahead of the Conservatives with 45% of the vote. Whilst all this really does is prove how horribly fickle and narrow-minded the British public can be, our happiness was refreshing. This mood of elation was perfectly captured by the lead single from "Stories from the City . . ." "Good Fortune," a hymn to happiness—its chorus runs *"And I feel like/ some bird of paradise/ my bad fortune/ slipping away/ and I feel the innocence of a child/ everybody's got something good to say."*

But, much like New Labour (who would go on to make painfully serious errors of judgement) this is almost pulling us into a false sense of security. Opener "Big Exit," runs, *"I'm scared baby/ I wanna run/ this worlds crazy/ give me the gun."* But she sounds far from scared—this is as strident and confident as anything from "Dry," with Harvey finally seeming at ease. Where her music was once about questions and uncertainties ("Is This Desire?") it was now about firm sentiments (This Is Love).

The sexual drive of her earlier works is also fully present. Harvey had been living in New York, a city she seemed to have fallen in love with, and captures the darker, more primitive side of the city's sexuality perfectly. "The Whore's Hustle and The Hustler's Whore," documents sleaze, prostitution and narcotics with a kind of glee, rather than disdain, whereas "This Is Love," places sex as a priority over the anomalies of the world (*"I can't believe lifes so complex/ when I just wanna sit here and watch you undress."*) News at the time, however, was more concerned with the ends of relationships than with the flowering of relationships—in this month, the House of Lords made a landmark ruling in the "White vs White," case, which involved a couple with assets exceeding £45 million, more than either needed for their requirements. It was held that the absence of financial need did not men departing from a more generous settlement for an applicant in big money cases. This, then, enabled the courts to make settlements reflecting the wealth of the parties, and not just their needs and requirements. It was decided then, that in all cases, regardless of division of assets against "the yardstick of equality of division." This was not to introduce a presumption of equality in all cases, but "to ensure the absence of discrimination,"—the example the BBC news report at the time used was "between a wage earner and a child carer, thereby recognising the non-financial contribution of the parent caring for children." Whilst all of this is positive, this politicising of relationships makes the upfront joy and sexuality Harvey brings to them all the more refreshing. Even the brilliantly mournful duet with Thom Yorke, "This Mess Were In," includes lyrics about *"sweat on my skin,"* chased with an orgasmic groan.

What Harvey managed with this record is remarkable—winning over many new fans with a more accessible sound, whilst retaining the quality that won her first wave of fans over. Perhaps selling more, but never selling out, the current climate was not enough to turn PJ Harvey into a product of the New Labour generation.

THE FALL—THE UNUTTERABLE   Nov 2000

November, 2000 saw the release of a new, hugely acclaimed album from The Fall, "The Unutterable." The album was recorded with the same line-up that had appeared on the previous album "The Marshall Suite," but by the point of "The Unutterable," the new line-up had had a year to gel, something which is quite apparent of the cohesion of "The Unutterable." Dave Simpson of The Guardian called it "a career peak," whilst Piers Martin of the NME said that "this is the most vital and relevant The Fall have sounded for a long time."

The rest of the year was bleak in Britain—on 29th December, Arctic weather conditions blighted the country, with heavy snow and temperatures as low as—13 degrees Celsius causing extensive gridlocking on the roads and railways. Driving was an ill-advised nightmare, making one track on "The Unutterable," "Way Out," about Mark. E. Smiths aversion to roundabouts, particularly well timed. After all, something that The Fall do very well is taking the mundane and making it thrilling—as a further example, one song on this album "Pumpkin Soup and Mashed Potatoes," is about exactly what the title suggests, and nothing more. As the nation was horrified by the racist murder of ten year old Damilola Taylor, drama did not seem positive. The everyday seemed safer; no news was good news.

Of course, there are livelier lyrical themes elsewhere. "Ketamine Sun," is a drug anthem, whilst "Dr Bucks Letter," is a tribute to the author Charles Bukowski which also dispraises superficial materialist modernity. The month of this albums release was peppered with stories of money—the attempted theft of £350 millions worth of diamonds from the millennium dome, Judith Keppel becoming the first person to win a million on the television show "Who Wants To Be A Millionaire?" and Rio Ferdinand becoming the most expensive football player ever in an £18 million transfer from West Ham United to Leeds United.

The press, then, were right—with a finger still firmly on the zeitgeist, The Fall really were as vital and relevant as ever.

MANIC STREET PREACHERS—KNOW YOUR ENEMY   Feb 2001

For a band to be classed as great, can they merely just make great records, or must they do something more? Either way, the Manic Street Preachers had by now firmly sealed their status. Their 1998 album "This Is My Truth Tell Me Yours," may have felt like they had matured to much as they ventured into Radio 2—friendly territory, but they made up for it in 2000 with the release of a fiery return to form, the stand alone single "The Masses Against The Classes." The artwork for this single was the Cuban flag—something which was fully capitalised on on February 17th, 2001, when the band became the first Western act to play Cuba, in a 17-pence gig for an audience of 5,000 including Fidel Castro. "We'eve just got a lot of respect for the Cuban people and the Cuban culture, and we wanted to do something really different this time," said bassist Nicky Wire, "and Cuba for me is the last symbol that really fights against the Americanisation of the world." This year, then, had already seen the band reaffirm their relevance through landmark actions—the album they released at time time, however, "Know Your Enemy," is a slightly hit and miss affair.

In spite of this, they were beginning to allude to their early days in a way which kept their original fanbase close. Even the old aesthetics returned—the sleeve of "Know Your Enemy," is a New Art Riot infused montage of words and paint splatters, whilst at the bands biggest ever gig, at Cardiff Millenium Stadium on the eve of the millennium, Nicky Wire kept the glamour stakes high a pink spray painted dress and glittery eyeshadow combination. The band who once told us "all rock'n' roll is homosexual," were clearly prepared to stand by their rebellion against gender norms, something which continued to be relevant as, on the 8th January, homosexuals finally received full equality when there age of consent was lowered to sixteen.

The news, however, was to be quickly wrapped up in political quagmire when, on 24th January, Secretary of State for Northern Ireland Peter Mandelson was forced to resign from the cabinet for a second time. This time, it concerned claims that he pulled strings to help billionaire Srichand Hinduya—who had been defending himself against criminal allegations in a long running corruption case involving an arms deal between Swiss company Bofors and the Indian government—secure a UK passport in return for a £1million sponsorship deal for the Millenium Dome whilst Mandelson was in charge of the project. However, such issues did not appear to affect the governments popularity—on 25th January, they scored 49% in the latest MORI poll, opening up a 20 point lead over their rivals. Considering the apparent lack of dissent, the Manics were still relevant, particularly being as blatantly political as they were—this album even goes so far as to entitle a song "Freedom of Speech Won't Feed My Children." The knack for keeping contemporary is very much there, as on the song "Baby Elian," they chronicle the recent news story of the Elian Gonzales dispute (a dispute over were a Cuban born child should be based—America or Cuba—which turned into an issue of international bureaucracy.)

International issues on the whole were becoming relevant to Britain—the conflict in Libya had hit us hard in the shape of the Lockerbie bomb in 1988, and the memories of this flashed back as a Scottish court sentenced Abdelbaset Ali Megrahi to life for the bombing (a second Libyan, Al Amin Khalyah Fhimah, was cleared.)

In spite of keeping largely relevant, there is a sense of effort on "Know Your Enemy," an awareness of keeping as interesting as their past. "My Guernica," is an angsty re-telling of TS Eliot's poem "The Love Song of J. Alfred Prufrock" (which gets a namecheck) a poem about the horrors of ageing which implies Wire's whole discomfort with the process. Songs like "Found That Soul," and "Intravenous Agnostic," are also full-throttle rock which attempt to recapture the bands early spirit.

On the whole, the Manics had always been a band who soundtracked crisis in Britain perfectly, and we certainly seemed to be sinking into that—on the 19th February, the foot and mouth crisis began, and the NHS received some terrible publicity when patient Tony Collins spent 77 and a half hours on a hospital trolley outside the toilets at the Princess Margaret hotel in Swindon. Whilst not on the level of their early works, "Know Your Enemy," sees the Manics react against the maturity of "This is My Truth . . ." in order to capture the moment ideally.

ELBOW—ASLEEP IN THE BACK   May 2001

It was easy to think that dissent was dead, but it was not. On the 1st May, the traditional anti-capitalist demonstrations were aggressive and forceful. The Right were also protesting—on the 16th May in Rhyl, a Countryside Alliance supporter threw an egg at deputy Prime Minister John Prescott. In a highly unprofessional but visually impressive move, Prescott turned round and punched him. Prescott was not always convincing in his claims he was the voice of the working-class North, but this act took the way anybody in the "real world" would have reacted and transferred it to be the political sphere. Unprofessional Prescott may have been, but its hard to have any sympathy for the protestor.

A rather more subdued, sensitive voice of the working-class North manifested itself this month in the debut album from the Bury band Elbow, "Asleep in The Back." It is full of yearning beauty and tragic, doomed love. The standout "Powder Blue," appears to chronicle the agonies of being hopelessly in love with a heroin addict ("I'm proud to be the one you hold/ when the shakes begin/ sallow skin, starry eyed, blessed in our sin") whilst "Red" runs "you burn to bright/ you live to fast/ this can't go on to long/ your tragedies starting to happen." Meanwhile, "Newborn," opens with a mournful lyric about "I'll be the corpse in you bathtub/ useless," before evolving into a crashing, multi-layered rock song.

"Asleep In The Back," then, is a largely bleak record. But the climate in which it was released was not completely bleak—on 15th May, medication prices fell due to a court ruling on the drug industry pricing policies, but there is still a distinct lack of health on this record—the moment of humour is called "Don't Mix Your Drinks." In contrast to their music, frontman Guy Garvey won a reputation as the funniest man in music. How easily he could divert from this in order to write an album like "Asleep In The Back," is a blessing.

It would be their 2008 album "The Seldom Seen Kid," a more optimistic record, which won over legions of fans and took home the Mercury Music Prize. These days, they are widely adored for a bigger, sweeping sound. But, for many, this upfront-indie debut remains their finest hour.

RADIOHEAD—AMNESIAC
AND
MUSE—ORIGIN OF SYMMETRY

Once a band is as well-established as Radiohead were by June 2001, newer bands are beginning to provide competition. Something that may have made this particularly problematic for Radiohead was the number of bands being labelled "the new Radiohead." This may be hard to believe about either of these bands now, but this was a label which had been given to both Elbow's "Asleep In The Back," released the previous month, and Muse's 1999 debut "Showbiz."

The month of June 1999 luckily cast away such labelling in a twofold manner. Firstly, because Muse' second album "Origin of Symmetry," proved they were a very different band to Radiohead, and because Radiohead's fifth album "Amnesiac," proved that there was no need for a new Radiohead. The original one really would do quite nicely.

The month of these album's releases was something of a landmark month politics also. The 7th saw a General election in which the Labour Party attained a second successive landslide victory. The election also saw notable new entrants to Parliament—the 34 year old Conservative David Cameron (obviously notable because of his future role—and exits, such as the retirement of former Prime Minister Ted Heath, aged 84. the lack of general success for the Conservative Party led to the resignation of their leader William Hague after four years.

The political climate may have remained largely the same, but music was all about progress. On "Origin of Symmetry," Muse frontman

Amy Britton

Matt Bellamy progressed their sound so much that he earned a new title—this generations guitar hero.

The opening of "Plug In Baby," and frantic breakdown of "Newborn" are perfect examples of his awe-inspiring musicianship.

Of course, Radiohead also have a guitar-hero in their line-up in the form of Johnny Greenwood, and "Amnesiac" sees a return to a guitar based sound after the electronics of "Kid A." However, both albums were recorded in the same period, during the same recording sessions. With regards to the decision to release two albums rather than one, Thom Yorke said that "they are separate because they cannot run in a straight line with one another. They cancel each other out as overall finished things . . . in some weird way I think Amnesiac gives another take on Kid A, a form of explanation. Something traumatic is happening in Kid A . . . this is looking back at it, trying to piece together what has happened." About the differences with the previous record, he said, "I think the artwork is the best way of explaining it. The artwork to Kid A was all in the distance. The fires were all going down the other side of the hill. With Amnesiac, you're actually in the forest whilst the fires happening." This sense of being in the midst of something frightening and aggressive was reflected in the June 25th race riots in Burnley, which saw 200 whites and Asians embroiled in vandalism and arson. The riots were started by whites, who seemed to place a ridiculous amount of importance on were people came from. Perhaps a classical theology influence was something we could benefit from. When talking about "Anmesiac," Thom Yorke said, "I read that the Gnostics believe when we are born we are forced to forget were we come from. I thought this was really fascinating. Its like the river of forgetfulness. It may have been recorded at the same time but it comes from a different place I think. It sounds like finding an old chest in someone's attic with all these notes and maps and drawings and descriptions of going to a place you can't remember. That's what I think anyway."

In between the release of "Kid A," and "Amnesiac," both Thom Yorke and drummer Phil Selway had become fathers. This album is dedicated to both of thems sons, and songs like the dreamlike

"Pyramid Song," ("*we all went to heaven in a little row boat*") are almost like complex lullabies. But this is still an album with relevance in the wider world.

As a second term for Blair implied a lack of progress in politics, "Amnesic" and "Origin of Symmetry" proved it was still very much present in the musical sphere.

"THE EDGE OF PSYCHEDELIA":
SUPER FURRY ANIMALS—RINGS AROUND THE WORLD
AND
THE BETA BAND—HOT SHOTS! II

After June had seen terrible race riots in Burnley, history repeated itself as this sparked a wave of race riots throughout the country. Firstly, on the 7th July, two people were stabbed in race riots in Bradford, West Yorkshire. Then, on 20th July, rioting broke out in Brixton following the fatal shooting of Derek Bennett, a 29 year old black man, by armed police in the area. 27 people were arrested and three police officers injured. In a backwards looking world apparently frightened of a range of colour, it is fittingly refreshing that this month saw the release of two albums at the edge of psychedelia—the Super Furry Animals "Rings Around The World," and The Beta Bands "Hot Shots II."

What both albums are is a reaction against previous works. The Beta Band's debut album was, to critics and fans alike, glorious; the droll delivery and inventive musicianship on songs like "Dr. Baker," and "To You Alone," had rightly won them acclaim. The band themselves, however, hated the album, going on to deride it as "rubbish" and use the follow up as an attempt to make up for it.

"Rings Around the World," also reacts against the Super Furry Animals's previous works—were 1999's "Guerrilla" had been "self-consciously disposable, happy," "Rings Around The World" tackles a broader, often heavier range of themes. The song "Presidential Suite," a look at Russia and United States presidents Boris Yeltsin and Bill Clinton, "takes a reflective look at the decadent nineties," during the Lewinsky scandal asking, "if we really need to know he came inside her mouth?"

Matters of political scandal, however, weren't exclusive to the "decadent nineties." On the 19th July, Jeffrey Archer was sentenced to four years in prison for perjury and perverting the cause of justice. The basis of the allegations originated with Ted Francis, a friend who claimed Archer owed him money, and Angela Peppiatt, Archer's former personal assistant. They stated that Archer had fabricated an alibi in his 1987 trial and were concerned that he was unsuitable to stand as Mayor of London as he planned to do. Peppiatt had kept a diary of Archer's movements, which contradicted evidence he had given during the aforementioned trial.

Clearly, the lyrics to songs like "Presidential Suite," were incredibly relevant, as were other moments on "Rings Around The World," for example, there are references to Peter Mandelson on the record. Elsewhere, "Juxtaposed with You," addresses social injustice and is about "house prices going up and people being left behind by the super rich." The title track, meanwhile, is based on an idea put forward by the father of Gruff Rhys' girlfriend, and is about "all the rings of communication around the world. All the rings of pollution, and all the radioactivity that goes round." A personal interest in many global issues colours the whole of this record—such as "Run, Christian, Run!" a reflection of guitarist Huw Banford's interest in doomsday cult websites.

The lyrics on "Hot Shots II" are more oblique, but it is still incredibly exciting. The quirky beats of opener "Squares" set the scene perfectly.

After all, through a riot colour and invention, both The Beta Band and the Super Furry Animals had reacted against themselves to make hugely relevant records.

NEW ORDER—GET READY   Aug 2001

One of the hardest things about writing this book is deciding what is eligible for inclusion. Whilst any good writer has the objectivity to see the wider picture of what is relevant, obviously to a point, personal taste does come into it. And thus, I put forward one of my more controversial musical opinions—New Order's 2001 album "Get Ready," is by far away my favourite album of theirs.

Excellent lead single "Crystal," sets the scene perfectly, a generous slab of guitar driven indie which dispels their usual synths in order to take them back to their Joy Division roots. *"Here comes love/ its like honey/ you can't buy it with money,"* sings Bernard Sumner in the chorus—a pretty clichéd lyrics, yes, but an apt one for an age of excess spending. As privatisation remained king, it seemed you could put a price tag on anything. Here, New Order are reminding us that you can't.

It was this climate of excess privatisation that made the events of 7th August, 2001 such a brilliant landmark—the government had taken the unprecedented step of nationalising a private hospital on Harley Street. The move had cost £27 million, but it was a wise one—the government needed to get back into favour after problems the previous month, when Gwyneth Dunwoody and Donald Anderson had been sacked as chairs of select committees on transport and foreign affairs.

Because the truth is, when you've fallen out of favour, the best thing to do is not rely on spin, but to put forward a move which will win the public back over and make up for previous errors. This is not exclusive to politics—and, after a critically subdued few years, this is just what New Order had done with "Get Ready."

SPIRITUALIZED—LET IT COME DOWN   Sept 2001

September, 2001 is a date nailed to history. Or, more specifically, September 11th 2001 is a date nailed to history. This was the day which saw the terrorist attacks on New York's World Trade Centre; the footage was like nothing we had seen before as hijacked planes brought the twin towers crashing down. The visuals looked more like special effects than real life. In a prompt reaction, over in the UK One Canada Square (the UK tallest building) and the London Stock Exchange were quickly evacuated. Tony Blair immediately cancelled a speech he was due to give to the TUC, and pledged to stand "shoulder to shoulder," with the Unites States.

The relationship between Britain and the United States perhaps informed our grief stricken reaction to the attacks a little to much. In his stand-up set, British comedian Stewart Lee summed up the response perfectly by talking about being abroad during the attacks and thinking that they had initially happened "somewhere like Columbia," before saying "then I realised, it happened in America, were English speaking people lived, and the true extent of the tragedy hit me."

It is true that the British would never show the same sympathy for the thousands who suffer and die at the hands of political despotism in more far flung nations every day. But none the less, the nations shock and grief was very real. On 13th September, the Queen ordered the changing of the Guard ceremony to be paused for a two minute silence, following the playing of the American national anthem. Last time there had been a wave of national mourning, it had been following the death of Princess Diana, which had coincided with the release of Spiritualized's heartbreaking album "Ladies and Gentleman we are Floating in Space." This second wave coincided with the release of their album "Let It Come Down"—they were becoming the unofficial soundtrack of mourning.

However, where "Ladies and Gentlemen . . ." really was full of grief following Jason Pierce's personal heartbreak due to his break up with Kate Radley, "Let it Come Down," is more like comfort and consolation. It is a largely orchestral work, influenced by Phil Spector-style production, and this alone makes it feel uplifting. The way this sound was put together makes it even more remarkable—Jason Pierce is unable to read music, so he wrote all the orchestral parts for the album by singing them into a portable tape recorder, transcribing them into a piano, and then helping the musicians turn these into their specific parts. The lead single "Stop Your Crying," is like a security blanket of a record, perfectly timed for the grief of 9/11. *"Nothing hurts you like the pain/ of someone you care about,"* sings Pierce with heartfelt understanding.

However, this record evokes senses other than deep emotion—"12 Steps" is a blatantly funny attack on drug rehabilitation systems, with the famously drug addled Pierce singing "ain't gonna worry about finding Jesus Christ/ I'd rather spend my cash on vice." If recent events were going to leave us all searching for something deeper in life, there was a sense Pierce was probably going to be immune to this.

Politics at home were also newsworthy, as Iain Duncan Smith took over as leader of the Conservative Party. But the shockwaves from 9/11 were so vast, everything else seemed to fade into insignificance.

IAN BROWN—MUSIC OF THE SPHERES

It was a difficult age for British music. Firstly, the wave of glorious sounds coming over from the States made our music seem insipid—this year had given us the albums "Fever To Tell" by the Yeah Yeah Yeahs, "White Blood Cells" by the White Stripes and the hugely significant "Is This It," by The Strokes, which would have a profound effect on the musical landscape. Secondly, the post 9/11 age was difficult to soundtrack. Censorship was coming down hard on potentially upsetting records (Radio One even went so far as to ban Hot Hot Heat's "Bandages," a song clearly about self-harm, for fear of causing war-related upset!), but nobody wanted to appear glib. There was a need to find the right soundtrack. Had their been anything earlier in the year which could capture it? Tom McRae's "End Of The World News," was a candidate, now sounding prophetic. Or there was the option of embracing escapism instead—the year had seen albums such as "Vibrate You," by King Adora, a glamorous four piece who promoted sex, sleaze and Juliet Bravo. For musicians recording and releasing now, though, it was still difficult. For example, having always been the voices of urban social politics, Pulp chose an escapist tact which saw them embrace nature and the rural. However, as Britain tagged along with America in its fruitless, widely condemned invasion of Afghanistan and Iraq, there was one album released which featured THE lyric of the post 9/11 age. The album was Ian Brown's "Music Of the Spheres." The standout song—and lyric—was the blisteringly intelligent F.E.A.R. Every single line in the song spells FEAR, opening, "for each a road/ for everyone a religion," not once letting go of this concept or repeating itself. In short, fear was unescapable, and there were many different ways of spelling it out.

The invasions raised a lot of ethical questions—George. W. Bush justified them by weakly claiming God had told him to order them.

Kofi Annan was also quick to label them "illegal." But many still supported them, due to the overwhelming fear of terrorism. This was exacerbated by the fact we appeared to be producing home-grown terrorists—on 22nd December, the British born terrorist Richard Reid attempted to blow up American Airlines Flight 63 from Charles De Gaulle airport in Paris to Miami International airport, using explosives hidden in his shoes. We had not felt this paranoid and terrified since the cold war days.

The fear was inescapable; Ian Brown's lyric still stands today as the song which truly captured this time.

"BRITAIN FIGHTS BACK":

THE COOPER TEMPLE CLAUSE—SEE THIS THROUGH AND LEAVE AND

IKARA COLT—CHAT AND BUSINESS

The wave of exciting new guitar bands was clearly a good thing. The NME, an ardent supporter and chronicler of the movement, dubbed it "the New Rock Revolution," and surely anybody would have been happy to fight for this cause. But the distinctly American sense of the revival was still dominant—New York's The Strokes had been the ones to start it all, with a sound that evoked New York's history in its resonance of new wave bands like Television.

However, we needed this jolt from our neighbours. British music had become horribly dull and uninspired as bands like Travis and Coldplay reigned. This was soon shaken up by a new movement (sometimes dubbed "the scene with no name") which produced many bands now largely forgotten, but at the time blisteringly relevant and exciting.

At the beginning of 2002, two of these bands, Ikara Colt and the Cooper Temple Clause, released their debut albums. There was something of a sense of relief in Britain, as, on the 14th January, the end of the Foot and Mouth crisis was announced after 11 months. But this does not make the aggression of such bands any less relevant, as we will go on to see.

Whereas much of the music in the new American Rock Revolution drew its influence from garage rock and new wave, the British wing was closer to the sharp, jerky stylings of post-punk. Ikara Colt were the closest thing a band has ever come to the sounds of The Fall.

(The post-punk revival would continue with Franz Ferdinand, and Stateside with The Rapture and Radio 4.) Post-punk had captured the dillusionment of Thatcherism—this time, it was the soundtrack of a Britain which felt sold out as we continued to fight in Iraq and Afghanistan—a conflict that 70% of the British public did not want us to be involved in. There were other matters of misery for certain individuals as well, as on the 19th February, Ford ended 90 years of British car production with the loss of more than 2,000 jobs after the last Fiesta was made in Dagenham. Business was a cruel world; the harshness of capitalism seemed to manifest itself in the misery of the workers. The vileness of the corporate machine and the cut-throat business world is perfectly captured by The Cooper Temple Clause on one song on "See This Through and Leave," "Who Needs Enemies?" which references boardrooms and function rooms, twinned with the opening line *"my oh my I'm seeing the potential/ now lets just see what we can do/first we'll try and teach you how to mingle/ then we'll teach you how to kill."* Meanwhile, Ikara Colt may have called their album "Chat and Business," but seemed refreshingly unconcerned with such music-business staples as the charts—"Chat and Business" came with a set of stickers for the listener to complete the artwork with, but these were deemed to be a free gift, making the album ineligible for the charts.

Other debut albums reflected the new British rock revival were released this year—for example, The Music, who bought an epic musicianship to the scene, and The Coral, who added a quirky sea-shanty inspired twist—but for me it is the full-throttle feel of the underrated debuts by Ikara Colt and the Cooper Temple Clause which really seemed to capture the moment.

BILLY BRAGG—ENGLAND, HALF ENGLISH   March 2002

Billy Bragg is a singer-songwriter largely associated with the eighties. And whilst, yes, he seemed tailor-made for protesting against Thatcher, he continued to be relevant long after her fall from power.

His work with the American band Wilco on the Woody Guthrie inspired "Mermaid Avenue" series of albums proved this; his 2002 album "England, Half-English," is also a perfect example. The time of this albums release was a positive time for the music scene. After an uninspiring few years, new bands were making the world exciting again, and on 11th March the first new BBC radio station in decades, radio 6 Music, was launched, a platform for more alternative music which would never have made it onto the playlists of Radio One or Two.

Bragg's reaction to this is the best it could be—rather than try and keep up with the new scene, he simply carries on in the same vein he has done for years, producing consistently excellent music. His old favourite theme of Britishness and just what it means to be English is more dominant than ever—and more articulate.

So, what is Britishness? Royalism is to often used as a symbol of the nation—in fact, the Royal Family can hardly be called a representative symbol. The Royals seemed to dominate the news for the first few months of 2002 all the same. On the 9th February, Princess Margaret died aged 71 after suffering a stroke. On 30th March, the Queen Mother died aged 101.

The true dominance of the Royals in the news though, lay not in these deaths but in the Queen's Golden Jubilee Celebrations. On the 29th April, as part of these celebrations, the Queen dined at 10 Downing

Street with the five living Prime Ministers who had served under her—Tony Blair, John Major, Margaret Thatcher, James Callaghan and Edward Heath. Never before had their been a room so full of people who both misunderstood and damaged the British public.

Englishness was coming to be something much broader, reaching beyond traditional ideas such as the outdated Royal Family. The title track on "England, Half-English," runs *"I'm a great big bundle of culture tied up in the red white and blue/ I'm a fine example of your Essex man/ And I'm well familiar with the Hindustan."* In Bragg's modern Britain, there is no room for racism, which was still rife across the nation as the BNP continued to make their voices heard. Their latest headline-grabbing statement was their decision to support Denmark in that years World Cup as their team was all white, whereas the England team included black players (they did not benefit from this decision—England beat Denmark 3-0 in the second round.) The truth is, the things we widely regard as British were not, not fully, as outlined on "England, half-English,"—*"Dance with me to this very English melody/ from morris dancing to Morrissey/ all that stuff came from across the sea/ Britannia, she's half-British, she speaks Latin at home/ St. George was born in Lebanon, how he got here I don't know."*

He is so right about this. After all, even the Royal family can't be called pure English. Speaking of which, the Golden Jubilee celebrations continued in an often surreal way—on June 3rd, the "Party at the Palace," took place at Buckingham Palace. As musicians such as Ozzy Osbourne participated, it was a moment of feeling let down by musics former rebels. Somebody with Bragg's integrity would never have been involved.

Of course, as ever, Bragg's contemporary relevance stretched beyond this issue and reached into wider, political issues. One of the most angry songs on "England, half-English," in this respect is "NPWA" which opens with the verse *"I grew up in a company town/ And I worked real hard til that company closed down/ They gave my job to another man/ on half my wages in some foreign land/ And when I ask how can this be good for our economy?/ I was told nobody cares/ so long as they make money when they sell their shares."* This mixture of protest and storytelling evolves into full-blown political dissent with the later verse *"the ballot box is no guarantee/ that we achieve democracy/ our leaders claim the victory when only half the people have spoken/ we have no job security in this global economy, our borders closed to refugees but our markets forced open,"* twinned with a typical Bragg rallying-chorus *"can you hear this? Are you listening? No power without accountability!"*

Such dissent was perfectly timed in age of often incompetent, unpopular politicians (particularly the line "who are these people? Who elected them?) Stephen Byers resigned as Secretary of State for transport on 28th May, but people had wanted him to go long before. However, in his resignation statement, although he admitted making mistakes he denied the often repeated allegation that he was a liar who often misled Parliament. He instead said he was resigning because the government he supported was being damaged as a result of his prescence in the cabinet, probably the most honest thing he ever said.

If there were political problems in this country, then they were nothing compared with overseas. The despotic rule of Mladic over Bosnia and Herzigova required the International Community to have a High Representative for this nation—on 27th May our own Paddy Ashdown, former leader of the Liberal Democrats, was appointed in this positions.

This was not some turning point in the UK becoming something more international. As "England, Half-English," shows, we already were.

"HELLO TOMORROW":

OASIS—HEATHEN CHEMISTRY

AND

PRIMAL SCREAM—EVIL HEAT

The previous year had seen the end of a musical era when the iconic Creation records closed down. Its final album release had been Primal Scream's brilliant "XTMNTR"; its biggest seller Oasis "(Whats the Story?) Morning Glory." These former Creation acts who had helped to define the previous decade (or, in Primal Scream's case, two decade) now had to prove that they could soundtrack the next generation too. Could the albums they released in the summer of 2002 do so?

The bands were in somewhat different positions—Primal Scream's previous album, the aforementioned "XTMNTR," was a complete classic which showed them at a career peak. It was their best album since "Screamadelica." By contrast, Oasis had been somewhat underwhelming of late—their third album "Be Here Now" was widely considered downright awful, and its follow-up "Standing On The Shoulders of Giants," hardly thrilled the world. It is perhaps no surprise, then, that Oasis' "Heathen Chemistry," is a step up and Primal Scream's "Evil Heat," is a step down. These albums were released in a different world to their previous records—post 9/11, everything seemed different. In the weeks prior to 9/11, with remarkably bad timing Primal Scream had been playing a song entitled "Bomb The Pentagon." Heavily edited, it instead appeared on "Evil Heat," under the title "Rise." Rather than letting the issue die quietly, in a Heathen Chemistry—era interview Liam Gallagher referenced his former labelmates "Bomb the Pentagon," when talking about 9/11, joking "anyway, it was the Scream that did it . . . never mind Al-Queada, I've told 'em to look out for a skinny Scottish fucker 'havin it large."

All the controversy over "Bomb The Pentagon," can't distract from the weaknesses of "Evil Heat"—lead single "Miss Lucifer," is faintly ridiculous, and it also includes the disastrous decision to cover Lee Hazlewood's brilliant song "Some Velvet Morning," the thin, breathy voice of Kate Moss in the Nancy Sinatra role draining the song of its original latent but potent sexuality. At least Oasis were showing reheated blood—the lead single "Hindu Times," sounded fresh and revitalised, with a video which addressed the contemporary post 9/11 world in which "everybody is getting high off bombs, rather than pills."

The problem now was that the band were such a part of the musical establishment that they could no longer seem controversial. Primal Scream were also often accused of selling out—having a Kate Moss vocal on the record, plus the fact that Bobby Gillespie was now in a serious relationship with Alexander McQueen and Dazed and Confused stylist Katy England and thus was often seen at high-fashion events, led to accusations of "shameless Met Bar starfucking," (to quote one letter to the NME which summarised the general feeling.) However, Gillespie still showed potential for controversy. "Evil Heat"'s "Skull X" featured a child chorus chanting about death camps (children and death being more controversial than ever in the month which saw the murders of ten year old girls Holly wells and Jessica Chapman) and their Glastonbury performance saw Gillespie scrawl "Make Israel History," over a stage banner. He refused to apologise for the incident, simply saying that he supported Palestine and that was not grounds for apology, and a misguided press accused him of Nazism. In the same month as "Evil Heat", Liam Gallagher contributed a vocal on "insane men preaching the Fuhrer" to Death in Vegas' "Scorpio Rising," which was cut by over-zealous censors.

So no, being a part of the establishment did not stop anybody from being relevant. After all, there is no bigger establishment than the Church of England and on 23rd July, Rowan Williams was elected to be George Carey's successor as Archbishop of Canterbury. He joked at the time that he was surely the first "hairy leftie," in the role—and his unashamed left-wing views made him a breath of fresh air. Perhaps his role was a sign we were all ready for tomorrow. Those of the previous generation would just have to keep up.

THE LIBERTINES—UP THE BRACKET   Oct 2002

The revival of exciting guitar music was obviously a good thing, but the movement was void of its defining ringleaders. Until now . . .

The revival as a whole could be partly attributed to the iconic Rough Trade label; their first signing after re-establishing themselves was the band that started it all, The Strokes. But the music press were keen to find a British equivalent—luckily, Rough Trade was soon able to give us that also. This band was the Libertines, a band every inch as free-spirited and excessive as their name (drawn from Marquis De Sade's stomach-churning erotica collection "The Lusts of The Libertines,") suggests. The band had first grabbed attention with "What A Waster," a song produced by former Suede guitarist Bernard Butler, that was so rife with profanity that it received no airplay. The language was no the only problem—a reference to the Taliban was a little to topical for the press's liking. Whilst media reception was thus generally lukewarm, the support of Radio One's Mark and Lard and an enthusiastic NME was immediate.

The hearts of the band, Carl Barat and Pete Doherty, shared the duties of songwriting, vocals and guitar. They also had an intense stage dynamic which saw guitar wires entangle, their microphones shared, Ronson and Bowie style, and lively banter. They had managed to draw a great deal of attention to themselves for a sustained period to the release of their debut album. How relevant were they by the time of the albums release?

October ("Up The Bracket" release date) had seen a chain of political events and reforms. On the 1st, main provisions of NHS reform and Health Care Professions Act came into force, which included the renaming and merger of existing NHS regional health authorities; to form twenty-eight new strategic health authorities, and introduction of Primary Care Trusts to be responsible for the supervision of family health care trusts.

As one reform cam into affect, however, others crumbled. On 14th October, once again the Northern Ireland Assembly was suspended. This was due to an alleged Provisional Irish Republican Army spy-ring and intelligence gathering operation based in Stormont, the Northern Ireland Parliament building, in the incident known as "Stormontgate."

The Northern Ireland Assembly seemed increasingly unpredictable. Finally, after years of the drab and predictable, music was following the same path. The Libertines often took this unpredictability to far, lapsing into the shambolic, but this was merely part of their appeal. The biggest manifestation of this unpredictability and excitement was in the "guerrilla gigs" which took place in Barat and Doherty's shared home; these saw 112a Teesdale Street, Bethnal Green, transformed into the "Albion Rooms." William Blake's "Albion," poetry was an enormous basis for the bands image—one track on "Up The Bracket," "The Good Old Days," runs "... *the Albion sails on course/ so man the decks and hoist the rigging/ the Pigmans found the source.*" (Pigman was Barat's nickname for Doherty; cliquey, personal intertextuality peppers the record throughout.) Literature on the whole seemed to be of huge importance to the band, to the point were many credited them with inciting a mass interest in poetry, particularly Romanticism. Education at the time was a complex issue—Estelle Morris resigned as Secretary of State for education, explaining she did not feel up to the job—but The Libertines were going some way to being a generations educators.

The standout track on "Up The Bracket," is "Time for Heroes," a hymn to being working-class which was riots. References to the socialist group The Wombles, a Keatsian line about *"its not right for young lungs to be coughing up blood,"* and a classic line about *"there's fewer more distressing sights than that of an Englishman in a baseball cap,"* come together to make an indie classic. The album was produced by Mick Jones of The Clash; his support of the band was surely beneficial.

On the 12th December, a MORI poll put Labour four points ahead of the Conservatives on 37%—clearly, the illegal war on Iraq had not affected the Party's popularity—although perhaps it was just an understandable case of not wanting the Conservatives. Any recent controversy attached to the Labour Party was relating to outside causes—on 10th December, Cherie Blair apologised for the embarrassment she caused in buying flats with the help of convicted fraudster Peter Foster.

Labour had come to power with a seeming desperation to be relevant to the young, but the War had alienated them. At least, with the flowering of the new "urch" (Urban Revolutionary Cultural Hero) scene around The Libertines, young people finally had something to belong to again.

ASIAN DUB FOUNDATION—ENEMY OF THE ENEMY   Feb 2003

On the 15th February, 2003, more than 2million people demonstrated against the Iraq War. This was the largest demonstration in British history. The issue also created internal dissent for the government—on 27th February, 122 Labour MP's voted against the government in a debate over the Iraq War. Nobody can deny that there was a voice of mass dissent, and on an enormous scale, but the problem was that nobody seemed prepared to listen.

One band who understood the good that an active role can have, however, were the already established Asian Dub Foundation, who used music in conjunction with education and social work for youth in the East End of London. There music widely explores cultural politics and the politicization of the term "Asian," reconnecting it with an anti-colonial history, as well as an ongoing struggle against racism.

In spite of their long-term place in music, they had never been more relevant. The post 9/11 environment had spawned "Islamophobia," racism was more rife than ever. The beginning of this year had seen incidents of terrorism completely unrelated to ethnic minorities (Richard Colin Reid was sentenced to life imprisonment by a US court, and the Protestant Ulster Defence Association Belfast leader John Gregg was killed by a loyalist faction) but minorities were still discriminated against in a way they had not been for years.

The London Congestion Charge was also complained about by many; individuals ignorance over the wider issue of chronic pollution was in line with a failure to see that, with all the Asians in the world, a handful of terrorists could hardly be seen as representative. Asian Dub Foundation had never felt more relevant.

THE KILLS—KEEP ON YOUR MEAN SIDE   May 2003

The 12th March, 2003 saw the Iraq Disarmament crisis, in which British Prime Minister Tony Blair proposed an amendment to the possible 18th UN resolution, which would call for Iraq to meet certain benchmarks for disarmament. The amendment was immediately rejected by France, who promised to veto any new resolution. Britain was about to make itself very unpopular indeed. The post 9/11 world was supposed to have ushered in a new age of gentleness and kindness; the problem with this was that it all seemed a bit contrived, as if we were being forced to be nicer to each other. This is what makes the nastiness and misanthropy of The Kill's debut "Keep On Your Mean Side," such a sharp piece of musical rebellion.

The band had an interesting back-story—its separate members, Jamie Hince and Alison Mosshart (or "Hotel" and "VV" to use their stage names) had already won acclaim with previous bands (Hince with Fiji, Scarfo and Blyth Power, Mosshart with Florida punk band Discount.) The pair first met when Mosshart heard Hince practicing in the hotel room above hers. This spawned an immediate, intense songwriting partnership. The problem here was obviously the distance, with Hince's London base and Mosshart's Florida base. For months, the pair air mailed tapes across the Atlantic, a huge test of patience for both of them as it would take weeks to receive each others tapes. As a consequence, Mosshart moved to London. The decision to follow America in the war showed that the Anglo-American relationship could have some unpleasant dividends, here on a small sale, it was giving birth to something more positive.

The album which resulted from this is consciously low-key. Whilst immediate fan Bobby Gillespie had drummed for them in some live shows, the album included no musicians other than Hince and Mosshart. The album artwork was also photographed in a photo booth, as opposed to using professional photography. The band had also turned down major label offers, eventually signing to British independent label Domino. The lyrical themes crackle with misanthropy and dark sexuality—a key track is "Fuck The People," a tribute to the Situationist—inspired rebels Florence Rey and Audry Maupin, nineteen year old Guy Debord acolytes who, on 4th October 1994 had sprayed police with tear gas, stolen their firearms and hijacked a taxi, ordering it to be drove to the Place de la Republique. A resulting police shoot-out resulted in the death of Maupin and a sentence of 20 year imprisonment for Rey (she was discreetly liberated last year instead.) Rey and Maupin became heroes for disaffected French youth, but there was no reason why the disaffected British youth could not appropriate such heroes. After all, there was plenty to be disillusioned by as events in Iraq unfolded. On 22nd March, Tomahawk missiles fired from Royal Navy submarines took part in a massive air and missile strike on military targets in Baghdad. On 6th April, British forces captured the city of Basra. Events came to a head three days later when a statue of Saddam Hussein was toppled, a symbol of Hussein's rule ending. But the errors of the war were still glaring—the argument that it was just blood for oil was reinforced by our failure to find any weapons of mass destruction, something Russian president Vladmir Putin mocked us for in the 29th April summit.

With the young British public driven by anger and disillusionment, the dark private world that The Kills built around themselves was perfectly timed.

BLUR—THINK TANK

AND

RADIOHEAD—HAIL TO THE THIEF

The beginning of May saw elections in Wales and Scotland. In Scotland, the Labour and Liberal Democrat coalition led by Jack McConnell won a majority of the seats and remained in power. Elections were something of a hot topic, with American president George W. Bush having been elected through what some saw as highly undemocratic means. The votes for the state of Florida had been collected by Bush's brother Jeb, and registered as a priority over the other states. This was seen as vote-stealing; anti-Bush campaigners took on the slogan "Hail To The Thief," which would become the title of Radiohead's sixth album.

Radiohead were not the only major act to release an album at this time. Blur also released "Think Tank," their seventh album and their first without Graham Coxon.

With "Think Tank," and "Hail to the Thief," Blur and Radiohead showed that they were every inch as relevant as they had been in the 1990's by producing what were the bands most political albums. Their titles alone gave clues to the politics within. Whilst the title of "Hail to The Thief" is largely linked to anti-Bush activism, Thom Yorke was quick to emphasise it wider political context of the slogan, citing its use during the 1888 election. It was the right kind of environment in which to get political—on the 29th May, Andrew Gilligan broadcast a report on the BBC Radio 4 "Today" programme stating that the government claimed in its dossier that Iraq could deploy weapons of mass destruction within 45 minutes knowing the case could be dubious. A political storm obviously ensued. Gilligan's source for this was weapons expert Dr. David Kelly.

On the 15th July, Dr. Kelly appeared before the House of Commons. Foreign Affairs Select Committee to answer questions about the information he had given to Andrew Gilligan. Just three days later, he was found dead near his home in Oxfordshire, people suspecting that he had committed suicide. There was clearly far more to this story than there had first appeared—on 20th July, the BBC confirmed that Kelly had been the main source for the original, controversial report that had sparked such a rift within the government.

This was not a death which could be without enquiry, and on 1st August, Lord Hutton opened the enquiry into Dr. Kelly's death.

Hutton wrote in his report that further investigation of complaints against the government were unnecessary; there was speculation that the report and the enquiry were more to clear the government than bring about justice for Kelly. Many felt as though this was an enormous whitewash. Andrew Gilligan resigned because of his part in the affair, as did two other BBC staff.

For all the political quagmire and controversy, there is a huge tragedy at the heart of this. British ambassador David Broucher recalled a conversation with Kelly at a February 2003 Geneva conference, in which he had asked Kelly what he would do of Iraq was invaded and Kelly replied, "I will probably be found dead in the woods."

Further evidence emerging from the enquiry exacerbated the tragedy of it all. The wording of the dossier, at the suggestion of Alistair Campbell, had been altered to present the strongest possible case for war. David Kelly had also had direct contact with dissenters within the Defence. Intelligence Staff had communicated their reservations to the press. The most marked men in all of this were Alistair Campbell and Geoff Hoon, who had actually said that they wanted Kelly's name making public. In spite of this, the Hutton report cleared the government of any wrongdoing.

The sounds of political dissent on "Hail To The Thief" and "Think Tank," seemed to have been tailormade for the distaste felt by many over all of this. Both are enormously interesting records in many different respects, right down to their artwork. The cover sleeve of "Think Tank," is a beautiful painting by the then-unknown artist Banksy, whilst "Hail To The Thief," is a road map with words and phrases replacing places. This is a nod to the British administrations ill-fated 2003 plan for peace between Israel and Palestine.

For all the politics on "Think Tank" and "Hail to the Thief," they also have moments of reflective beauty, particularly in their lead singles. Radiohead's "There There" opens with the beautiful line, *"In pitch black I go walking in landscapes,"* whereas Blur's "Out Of Time," is an understated ballad which ranks as one of their finest moments, running, *"you've been so busy lately that you haven't had the time/ to watch the stars spinning/ gently out of time."* Perhaps, then, these albums are perfect reflections of a time of serious politics enveloping the terrible tragedy of one individual.

"DREAMING AND REACHING":
PATRICK WOLF—LYCANTHROPY
AND
SPIRITUALIZED—AMAZING GRACE

In the 18th September by-election for Brent East, Sarah Teather of the Liberal Democrats took the seat after 29 years of Labour's control. After the shocking whitewash of the Hutton Enquiry, had people grown disillusioned with Labour? On the 26th June, prior to the enquiry, the latest MORI poll had put Labour and Conservatives equal with 35% of the vote. The Iraq issue as a whole was proving problematic for Blair's Labour.

The role of music in this time of dissatisfaction was to provide escape and give people some faith in the incredible things that talent could achieve. Two key albums for this were Patrick Wolf's debut "Lycanthropy" and Spiritualised's gospel-infused "Amazing Grace." Both of these records were the creations of incredibly talented people unafraid to use and flaunt this talent. "Lycanthropy" had been eight years in the making; the prodigal multi-instrumentalist Wolf having been just a child when he began work on it. Both are albums which are unafraid not just of flaunting the talents of their creators, but also of controversy. On "Amazing Grace," Pierce once again derives humour and insouciance from his drug habit with this take on The Crystals "He Hit Me (It Felt Like A Kiss)", "She Kissed Me (It Felt Like A Hit.)"

Wolf, meanwhile, showed he could be even more controversial. One track on "Lycanthropy," "The Childcatcher," tells the story of a boy targeted by a paedophile. As children grew increasingly prized and protected in society—this year had seen the appointment of the first ever Minister for Children, Margaret Hodge, paedophilia was treated with such revulsion that it was simply not seen as a fitting subject for music.

The boldness of "The Childcatcher," should not distract from the brilliant complexity of other lyrical themes on "Lycanthropy"—the title track examines gender dysphoria through abstract lyrics. The bisexual Wolf was himself androgynous, but in a fantastical, proper-pop star way, not really seen since the like of David Bowie. Androgyny had once been a staple of the musical aesthetic, but ever since the lad culture of the nineties it had died out somewhat. However, there were still other nods here and there—in the same month "Lycanthropy" was released, the Manic Street Preachers released a b-sides collection. By giving it a leopard print cover and calling it "Lipstick Traces," they showed a willingness to nod to their androgynous past.

Patrick Wolf and Spiritualized were not the only bands progressing through ambition—The Cooper Temple Clause's "Kick Up The Fire and Let The Flames Break Loose," was so heavy and full-on it made their debut seem like a warm-up, and Muse's third album, "Absolution," was their most ambitious yet. Clearly, this was the theme for the year. But what most marks out "Amazing Grace," and "Lycanthropy," is their mix of escape and reality. The way they go against convention is almost a musical dissent.

Not that dissent was dead in the wider world—when George. W. Bush visited London for a state visit he was greeted by massive protests. There was clearly a strong dislike Bush and thus of Blair for blindly following him in his catastrophic decisions, but the British public did not know were else to turn. After all, if the main alternative was the Conservative Party, then what hope was there for us? As it happens, the Conservative Party were falling apart once again as on 29th October, Iain Duncan Smith resigned as leader after just two years. The party also displayed its typical regressive attitude when, on the 26th November, the Shadow Home Secretary David Davis called for the death penalty to be reintroduced. The overturning of two murder convictions on 20th December shows just how wrong he is there.

But as our politicians looked backwards, at least we could say our musicians were looking forwards.

"BRITAIN SHARPENS UP":

FRANZ FERDINAND—FRANZ FERDINAND

AND

THE FUTUREHEADS—THE FUTUREHEADS

The supposed "new rock revolution," which had swept Britain was actually more of a post-punk revival, which has never been the most accessible of genres. However, this use of jerky guitar sounds and spiky rhythms was to gain new pop sensibilities with the release of two extremely accessible, eponymous debut albums from The Futureheads and Franz Ferdinand. Pop music at this time was dying a death; the charts barely seemed worth comprehending. Even that great British institution, "Top of The Pops" was struggling—although at least the BBC showed some ethics over the programme. Coca-Cola was the sponsor of the music charts, but on 3rd January the BBC cancelled the appearance of Coca Cola in the sponsorship credits of "Top Of The Pops" as they feared promoting unhealthy products to young people. Coca-Cola's lack of ethics (extending to the murders of two union workers) meant this was not just a question of health; avoiding promoting this product was the best thing the BBC could do. After all, they were in a difficult place on the whole—on the 15th February, the government were reported to have drawn up plans to break up the BBC in the wake of the Hutton Enquiry.

The history of the BBC is touched on on one song on "Franz Ferdinand," "Matinee,"—*"I'm on BBC Two now/ telling Terry Wogan how I made it."* Whilst the bands early interviews show a fixation with Wogan (in particular a desire to see him "drink brandy out of a virgins arsehole") what this lyric really symbolises is ambition and confidence. Other lyrics include "*Ich dans heisse su) per-fantastique! I drink champagne with smoked salmon!*" and "*I *am the new Scotch gentry!"* ("Darts of Pleasure," and "Shopping for Blood" respectively. By contrast, the Futureheads lyrics deal very much with the ordinary, everyday world of nine-to-five work. This seemed to capture the sense of dreary disillusionment people felt in their day to day lives, something exacerbated by an increasing lack of faith in Tony Blair. Even members of his own party were turning against him. On 27th January, he only narrowly defeated a rebellion within the Party over the Higher Education Bill, a highly controversial bill to reform higher education funding, including the introduction and variable tuition fees, by just 316 votes to 311. It was an increasingly difficult time for the government in the wake of Iraq anyway. On 3rd February, an independent enquiry to examine the reliability of intelligence on weapons of mass destruction in Iraq, to be chaired by Lord Butler, was announced. Then, on the 21st February, Blair found himself under enormous pressure from human rights groups because of the governments sweeping powers under the Anti-Terrorism Crime and Security Act, which allowed the detention of 14 foreign terrorist suspects in the UK at what had been described as "Britain's Guantanemo Bay."

Events in Britain were certainly cause for concern' negative events far outweighed positive events—Richard Desmond, owner of The Express, bid for and saved "The Telegraph," making something of a Conservative paper empire, whilst the drowning of 21 Chinese cockle picker on Morecombe Bay shocked the nation and raised serious questions. Current affairs was not, at this point, the flat and lifeless field that it could sometimes be, but this was not a good thing.

Excitement in the news came to a head with good old-fashioned spy stories. On the 25th February, Katherine Gun, formerly an employee of British spy agency GCHQ, had a charge of breaching the Official Secrets Act dropped after prosecutors offered no evidence, apparently on the advice of the Attorney-General for England and Wales. Gun had admitted leaking American plans to bug US delegates to a newspaper. The next day, the former Cabinet Minister Clare Short alleged on the BBC "Today" programme that British spies regularly intercept UN communications, including those of Kofi Annan.

(Incidentally, the crossover song from "Franz Ferdinand" was "Take Me Out", a story of two snipers spying on each other.)

All this controversy was, naturally bad for the governments popularity. On 11th March, Tory and Labour support was equal on 35% for the second time in nine months, raising the spectre of a hung parliament at the next general election which was expected within a year.

Post-punk had always thrived on environments of uncertainty. 2004 was a perfect time, then, for the genre to "go pop."

"ESTABLISHED, NOT ESTABLISHMENT":
GRAHAM COXON—HAPPINESS IN MAGAZINES
AND
MORRISSEY—YOU ARE THE QUARRY

The wave of new guitar bands which had emerged in recent years should not distract from the fact the established "indie icons" were still very much a force to be reckoned with; something truly reinforced in May 2004 with the release of new albums by Graham Coxon and Morrissey.

The previous month, Tony Blair had announced a change in government policy—there was to be a referendum on the proposed EU constitution. It seemed to matter little what policies he changed now, though—the damage had been done. If there was one song this year that really captured the anger of the nation is was Morrissey's lead-off single from "You Are The Quarry," "Irish Blood, English Heart," a tirade against the current state of England. "*I've been dreaming of a time when/ to be English is not to be shameful,*" runs the bitter chorus, twinned with verses about yearning for Englan "to be sick death of Labour and Tories." The song urges rebellion as Morrissey tells us how "*no regime can bind or stifle me,*" and "*I will die with both of my hands untied.*" It is his certainly one of his most political songs, and after the thin ground skated on in some of his more nationalistic works, it was risky ground—but it paid off. After a period of making complex and thus largely ignored works, "You Are The Quarry," bought him back to public attention. (The song "First Of The Gang To Die" from this album also ranks amongst his classics.)

"Happiness is Magazines" also saw Coxon become more commercially viable—his solo albums had always been demanding than his work with Blur. However, the roles seemed to have switched—Blur's most recent album "Think Tank," was their least accessible, whereas now Coxon was embracing guitar driven, upfront indie with a potentially wide fanbase. It also spawned his biggest hit as a solo artist, "Freakin' Out," with such wry lyrics as *"nothing to do, nothing to say/ la la la la la lay."* In an age when there was nothing the government could do or say to win back the public after the mess they had created, then this was all to apt.

Both Morrissey and Graham Coxon may have been better known for their work with previous bands, but May 2004 certainly proved their worth as solo artists.

HOPE OF THE STATES—THE LOST RIOTS   June 2004

The recent failures of New Labour became increasingly apparent. The European, local and regional elections allowed the public to show exactly what they thought, and the results reflected badly on the government, with Labour losing many seats. (Somewhat ironically, Britain's biggest gainers in the European elections were the UK Independence Party, increasing from 3 to 12 MEP's.)

As the British public found themselves hating their own government, there was desperate need in the music world for a band who represented dissent, and whats more could put it forward articulately.

Luckily, there was such a thing—June 2004 saw the release of "The Lost Riots," the debut album by the intelligent, underrated The Hope Of The States. Their name was drawn from a 1930's paper on the state of mental healthcare in the US. Clearly, everything about this band related to intelligence and socio-politics. There was a time when a band with such openly left-wing politics as Hope Of The States may have been seen as faintly threatening, but Britain now seemed happy to lean to the left a little—on 11th June, "Red" Ken Livingstone won a second term as the Mayor of London. This willingness to embrace the Left drew a lot of critical acclaim and attention towards Hope of The States debut single, the excellent "Black Dollar Bills." Copies of "Black Dollar Bills" came in a Hessian sleeve, each one hand-sewn by members of the band wearing their working-class background on their sleeve.

It was not the sleeve which truly grabbed attention on "Black Dollar Bills," though, but the clear prominence of a brilliant new band, its heart being the guitarist Jimmi Lawrence and the vocalist Sam Herlihey.

On the 28th June, the Coalition Provisional Authority handed out sovereignty of Iraq to the Iraqi Interim Government, two days ahead of schedule. Whilst this was obviously a mark of progress, it did not make the Iraq issue any less contentious. On the 14th July, The Butler Inquiry released its report—which was mildly critical of the government in their use of intelligence relating to weapons of mass destruction in Iraq. The past year had seen a wave of anti-war songs as even the most inoffensive of musicians jumped on the bandwagon to condemn the way we had blindly followed America—but no song did it better than one song from "The Lost Riots," "The Red The White The Black The Blue." *"The red white and the blue has always been what lead you/ if you don't do something they'll steal it all from under you/ they'll beat us black and blue, their coming back to fight you,"* runs the chorus, each word stretched out and reinforced by Herlihy's distinctive voice.

In a complete sea of songs on the issue, "The Red The White The Black The Blue," stood out and is the one which has stood the test of time.

Of course, it would be unfair to suggest that their was no liberalism in the UK. On the 2nd July, the openly gay cleric, Jeffrey John, was installed as the Dean at St. Albans. Eleven days later, the Public Administration Committee of the House of Commons recommended massive changes to the British Honours System; including scrapping knighthoods and renaming Order of The British Empire to "Order of the British Excellence." However, these changes were never actually passed, simply talked about. Clearly, the outmoded idea of empire was something Britain wanted to cling on to. In short, there was very little to suggest that this could be a positive, forward-thinking age. It would be easy to say that at least to suggest that this could be a could be a positive, forward-thinking age. It would be easy to say that at least we had a new interesting voice of musical dissent, but Hope of The States did not run for much longer.

After the album was recorded, Jimmi Lawrence committed suicide by hanging himself. He left no note and his bandmates wrestled with explaining his decision. They would make one more album, the equally wonderful "Low," before splitting and recording under the name Chapel Club.

A short-lived band, then, but one that needs to be remembered. "The Lost Riots" is just that—a lost riot. This band were one of the key voices of musical anti-Blair feeling. If only for capturing a time, a place and a feeling, they are worth remembering.

THE LIBERTINEs

THE LIBERTINES—THE LIBERTINES　　　　　　　Aug 2004

The end of July, 2004 had been full of government decisions that seemed neither good nor bad; just strange, the work of a government lost for ideas. On the 23rd July, Tony Blair announced that Peter Mandelson was to become Britain's new European Commissioner. Whilst there were certain areas of politics that he had no doubt excelled in, putting him in the role of European Commissioner seemed somewhat risky given his track record of controversy, which in the past had seen him forced to resign from the cabinet twice, for separate scandals. But he was an ingenious master of spin, something New Labour relied heavily on, and they needed drastic ways of winning back favour—the New Labour dream had turned sour.

The other dream which was turning sour was the Arcadian dreams of the Libertines, all captured with heartbreakingly detailed honesty on their second, eponymous album. A rift in the band had been apparent for a long time now as Pete Doherty sank into crack and heroin addiction—the signs of which had been clear on their debut "Up The Bracket" on songs such as "Horrorshow," (*"it's a horrorshow/ come on down/ come on down, the horse is brown."*) The bands reputation for rock 'n' roll, hard living was what had made them interesting—now, stepping to deeply into this was what would tear them apart. Carl Barat and Pete Doherty's friendship, once intense, was now in ruins as Doherty broke into and stole from Barat's home, resulting in a six month sentence in Wandsworth Prison. Even in the midst of such actions, Doherty remained full of typical addicts denial and delusion, although this is ironically then used to create the feel of honesty on "The Libertines," particularly on the eventual moment of confession, "The Saga," which runs *"a problem/ becomes a problem, when you lie to your friends, and you lie to your people, and you lie to yourself/ and when it gets to hard to comprehend, you just pretend their isn't a problem.*" Pretending that there wasn't a problem had seemed to be something of a theme in recent years—or rather, pretending there *was* a problem, concerning the supposed hunt for weapons of mass destruction in Iraq. However, Blair now seemed very, very aware of his errors as the nation turned against him, and on the 1st October he announced his intention to resign as Prime Minister of the United Kingdom if Labour were to win the next general election, so he would not have to stand for a fourth term in the position.

The role of conflicts and wars in a Prime Ministers time can make or break them; the senselessness of the Iraq invasion had gone against Blair. It was no longer an age in which war was always a positive thing; anybody still carrying these ideas was hugely outdated in their thinking.

The role of history blends with the present on "The Libertines." "Last Post On The Bugle," could be about Doherty's own problems or conscientious objection in the First World War, whereas "Arbeit Macht Frei," sets one verse during the Holocaust and one in the present, before running, *"her old man/ he don't like blacks or queers/ but he's proud he beat the Nazi's/how queer."*

The biggest conflict with The Libertines was clearly with each other; this would be their last album together—but this very personal issue seemed very relevant to a nation disillusioned with wider conflict.

MANIC STREET PREACHERS—LIFEBLOOD

Whilst the Iraq War had done the government few favours and had left them increasingly unpopular, there had been few active voices of dissent in the public. The initial protests against the war had been strong, but beyond that there was little active protest. The biggest protesters against the government had been the "Fathers 4 Justice," campaign group, and they were often not as sympathetic as they made out—most of them were denied access to their children for very viable reasons. The other strong voices of anti-government protest was from the pro-hunting faction as on the 18th November, Parliament passed the Hunting Act 2004 banning fox hunting in England and Wales. Was it only unsympathetic corners of society prepared to protest against the government?

Any other instances of people standing up and saying "no" were rather unremarkable, because it was a tangent of things such as referendums (on 4th November, for example, a referendum was held in North East England on the establishment of elected regional assemblies. The majority of voters said "no" to the plans.) Perhaps music could be the true voice of the seemingly uncommunicated public feeling. After all, November 2004 saw the release of a new Manic Street Preachers album . . . surely, given their track record, they could provide a fierce form of dissent? Actually . . . no, not really. "Lifeblood," an album largely forgotten from the back catalogue, forsakes the political in favour of the personal. Whilst the album is not void of political history—there are songs with titles such as "The Love of Richard Nixon," and "Emily," about Emily Davison, but it is personal reflection which make up most of the songs—"Cardiff Afterlife," muses on former member Richey Edwards, whilst "1985" has them considering their past. The album also has a distinctly different sound to their previous albums, the introduction of keyboards and musical subtleties creating a soft sound that bassist Nicky Wire described as "elegiac pop," during the recording process. The problem was, it was not "pop" enough to sell many records.

Largely considered their weakest moment, "Lifeblood" appears to have vanished from the bands history. Part of the problem is clear—we were living in a difficult political age, were the Iraq war had ruined us, Council Tax needed a review due to some problems and inconsistencies, and Home Secretary David Blunkett resigned in disgrace after fast-tracking a visa for a nanny who he was having an affair. If any band could have soundtracked all this, it was the Manics. But with "Lifeblood," they chose a very different route which has left the album forgotten.

"INDIE GETS POLITICAL":

BLOC PARTY—SILENT ALARM

AND

THE OTHERS—THE OTHERS

2005 had not opened happily for the world. The Boxing Day Tsunami in Thailand (which had killed a significant number of Britons) had sent shockwaves around the world. New Years Eve celebrations all over the UK had fallen silent for two minutes as a mark of respect for those who had died in the tsunami. This terrible natural disaster dominated the news at length; political events were in danger of being overlooked. January 2005 saw the introduction of the Freedom of Information Act, and the Environmental Information Act, and the Environmental Information Regulations, but this passed many by.

However, as it happens, music was ready to be political again, as two London based politicised indie bands, Bloc Party and The Others, released their debut albums. Taking an anti-establishment tact was a wise move considering recent events. Both bands were angry in different ways—Bloc Party with subtle articulacy, the Others unrestrained and outspoken courtesy of controversial frontman Dominic Masters. And there were certainly lots of people in the news it was worth directing anger against. There were also those so preposterous that it barely seemed worth directing anger at them, something which manifest in two separate events on 13th January. One was the appearance of Prince Harry thoughtlessly wearing a Nazi military uniform at a private fancy dress party an unforgivable move considering it was Holocaust Remembrance Week; the other was Sir. Mark Thatcher being fined three million Rand (roughly equivalent to £265, 000) and receiving a four-year jail sentence after pleading guilty to supplying equipment to mercenaries for an attempted coup of Equatorial Guinea.

The targets for Bloc Party and The Others were somewhat broader than the likes of these. The Others quickly grabbed attention by chastising the rich; their song "This Is For The Poor," viciously runs "this if for the poor/ not you rich kids." Such "rich kids," would be the source of much disdain from Dominic Masters in interviews.

Like many other people, Bloc Party directed their anger at the Bush administration. ("We had a fight, we had a fight/ six out of ten, better luck next time/ just like his dad, just like his dad/ same mistakes, just so much younger," runs "Helicopter.") People even seemed to feel restless and dissatisfied in the realm of internal politics. On 15th January, Conservative MP for Wantage, Oxfordshire, defected to the Labour Party, and on a different level, five days later member of Scottish Parliament Carolyn Leckie was jailed for seven days for non-payment of a fine arising from a protest at Faslane Nuclear base.

No dissent could be felt more deeply than that of the masses though. Young people in Britain particularly felt this, or those who had emerged from the human-rights concerned generation. Human rights was coming to be a much-discussed topic in Britain once again—in January, four innocent Britons finally returned to the UK after being detained as Guantanemo Bay for three years.

Attitudes may have been getting more liberal (former culture secretary Chris Smith finally felt able to admit he had been HIV positive for 17 years), but actual events suggested otherwise. In reflection of this, the decline of working-culture also continued. The 26th January saw the closure of Ellington Colliery in Northumberland, the last remaining operational deep coal mine in North East England and the last to extract coal from under the sea. As the working classes were increasingly sidelined, "New Labour," being so little like Labour that they lacked a mainstream voice, maybe the formation of a new political party was the answer. However, the fulfilment of this was simply the creation of a new right-wing party, as Robert Kilroy-Silk officially launched the party Veritas in the wake of quitting UKIP after a failed leadership bid. The basis of Veritas was often was often anti-immigration policies, feeding on the wave of racism still sweeping the country in the wake of 9/11. Racism had reached such a level that when Yusuf Islam (formerly known as Cat Stevens) was denied entry to the United States, due to his conversion to Islam, both the Sun and the Sunday Times stated this was only fair—even though he had previously been awarded the Man for Peace award by Nobel Prize Laureates. The world of indie music has always presented a general anti-racism image, but on the whole is lacking in diversity itself. However, Bloc Party were one of a very small number of bands fronted by a black person (Kele Okereke) something which went happily unnoticed in a genre which prized sound over colour every time.

As well as racism, another unpleasant side-effect of the past 9/11 age was an increased sense of Big Brother. In February, the House of Commons passed the Identity Cards Bill at its third reading by 224 votes to 64, with a majority of 160, moving the bill to the House of Lords. Such increased surveillance meant that being outspoken was braver than ever. However, it could be argued that The Others Dominic Masters pushed this to far. Interviews in which he created an issue out of bisexuality (he had a transsexual partner), ranted against the rich and claimed that crack cocaine (which he smoked four times a week) was harmless outweighed the fact that he did have the ability to write great songs, such as his loving and genuine letter to Pete Doherty, "Stan Bowles."

February 2005 was also the month in which injustices of the past began to be corrected. On the 9th, Tony Blair issued a public apology to the 11 members of the Conlon and Maguire families who were wrongly convicted for the Guildford and Woolwhich IRA pub bombings. Then, on 15th, The European Court of Human Rights deciding on the "McLibel Case," ruled in favour of environmental campaigners David Steel and Helen Morris and their claim that their trial was unfair.

But these are just two events in a world that brimmed with injustice, reaching its peak on the 23rd of February when British soldiers were found guilty of abusing Iraqi prisoners.

In this world, we needed the media and culture to be politicised. Luckily, the indie music coming out of London went some way to fulfilling this.

MIA—ARULAR   March 2005

Many people can sing political songs. Not all can be seen as so deeply controversial and potentially antagonistic as MIA. Her ground-breaking, genre-defying debut album "Arular" considers identity, politics, poverty, revolution, gender, sexual stereotypes, war, and the conditions of the working class in London. Most striking, however, are her blatant references to key political movements, particularly the Tamil Independence movements (the Tamil Tigers being the most dwelled on) and the Palestine Liberation Organisation. This album, a mix of social storytelling and commentary incited debate on her "invigoratingly complex" politics—to the point were she was placed on the US Homeland Security Risk List. To earn a place on this list through lyrics alone is quite something, but it also reflects an age of heightened paranoia. On the 11th March, the Prevention of Terrorism Act received Royal Assent. This permitted the Home Secretary to make control orders restricting the liberty of named individuals.

The truth about MIA was, however, that she simply spoke the truth. However, it appeared in a way not felt since the 1950's, that this was simply unforgivable.

"SOCIAL HUMOUR RETURNS":
ART BRUT—BANG BANG ROCK 'N' ROLL
AND
KAISER CHIEFS—EMPLOYMENT

May 2005 saw a General Election, which kept the Labour Party in power, but recent events had damaged them somewhat and their majority was reduced to 66. There were significant additions to Parliament, largely the new RESPECT party, who gained their first MP in former Labour Party MP George Galloway, who gained the Bethnal Green and Bow seat from Labour. People were undeniably ready for something new and RESPECT's life-wing, anti-privatisation policies were a refreshing addition to parliament. The defeat of the Conservatives led their leader, Michael Howard, to announce plans to resign "sooner rather than later."

This slight rise on positivity in UK politics opened the doors for an age when sociology did not have to be treated with total seriousness, hence the attention given to two humour-infused albums—Kaiser Chiefs' "Employment", a commercial success, and Art Brut's "Bang Bang Rock 'n' Roll," a critical success.

The lead singles from both these albums brim with wry, well-observed humour. The Kaiser Chief's "I Predict A Riot," observes the nightlife in a certain part of Leeds, but could apply to so many areas of the UK, were people *"get lairy,"* and the *"girls run around with no clothes on . . . if it wasn't for chip fat they'd be frozen."* Many a small-town listener could identify with such lines as *"as I'm stood waiting for a taxi/ a man in a tracksuit attacks me."*

The lead single from "Bang Bang Rock 'n' Roll," is just as witty—"Formed A Band," a send-up of the aspirations of those who form bands. *"And yes! This is my singing voice! Its not irony! Its not rock 'n' roll! Were just talking . . . TO THE KIDS!"* shouts frontman Eddie Argos over the kind of brilliantly dominant guitar riff that is a key part of Art Brut's sound. *"Were going to be the band/ that writes the song/ that makes Israel and Palestine get along!/ Were going to write a song as universal as happy birthday, that everybody knows, so everybody can sing along, were going to take that song, and were going to play it for eight weeks in a row on Top of the Pops!"*

Whilst Argos is clearly being tongue in cheek, there was a belief that music could change the world. On 31st May, Bob Geldof announced plans to put on a "Live 8," concert, similar to Live Aid, to coincide with July's G8 summitt. In the meantime, Art Brut and the Kaiser Chiefs just seemed happy to make hugely entertaining music.

These albums were part of what was being classed as "Britpop part II." Art Brut's Eddie Argos was labelled "The new Jarvis," and the Kaiser Chief's Ricky Wilson "The New Damon." (The "new Liam" tag was given to Kasabian's Tom Meighan.) The original Britpop movement had thrived on British optimism, but the "New Labour" promise that spawned that had been shattered. So, was it applicable to the second wave?

Respect were on the rise, the Conservatives were practically obsolete and there were new signs of liberal progress on 17th June when the Ugandan-born bishop of Birmingham John Sentamu was named the new Archbishop of the Church of England. But the wider picture in Britain still showed us in a rut. This did not register Art Brut and the Kaiser Chiefs redundant, though, the type of humour they used was so cynical that it actually seemed perfect for an age of broken promises were cynicism was easily justified.

THE RAKES—CAPTURE/RELEASE   Aug 2005

By the summer of 2005, the East London scene was beginning to look tired. The break-up of The Libertines had left the scene without a ringleader and there was a wave of increasingly mundane bands breaking through. However, there was one standout band, who produced the sharpest and most socially relevant lyrics of all the bands. This band was The Rakes, who had stories through the eyes of the ordinary man, chronicling day to day life.

The news at the time was a mixture of ordinary people and immense power. On the 1st July, Tony Blair assumed the Presidency of the Council of the European Union, giving him an extra position of power which would lend weight to his role in the G8 summit.

As hosts of the G8 summit, the UK stated its intent to focus on the issues of global climate change and the lack of economic development in Africa. Blair planned to move beyond the Kyoto Protocol by looking at how to include key developing countries not included in it. The summit showed that the art of protest was well and truly alive as the citizen response was overwhelming. The Make Borders History Tour went around Glasgow illustrated the presence of borders and immigration control, roving anti-capitalist street parties took place, and a Counter Summit organised by the "G8 Alternatives," took place alongside a smaller event called G8 Corporate Dreams Global Nightmares. The efforts of the Make Poverty History Coalition also attracted much attention. The important role of protest in history is captured in one song on "Capture/ Release," "Strasbourg," about totalitarian rule in the Cold War era. ("On TV our friends smashed cement/ pulled down the bastards monuments.") "Strasbourg," is actually a wider story of a couple trying to break onto the Western side of the Berlin Wall; this is clearly the work of an intelligent and informed band. They flaunted their intelligence shamelessly, particularly their frontman, well-read physics graduate Alan Donohue, but also maintained both a down-to-earth normality reflected in their lyrics and a hardcore-drinking lifestyle typical of rock stars. Clearly, no matter what you wanted from your musicians, The Rakes somehow managed to fulfil it.

Something which did not fulfil its expectations in the long run was the G8 summitt. The USA's unwillingness to take action on global warming led environmental campaigners to label the result of the summit, "a very disappointing finale", whereas action against poverty was a non-starter—a debt relief bill was not approved by the IMF, the USA said it could not make a funding commitment, and the Western decision to privatise African water supplies increased their prices. The whole thing may as well have never taken place. The media also seemed to widely ignore these outcomes, having been distracted by the London bombings which occurred on the second day of the summit.

The bombings had thrown the capital into disarray—but only for a short period of time. The traditional British "keep calm and carry on" attitude showed its continuing role as people continued their normal lives the next day.

The day to day life of the British is something The Rakes tapped into; they played gigs in kebab shops and wrote songs like "Work Work Work Pub Pub Pub Sleep," (*"wake up smelling like the smoking bit of a Wetherspoons pub"*). But there is something to be said for this way of life—July, 2005 showed that there was nothing that could keep us from it—global terrorism was apparently no match for the British daily grind.

KATE BUSH—AERIAL Nov 2005

On 14th September, 2005, Secretary of State for Northern Ireland announced that the government no longer recognised the Ulster Volunteer Force's ceasefire, due to their ongoing fued with the Loyalist Volunteer Force, and recent violence against the police. The battle the UVF waged often seemed pointless, as they fought for something they already had. It was a movement which continued to look backwards—perhaps, in the musical realm, we needed figures from the past to re-emerge in order to soundtrack problems in Ireland as they had the first time around. Luckily, then, this year saw the return of Kate Bush after a twelve year absence from the music industry which she had used to devote her time to raising her family. As expected, anticipation was immense; the album could easily have collapsed under the weight of expectation.

Once delivered, "Aerial" lived up to the anticipation. Her first double album, it is a multi-layered, beautiful work encompassing a mix of genres. Like 1985's "Hounds of Love" album, it is split into two sections. The first disc has the subtitle "A Sea of Honey" and contains a list of unrelated songs on an impressive array of topics—"Pi" has her singing pi to its 137th decimal point, the utterly stunning "A Coral Room" deals with the loss of her mother and the passage of time, "Bertie" is an ode to her son and "Joanni" is based on Joan of Arc. All this would be enough for any other artist. But of course, there is nobody quite like Kate Bush and the second disc, "A Sky of Honey", themed around birdsong, is no less impressive. As we saw in a previous section, Bush's earlier album "The Hounds of Love," was released at the time of Handsworth riots. This latest album also appeared directly after some terrible race riots, this time in Birmingham between blacks and Asians. To give these riots some context, the majority of the Asian population in Birmingham are of Pakistani origin; the majority of the black population are of

Caribbean origin. The animosity which preceded the rioting appears to have been largely based on local economic rivalry combined with possible agitation from opposing criminal gangs. The alleged rape of a 14 year old Jamaican girl by an Asian shopkeeper (never proven) added fuel to the fire, leading to pickets being set up outside the shop in question, which led to an eruption of violence. In November 2007, four men were jailed for their part in the riots.

After soundtracking the Handsworth riots, Bush remained an important musician all these years later. Her world of birdsong and beauty is a retreat into peace and nature—and in a world of race riots and continued violence in Ireland, in which very little had changed since Bush's heyday, this was almost like a very beautiful kind of rebellion.

BABYSHAMBLES—DOWN IN ALBION   Nov 2005

The Libertines may have broken up in a sea of internal conflict and drug addled behaviour, but their fans were still very much in force. Pete Doherty had a huge support network and the end of The Libertines certainly did not mean the end of his career as something of a contemporary icon. But he was no longer simply an icon of modern teenage rebellion—he was now a regular fixture in the tabloid press due to his relationship with supermodel Kate Moss. Almost overnight he became one of the media's most divisive figures, the age old debate about appropriate role models had raised its head. Conservative leader Michael Howard even went so far as single him out personally in a speech, saying how appalled he was that the behaviour of a drug addict should be so prevalent in the media, and what a terrible worry it should be that young people seemed to adore him. The fact that Howard was talking as though this was something new shows how out of touch he was; it was certainly the right time for him to leave his position.

The Conservatives being the Conservatives, his replacement was no better. On 6th December, David Cameron the 39 year old MP for Witney in Oxfordshire, was elected their new leader, beating David Davis. Cameron was the same usual overpriveliged, right-wing Conservative, but a carefully constructed image saw him fall into favour. On 12th December, an IPSOS MORI opinion poll put his party two points ahead of Labour on 37%.

It was obvious with both Cameron's demeanour and some misguided ideas (such as the frankly bizarre "Hug A Hoodie" initiative) that he was desperate to reach out to younger voters. But he was as ill-informed as Michael Howard had been with his anti-Doherty speech. After all, all Howard had done was potentially glorify

Doherty even further—if the Conservatives hate somebody, then that can only accelerate their appeal to the left-leaning young.

The level of hero-worship directed at Doherty, however, is difficult to understand upon an initial listen to the frustratingly patchy "Down In Albion," the debut album by his post-Libertines venture Babyshambles. But the flaws lie more in Mick Jones' muddy production than in a lack of songwriting ability—standouts include "Fuck Forever" is bridge of *"New Labour/ and the Tories/are one and the same,"* summing of the feelings of a frustrated body politic, and "A Rebours," a nod to the JK Huysman novel which is a bitingly funny attack on selfish decadence—a novel which was certainly still relevant in 2005.

The albums best-known song, however, is "Albion," a reconstruction of William Blake's world of labouring and grime into something more traditional (*"gin in teacups/ and leaves on the lawn"*) twinned with the Britain that we know—for example the all too familiar *"violence at bus stops."*

In spite of its apparent intentions to be a loose concept album on Englishness, "Down in Albion" also has a fixation with French culture, such as the aforementioned "A Rebours" and the opener "La Belle a La Bete," inspired by Jean Genet's wonderful novel "Notre Dame De Fleur." A firm favourite of Doherty's, the novel is a provocative piece of writing and the song could also be were it not for Kate Moss's twee backing vocal. "Notre Dame De Fleur" was written by Genet whilst he was in prison and often attacks the flawed justice system he had fallen prey to. That was 1940's France, but still relevant—however, the UK did show some progress in terms of justice on 9th November when the government lost a key House of Commons vote on detaining suspects for 90 days without charge, in the report stage of the Terrorism Bill.

However, this was the sort of news which seemed increasingly sidelined by the media's fixation with celebrity culture; every week, fresh Pete Doherty stories emerged—a seemingly endless list of arrests, court cases, continued failed attempts to quit drugs (rehab,

Naltrexone implants) and a failure to show up on time for gigs or even attend at all turned him into a soap opera, widely loathed by people who had never even heard a note of his music.

Lessons in excess and its dangers were certainly being taught at this time, with the death of George Best, but perhaps as a nation we were all becoming more excessive—on 24th November, pubs in England and Wales were permitted top open for 24 hours for the first time, and drug addiction was rife.

For people like Michael Howard and the tabloid press to label Doherty as responsible for wider drug use is preposterous. Such behaviour was no longer just "typical rock star", but symbolic of a wider society. Doherty may have reached the status of an A-lister, but a bleak modern world meant he was actually very much an everyman.

ARCTIC MONKEYS—
WHATEVER PEOPLE SAY I AM, THAT'S WHAT I'M NOT

The beginning of 2006 was an odd mix of the predictable and the surreal. In the "surreal" vein, a media circus gathered around a whale discovered swimming in the Thames; in the "predictable" vein, Charles Kennedy resigned as leader of the Liberal Democrats, finally admitting what had been obvious for an extensive number of years—he had a drinking problem. His replacement was Sir Menzies Campbell, which raised eyebrows—surely Campbell was a little old for the job?

However, the voice of the young was very, very dominant in music if not in politics. The biggest debut album of the year was released in January; the rest of the year would definetly slow down in terms of musical excitement. The Arctic Monkeys had already gathered a dedicated following via their live show and the internet, setting the bar for their debut album high. When it arrived after much anticipation, it was a collection of realist stories reflecting the real world, given an extra dimension of realism by vocalist Alex Turner's heavily accented (Sheffield) vocal style.

For years, bands in the UK seemed to have been taking their cue from America, to the point were it appeared many of them really thought they were actually from America in terms of their image. This is something fiercely seized on by the Arctic Monkeys in the song "Fake Tales of San Francisco," in which the band attack those they were sharing bills with (*"The band are fucking wank and I'm not having a nice time . . . you're not from New York City, you're from Rotherham!"*). Nobody could accuse the Arctic Monkeys of trying to be anything other than British, as they blend Northern slang ("Mardy Bum," "by sound 'on it," on the huge hit "I Bet That

You Look Good On The Dancefloor") with realist stories. "When The Sun Goes Down," tells the story of a "scummy man" whose life as a pimp is depicted in a way far removed from the contemporary hip-hop glorification, whilst "The View From The Afternoon," soundtracks the kind of town that young people all over the world were familiar with (were *"theres only music so that there's new ringtones."*)

In February, the socialist President of Brazil Luis Inacio Lula De Silva made a state visit to the UK. We may have been accepting of other nations socialism, but we still steered clear ourselves—the latest MORI poll put New Labour on 42% of the vote. It would be easy to say, considering this, that the lack of a voice for the liberal, working-class young was compensated for by the straight-talking "Whatever People Say I Am, That's What I'm Not." Being young and being working-class are what define this album. But, as it went on to sell clearly its appeal went far, far wider.

MORRISSEY—RINGLEADER OF THE TORMENTORS AND CARBON/ SILICON—ATOM

As younger bands made their voices known, there seemed to be a fundamental flaw with the older, established icons. As opposed to being the faces of anger that they once were, John Lydon, Ozzy Osbourne et al all seemed to be turning into lovable eccentrics. However, there were glimmers of hope in the summer of 2006, notably in Morrissey's album "Ringleader of the Tormentors" and a new album from Mick Jones' latest (very angry) venture, Carbon/ Silicon.

Morrissey had shown a revival of his abilities on his previous album "You Are The Quarry," but this was accelerated even further on "Ringleader of the Tormentors," is only on the strength of "You Have Killed Me," its beautiful sensual lead single—his most romantic lyric since "Hand In Glove." The song is charged with a sexual undercurrent and the album as a whole is peppered with sex references, which certainly raised eyebrows considering he had always been noted for his celibacy.

Carbon/ Silicon were not as likely to draw attention, but were just as relevant. Consisting of Tony James (Generation X/ Sigue Sigue Sputnik) and Mick Jones (The Clash/ Big Audio Dynamite) the act are almost an experiment in musical Marxism. Catalysed by the internet and file sharing, they are willing to support file-sharing in the interests of spreading and sharing music, as opposed to making profit. Songs like "The Networks Going Down," ("*the networks going down cos I think for myself*") are attacks on mass corporations which showed anger was not just the preserve of the young. But what was there to be angry about? What did Britain's political landscape look like? On 5th May, Tony Blair reshuffled his cabinet, the dissident Jack Straw being replaced as foreign secretary by Margaret Beckett and Charles Clarke, who had been an unimpressive Home Secretary, dismissed from the role. These changes did not actually do anything for Labours popularity. On 30th May, an IPSOS MORI poll showed the Conservatives in the lead with 36% of the vote, two points ahead of Labour. Turning to the Conservatives was not a wise move on the UK's part, but going to the nearest solution seemed to be what people favoured over anger. The Conservatives were still horribly irrelevant—not even the election of a younger leader could change that. After all, as Morrissey and Carbon/ Silicon showed, relevance was not always about youth.

PRIMAL SCREAM—RIOT CITY BLUES   June 2006

The Labour Party were faltering. On 29th June, 2006, the Blaneau Gwent by-elections saw them defeated by independent candidates, and the Bromley and Chislehurst by-election was won by Bob Neill for the Conservative Party. At the beginning of the decade, Primal Scream had recorded the ultimate anti-New Labour album in the form of "XTNMTR", but as the nation appeared to have grown wise to New Labour, musical dissent did not seem as groundbreaking. As a consequence, Primal Scream's 2006 album "Riot City Blues" is a straightforward, often tongue-in-cheek rock album. (Typical lyrics—"she got her wings giving head to a priest/ the fucker choked on his rosary beads.") Rather than be political, it is vaguely personal, as Gillespie pens tributes to his friends such "Suicide Sally and Johnny Guitar," inspired by Kate Moss and Pete Doherty. Whilst the song which would become best-known from this album is "Country Girl," for me the standout is "Dolls", a collaboration with The Kills Alison Mosshart crammed with rock 'n' roll clichés and all the more entertaining for it. There is an air of frivolousness to "Riot City Blues" that makes no effort to reflect the political landscape—or does it? Politics had become so debased that it was losing seriousness; on 17th July, George. W. Bush greeted Tony Blair with the phrase, "yo, Blair!"

It is also important not to be to harsh on Primal Scream. Whilst this album felt frivolous, Bobby Gillespie still made his politics clear in interviews, particularly concerning his pro-Palestine viewpoint. As on 18th July 180 British citizens were evacuated from Lebanon due to the growing crisis between Hizbollah militants and Israel, issues in the Middle East suddenly felt closer to home.

At least, even if it was not reflected in their music, the return of Primal Scream meant that someone was there to speak articulately on the issue.

THOM YORKE—THE ERASER July 2006

For over fifteen years Radiohead had been one of the most worthwhile and interesting bands in Britain; so why exactly did Thom Yorke feel the need to release a solo album in 2006? He explained this decision clearly at the time by saying, "I've been in this band since we left school and never dared to do anything on my own, and it was like 'this is getting stupid.' It was like 'man, I've got to find out what it feels like,' y'know? And it was good. It was a really good time." It was a good time for the listener as well; "The Eraser" is a hugely accomplished, excellent album, largely inspired by the issue of climate change (Yorke was a spokesman for Friends Of The Earth's "The Big Ask" campaign to reduce carbon emissions). Climate change was becoming an increasingly dominant issue this year—on 30th October, the Stern Review, a 700 page report on the economics of climate change by Nicholas Stern was published by the government. It stated that climate change was the greatest and widest-ranging market failure ever seen, presenting a unique challenge for economics. The review provided prescriptions including environmental taxes to minimize the economic and social disruptions. The Stern Review's main conclusion is that the benefits of strong, early action on climate change far outweigh the costs of not acting, pointing to potential impacts of climate change on water resources, food production, health and the environment. According to the review, without action, the overall costs of climate change would be equivalent to losing at least 5% of gross domestic product each year, now and forever—which could easily increase to over 20%. In return, the review proposes that 1% of global GDP per annum is required to be invested in order to avoid the worst effects of climate change.

The Stern Report was the most widely discussed of its kind, evoking debate everywhere. The climate change theme on "The Eraser" certainly felt relevant.

There are other issues in politics tackled on "The Eraser" to heartbreaking effect; namely "Harrowdown Hill" about the death of Dr David Kelly. In an interview with The Observer, Yorke said that "Harrowdown Hill" was "the most angry song I've ever written in my life," and stated that he would not discuss the background of it, saying that, "its not for me or for any of us to dig this up. So it's a bit of an uncomfortable thing." In a further interview with The Globe and Mail, Yorke said that "he had been feeling really uncomfortable about that song lately," but felt that "not to write it would probably have been worse." Yorke was particularly cautious when it came to the feelings of Dr. Kelly's family—he seemed to be showing far more sensitivity to the issue than any of the characters initially involved ever could. A tortured lyric of "I can't take this" reminds us how, in the middle of the political whitewash and media backstabbing, there was one man—one mans life—caught in the middle of it. The issue of the invasions which had sparked this in the first place also still dominated the news as on 2nd September the RAF Nimrod crash in Afghanistan killed fourteen personnel in Britain's worse single military loss since the Falklands War.

In a world in which doom and gloom prevailed, Thom Yorke showed his solo voice to be every inch as honest and relevant as his work with Radiohead.

KLAXONS—MYTHS OF THE NEAR FUTURE   Jan 2007

The opening of 2007 saw two days strike action hit Central Trains, affecting many parts of England, especially the East and West Midlands. People still clearly knew how to take power into their own hands, something which is not merely inspirational but almost reassuring considering the general astonishing incompetence of the government at the time. John Reid, a man noted for making a mess of every position he had been in, faced mounting problems including prisoner escapes and the absconding of those under Control Orders. With the UK in turmoil, people were searching for a new escapist scene to hold on to, hence the emergence of "nu rave," which attempted to capture the ecstasy-fuelled glory of the original rave scene. It all turned out to be a bit of a great white hype, over fairly quickly and producing little outstanding music—but the genre's key album, The Klaxon's "Myths of the Near Future," stands alone as a modern classic, sounding like nothing else that there had ever been before. Like so many previous bands, one of the biggest influences on this album is the science fiction author JG Ballard—the albums title is taken from a short story collection of his, which features such fantastical stories as that of a man in love with a mannequin who used to be a real woman, whilst the crossover hit "Golden Skans" is also inspired by a novel of his.

Whilst interviews saw the band discuss a love of maths, and they all have philosophy degrees, literature does seem to be the main intellectual influence on this album—"Atlantis to Interzone" (host to one of the best guitar breakdowns since Radiohead's "Paranoid Android", has a William S. Burroughs influence, whilst "Gravitys Rainbow" draws it title and inspiration from Thomas Pynchon's famously baffling postmodern novel. Whilst the original rave scene had just been about having a good time, the Klaxons were ensuring that this time around there was a great deal of intellect added to it.

Their take on escapism also involves a surprising amount of darkness. "Isle of Her" is inspired by the Mayan prophercies, and covers cannibalism and Cyclops, "Four Horsemen of 2012" has an apocalyptic theme and the standout "Magick" is about the works of the famous Satanist Aleister Crowley—its accompanying video equally gleefully sinister, with two members of the band turning the third into a victim of Satanic practice.

A melting pot of sounds and themes, but always miles from reality, this Mercury music prize winning album allowed escapism from a dull nation through a riot of colour and originality.

"STARTING OVER":
THE FALL—REFORMATION POST TLC
AND
PATRICK WOLF—THE MAGIC POSITION

On the 1st February, 2007, Defence Secretary Des Browne announced that the UK forces in Southern Afghanistan would be boosted by 800. In short, we showed absolutely no signs of even thinking about ending this conflict. Proposed military expansion of the Trident missile system caused a revolt within the Labour Party. Both Stephen Pound and Chris Ruane resigned—and there was a particularly significant resignation from Nigel Griffiths as Deputy Leader of the House of Commons over the issue.

As military conflict dragged on and on, many were left thinking that surely it was time to start over. If politics was not prepared to refresh itself, then at least music was.

The previous year, in a short interview with "Another Magazine" (the new sister publication of Dazed and Confused) the frequently dark and inaccessible Patrick Wolf said that his next ambition was "to be a pop star . . . but a good one." He seemed like the least likely person on Earth to fulfil this, but he certainly captured a great deal of pop sensibility on "The Magic Position," particularly on the title track. Whilst this does not extend to the whole album, he had shown a willingness and an ability to embrace something new.

The Fall were also embracing the new, but in a more "expected" manner—their latest album "Reformation Post TLC," saw yet another line-up change. It was their 26th album, but the new line up kept the sound as fresh and vital as ever (The line up consisted of Tim Presley, Rob Barbato, Orpheo McCord, Dave Spurr and the potential cog of interband harmony, Mark. E. Smith's new wife Elena.)

Mark. E. Smith was clearly happier with this line-up than the previous one—"post TLC" means "post traitors, liars and cunts." And "traitors, liars and cunts," certainly seemed a part of everyday life, particularly in relation to the cash for honours allegation. On the 1st February, Downing Street revealed that Tony Blair had been interviewed as a witness by police on the 26th January in connection with the cash for honours allegations. As it appeared we were unable to trust those in government, "The Magic Position" and "Reformation Post TLC" were ideal albums for the time—the sounds of refreshed and revived acts coming across as hugely positive through the medium of starting over, but still with that edge of darkness which had first bought them to attention in the first place. It was a good time for eccentricity and theatricality—Gruff Rhys' solo debut "Candylion," made him seem like a modern Syd Barrett, whilst the Horror's debut album "Strange House" revived goth not just to the point of being acceptable, but being fashionable. In the midst of all this, though, nobody was coming across as more genuine or effective than Patrick Wolf and The Fall.

MANIC STREET PREACHERS—SEND AWAY THE TIGERS May 2007

On and on and on. That was the sense surrounding the conflict in Iraq. On 5th April, four British soldiers had been killed in a bomb blast near the Iraqi city of Basra, whilst ten days later two UK military helicopters collided near the town on Taji near Baghdad, killing two soldiers.

As the initial stages of the Iraq war had seen a massive wave of anti-war, dissenting songs, the Manic Street Preachers had gone against the grain to release their most apolitical album, "Lifebolood." Anyone worried that they had been drained of their abilities would, however, have had these fears alleviated by "Send Away The Tigers", an album which failed to fully reacquaint them with previous levels of commercial success but did bring them back to critical acclaim. The return of politics is instantly apparent—the sleeve features a quote from the controversial artist Wyndham Lewis which runs "when a man is young, he is usually a revolutionary of some kind. So, here I am, speaking of my revolution." Naturally, this follows into the music itself. The song "I'm Just a Patsy," draws its title from Lee Harvey Oswald's denial of the murder of John. F. Kennedy, whereas "Rendition," concerns global systems of human rights violations. Human rights was, after all, an important topic in the press at time, particularly with the dominance of The Terrorism Act. On the 24th April, British anti-terrorism police arrested five people in London and one in Luton for alleged breaches of the Terrorism Act. Issues of human rights in relation to justice were particularly hazy, especially with justice itself becoming so complicated. This is reflected in events on 9th May, in which the Ministry of Justice came into existence in the UK, reorganized from the Department of Constitutional Affairs and taking over some responsibilities from the Home Office. But all there extra "ministries" which were emerging felt strangely "1984"-esque . . . was there actually anything good happening in the world?

Yes, there was. On 23rd May, the government announced a carbon emissions trading scheme, the Carbon Reduction Commitment, that would apply to hotel chains, supermarkets, banks and other large organisations. This was clearly a step forward. Another progressive step, in a different way, occurred the next day when Jenny Bailey became the first transsexual mayor in the UK. The optimistic, upbeat sounds on "Send Away The Tigers" then, were not completely incongruous. (A key track for this is the lovely call and response duet with Nina Persson of the Cardigans, "Your Love Alone Is Not Enough.")

If anything is to be noted about politics in May 2007, though, it is that they brimmed with life, excitement and change. The Foreign Office in particular had to deal with an intriguing case—on 28th May, they submitted a formal request to the Russian government for the extradition of ex-KGB agent Andrei Lugovi to face charges over the murder of his former colleague Alexander Litvinenko in London. Whilst the murder of Litvineko was obviously terrible, exciting espionage stories did not usually take place here in the UK. Other news stories may have been less dramatic, but still reflected a changing world. On 16th May, Alex Salmond had been elected first minister for Scotland in the Scottish Parliament, the first person from the Scottish National Party to hold the post. Supported by the Scottish Green Party, his party would form a minority administration. However, the biggest political story this month occurred on the 10th, when Tony Blair asked Labours National Executive Committee to seek a new party leader, announcing that he would officially step down as Prime Minister on the 27th June. This was a wise move; not only had the Iraq war made him unpopular, but a new economic downturn was also affecting him. His terrible decisions, courtesy of him personally and various cabinets, made him potentially our worst ever Labour Prime Minister. Hopefully, his departure would usher in a new age. There was also progress in Northern Ireland on 8th May in which the formation of the power sharing Northern Ireland Assembly. As Britain as a whole prepared to move into an optimistic new era, with "Send Away The Tigers" the Manic Street Preachers showed they were ready to move into theirs.

PART TWO

SECTION TWO

THE GORDON BROWN YEARS

RADIOHEAD—IN RAINBOWS
Nov 2007

The final MORI poll of Tony Blair's reign as Prime Minister had put his Labour government three points ahead of the Conservatives on 39%. The party's new leader, Gordon Brown, had the task of maintaining. Whilst Blair took on a role as a Middle East envoy—to the disbelief of many—Brown unveiled his new cabinet, a female-centric government including Harriet Harman as deputy leader and Jacqui Smith as the first female Home Secretary. Initially, this cabinet managed to hold on to Labour's popularity. The first MORI poll of Gordon Brown's reign, on July 12th, put his government six points ahead of Conservatives on 41%. A later MORI poll on 26th September then put them at 48%, with a 20 point lead over the Conservatives, sparking media reports that Brown would call a general election within the next few weeks in order to form a term of parliament until the end of 2012. However, they say that a week is a long time in politics and thus a month is even longer—an October 31st MORI poll saw Labour fall behind the Conservatives for the first time in a MORI poll since Gordon Brown became Prime Minister, as their 35% showing put them five points off the top.

If the British were growing more disillusioned with politics, they had a reason to have some faith in the music industry—for Radioheads latest album, "In Rainbows," those who downloaded it only had to pay what they thought it was worth.

So, how much is it worth? The content is certainly as interesting as to be expected from one of Britain's greatest bands. The singles are incredibly strong—"Nude" is a beautiful piece of slow burn yearning, "Jigsaw Falling Into Place," is based on asset of observations and different experiences witnessed by Thom Yorke during his weekends out drinking, and "Bodysnatchers" is inspired by Victorian ghost stories and Yorke's feeling of "your physical consciousness trapped without being able to connect fully with anything else." It was recorded when Yorke was, in his own words, "in a state of hyperactive mania"—and it certainly shows.

The album was a typically painstaking process. On "All I Need," Johnny Greenwood wanted to recapture the white noise generated by a band playing loudly in a room, a sound which never occurs in the studio. His solution was to have a string section play every note of the scale, whilst blanketing the frequencies. Thom Yorke has also described the process of recording "Videotape" as "absolute agony," stating that the song went through "every possible parameter." (Eventually, Yorke left the studio one day to find that Johnny Greenwood and producer Nigel Godrich had stripped the song down to the version found on the album, a minimal piano ballad.)

Talking about the album as a whole, Yorke had said that its lyrics are based on "that anonymous fear thing, sitting in traffic, thinking, 'I'm sure I'm supposed to be doing something else.' Its similar to 'OK Computer' in a way. It much more terrifying." He has also said it "is about the fucking panic of realising your going to die! And that any time soon I could possibly have a heart attack when I next go for a run." As the age of heightened paranoia continued, accelerated by attempted terrorist attacks on Glasgow airport, this was a fitting theme. However, Ed O' Brien said of the lyrics that "they were universal. There wasn't a political agenda. Its being human." This is also relevant, given the dominance of "personal" news stories, such as the disappearance of Madeline McCann, over the political at the time.

So, then, this album is definitely worth something. It showcases everything that is great about Radiohead—their ability to progress whilst, unlike other bands who had been together this long, maintaining the same line-up. In an age of the transient (Sir Menzies Campbell resigned as Liberal Democrat leader after little more than a year), Radiohead were showing the power of longevity.

BABYSHAMBLES—SHOTTERS NATION Nov 2007

On the 1st November, London's Metropolitan police service was found guilty of endangering the public following the fatal shooting of Jean Charles De Menzes, an innocent Brazilian who officers mistook for a suicide bomber. This terrible act of police incompetence did little for their public image; but as part of the establishment they had always been decidedly unpopular in rock 'n' roll anyway. The two had been in conflict since the Sixties, when the Rolling Stones had been public enemy number one. The current band for such a title was Babyshambles, who had faced a series of lucrative requests for oft-fabricated offences, such as snorting cocaine from a Macdonalds counter. The media coverage of the bands reckless behaviour was overshadowing the music greatly—thankfully, critics were silenced and the media distracted when their second album, "Shotters Nation" redeemed their patchy debut. The best decisions they had made involved the participants—guitarist Patrick Walden had been replaced by the brilliant, renowned ska guitarist Mick Withnall, and production duties saw Stephen Street, the production genius behind The Smiths and Blur, take over from Mick Jones. Their bass player Drew McConnell was also now renowned as an indie hero for his tireless campaigning against racism. As racism crept back into the mainstream—Nigel Hastilow, a Tory candidate due to stand for Halesowen and Rowley Regis at the next general election, resigned after coming under heavy criticism for his claims that Enoch Powell had been "right"—now was as good a time as ever for this.

Of course, no matter who else is involved in Babyshambles, Pete Doherty is the central focus of the band and he himself had undergone some worthwhile changes. Newly drug-free and having split from Kate Moss, there was now nothing to make him a tabloid favourite, thus putting the focus back on the music.

It was obvious that the band had been refreshed and revived upon hearing lead single "Delivery", a Kinks-esque slice of competent writing which far surpasses anything from their debut. As an act expected to be shambolic and scandalous were proving to be neither of these, those we actually expected some competence from—the government—were going in the opposite direction. On 20th November, the Child Benefit Data scandal saw HM Revenue and Customs admit it had misplaced two computer discs which contained the records of child benefit claimants data, inlcluding bank details and national insurance numbers, leaving up to 7.25 million households susceptible to identity theft. The issue of loans to the government also created scandal—on 26th November, "Donorgate" saw Labour Party official Peter Wyatt resign over loans received by the party from David Abrahams. The Labour Party had been disgraced, the Conservatives were still the Conservatives and thus the less said the better, and the Liberal Democrats were still not much of a viable alternative—on 18th December, Nick Clegg won their leadership election. Clegg was a confused jumble of carefully presented image mixed with not knowing when to stop talking, with typical Liberal Democrat "right-leaning masquerading as liberal" policy.

People had been disillusioned with politics for so long that all this was almost to be expected. But, with "Shotters Nation," we learnt the possibility of recovery from past mistakes. The album may have had Henry Wallis; "Death of Chatterton" as its artwork, but there were at least glimmers of hope that it was not set to be a footnote in any kind of similarly tragic story.

LAURA MARLING—ALAS, I CANNOT SWIM
AND
MYSTERY JETS—21

Corruption and scandal have always been a part of politics, and the beginning of 2008 saw it accelerate with a series of incidents, showing both of the main parties to be questionable. Irregular donations was one issue which continued to plague the Labour Party—on 24th January Peter Hain resigned as Secretary of State for Work and Pensions over the issue. Controversy for the Conservatives, meanwhile, manifested itself when on 31st January their MP Derek Conway was suspended from the House of Commons for 10 days over payments made to his son from his parliamentary allowances. With such levels of corruption in the world, it was an ideal time for the emergence of honest songwriters whose attitude would have felt downright refreshing in a sea of lies. Step forward, then, ultra-talented teenager Laura Marling and her album "Alas, I Cannot Swim." The strength of songwriting here is truly impressive. "New Romantic" looks at the turmoil of romance with a partner who "puts on Ryan Adams," to force her guard down; its tragic chorus of "I feel sorry for whichever man/ should meet my sorry state," setting the tone perfectly. Love in Marling's world veers between gothic ("Night Terror") and cynical ("Ghosts") but it is always beautiful, sounding like the slow sounds of loss. Slow losses were something of a theme in the UK, the most notable being the coal industry—25th January saw the official closure of the Tower Colliery in the Cynon Valley, the last deep coal mine to be worked on in Wales.

Marling is also a presence on the Mystery Jets second album "Twenty One," adding a gorgeous guest vocal to the track "Young Love." The Mystery Jets had attracted attention three years previously with their experimental and interesting album "Making Dens." Notably eccentric, they hailed from Eel Pie Island (a haven of eccentricity) and the line up had originally included brothers Kai and Blaine Harrison . . . and their father Henry. Blaine Harrison, a spina bifida sufferer, was also the first disabled frontman since Ian Drury, but this issue was refreshingly never dwelled on by either the band or the music press.

On "Twenty-One," the band created something almost like a crossover record with "Two Doors Down," an uplifting parody of the eighties, its accompanying video depicting the band in pastel suits, singing against neon backdrops. Whilst it is not a political song per se, the extent of the recession we were sliding into (Northern Rock being the most notable disaster) meant it felt like we were back in the eighties, making this quite timely. The excesses of the eighties were also still very much in existence—on 9th January, Israeli diamond magnate Lev Leviev bought a new build house in Hampstead, London for a record £35 million.

The miniature scene which Marling and the Mystery Jets were a part of (it also included Larrikin Love, the Maccabees and Noah and the Whale) was refreshingly low scale and unassuming in comparison—but, then again, it is the role of any goof alternative scene to do things a little differently.

THE KILLS—MIDNIGHT BOOM   March 2008

2008, as we are learning, was not without its political disasters, something which hit its peak in May when the famously incompetent Conservative Boris Johnson was voted mayor of London. The fact that Johnson had always been regarded as something of a comedy figure did not reflect well on the British publics voting decisions, favouring a supposedly amusing personality over competence and policy. In a different way, music can be affected by such factors, too—this was the year that The Kills came to public attention, not for their music but for their personal lives (Jamie Hince was now in a relationship with Kate Moss).

This should not distract from the fact that their third album, "Midnight Boom," is a return to the brilliance of their debut "Keep On Your Mean Side," after a slightly disappointing second album, "No Wow." Largely influenced by the documentary "Pizza Pizza Daddy-O," about children's playground chanting games, the album has the feel of a series of these kinds of chants. However, this does not wipe out the nasty sexuality which first bought them to attention; "Cheap and Cheerful" is particularly carnal, with its chorus of "I want you to be crazy 'cos you're boring baby when your straight," whilst the clap-along rhythms of "Sour Cherry" express a joy in being pat of a darker counterculture.

The biggest leap of progress on this record, though, is in Alison Mosshart's voice. Whereas before it had just been about its sexuality, by the time of "Midnight Boom" it appeared to have gathered a new level of strength—"Tape Song" and "Last Days of Magic" are notable examples of this.

The 1st May also saw local elections with worrying results. The BNP made gains and the Conservatives were ahead on 44% of the vote.

If these elections were anything to go on, the mainstream was about to be worth more disdain than ever. In spite of press attention, The Kills seemed happy to remain consciously counter-culture. For this, we needed them more than we had ever needed them before as the alternative world accelerated its appeal.

PRIMAL SCREAM—BEAUTIFUL FUTURE   July 2008

There's nothing like a downturn to affect a government's popularity. On 18th July, it continued to hit Labour hard when the latest MORI poll put the Conservatives 20 points ahead with 47% of the vote. With an election due within the next two years, or possibly the following year, David Cameron was well on course to become the UK's next Prime Minister. With an economic crisis beginning, fears of a recession and mass unemployment rising, it was widely expected that Labours struggle would cause Cameron's popularity to grow. Further bad news for the economy showed that it contracted by 0.1% in the second quarter of the year—ending 16 years of unbroken growth.

The unpopularity of Labour continued into the second half of 2008, when the 14th September IPSOS MORI poll put them 16 points behind the Conservatives. The economic situation was clearly desperate—on 8th October, the government announced a bank rescue package worth some £500 billion as a response to this ongoing financial crisis.

Perhaps, then, there is some level of irony in Primal Scream entitling their 2008 album "Beautiful Future," something which there really did not seem much hope of. For some, the idea of any future seemed obsolete, particularly those hit by the wave of unemployment. Notable catastrophes were the end of Woolworths and MFI. For pessimists, the decision of Primal Screams to entitle the lead single "Can't Go Back," was far more fitting.

"Can't Go Back," is a blistering slice of rock 'n' roll—nothing new, but still loud and exciting enough to grab attention. But "Beautiful Future," as a whole is rather patchy. In this respect, it is an album reflecting how people felt about the government—starting off promisingly but going on to disappoint. As with "Evil Heat," the politics was found more in the bands interviews than music, but the nation seemed unconcerned with liberal politics as well seemed to happily accept the Olympics bringing tourism to the unethical nation of China. With such things occurring, we really needed articulate, political bands like Primal Scream—but we needed them to be more consistent musically. At the time of writing, this was their most recent album. Lets just hope, by the time you are reading this, they will have released something to match the glories of "Screamadelica" or "XTNMTR."

PETER DOHERTY—GRACE/WASTELANDS

As the decade began its final year, the conflict in Afghanistan which had defined it continued. On 1st January, 2009, a British Soldier from 6th Battalion the Rifles, later named by the Ministry of Defence as Sergeant Christopher Reed, was killed in an explosion in Southern Afghanistan, bringing the total number of British forces to die in the conflict to 138. This set the scene for a period heavy on fatalities—by the end of February, the total number of deaths had reached 179. But the time lapse since the start of the war meant that artistic references to it were fading—the danger was that it had all already been said, and would thus look somewhat passé.

This problem was dealt with most eloquently by Peter Doherty, who looked back to the past to address the issue of war—bringing wars in general into consciousness without having to reference Afghanistan. His song "1939 Returning," a highlight of his debut solo album "Grace/Wastelands," looks back at the second world war before transporting the characters involved to the present day—with this being the kind of technique more expected from a novelist than a songwriter, on the whole this is the album that finally fulfils all his literary allusions, as well as proving his critics wrong. Largely casting off the pity-me approach and hard drug references in favour of an archaic lyricism, and with an excellent "supporting cast"—production by Stephen Street, guitar by Graham Coxon and a guest vocal from One Dove's Dot Allison—this album won over many, including his former nemesis, the tabloids. After all, these days Britain had bigger things to worry about than the exploits of a celebrity drug addict. The nations financial crisis was instead the main concern. By the 5th February, the Bank of England had made eight reductions in interest rates since October, making them the lowest they had ever been in the banks 300 year history. On 14th January, the government unveiled a £20 billion loan guarantee scheme for small and medium sized businesses to try and tackle the crisis. On the same day, Gordon Brown appointed former banker Mervyn Davies as the Trade and Investment Minister. Five days later, the government announced further assistance for the banking sector, measures including to government insuring bad debts and increasing its stake in the Royal Bank of Scotland. However, the measures made little impact on the stock market, with banking stocks falling across the board. Worse still, it did not look as if things were going to get any better, as on the 28th January the IMF projected that the UK economy would shrink by 2.8% in the following year, the biggest in any developed nation.

Doherty had lyrically tackled the issue of poverty before (on the Libertines "Death On The Stairs") but rather than reflecting on economic problems on "Grace/Wastelands," he opts for a more escapist world. Opening track "Arcady," taking its cue from vaudeville play "The Arcadians," imagines a perfect, Arcadian world, miles away from what we were actually living in. In fact, nearly all of the lyricism on this album feels old-fashioned; no bad thing. Recorded at his home in beautiful rural Marlborough, Wiltshire, it sounds cut off from contemporary urbanism. In a world were "progress" seemed to mean destroying the natural world (a fifth runway proposed at Heathrow airport invited protest) this seemed hugely refreshing. Doherty's new embracing of nature even sees this album feature a tribute to the elements, "I Am The Rain."

The albums title clearly nods to TS Eliot. As extreme weather conditions plagued the UK, we were in something of a wasteland ourselves—one perfectly soundtracked by this sparse album, to convert even the harshest of critics.

THE HORRORS—PRIMARY COLOURS   April 2009

Two years previously, garage rockers The Horrors had made themselves known with their debut album "Strange House," a fun bur opinion dividing album. Whilst they attracted a devoted following called The Horribles and sparked a goth revival in fashion, it still all felt very style-over-substance. Songs like "Count in Fives" showed potential, but many did not take the band seriously. Which is why their second album, the truly incredible "Primary Colours", was such a revelation.

Firstly, let us give "Primary Colours" some context. Britain was still dominated by financial problems—unemployment was above 2, 000,000. On 7th March, the government took a controlling stake reported to be 65% in the troubled Lloyds Banking group. Toxic loans totalling £260billion would be insured by the government as part of the deal.

Rather than stick to the minimal sound of their debut, The Horrors kicked against the recession by recording a series of lush, complex soundscapes which seem to envelope the listener. Critics were quick to compare it to My Bloody Valentines "Loveless," a fair comparison.

It does not take long for the listener to realise what an enormous leap up from "Strange House," "Primary Colours" is. Opener "Mirrors Image," opens with a whirl of sound before drawing in the listener with Faris Badwan's winding vocal. (He had previously been known as Faris Rotter as the band used comic pseudonyms, but now reverted to their real names as they became more about the music than the image. The sharp gothic look of before was also swapped for a more fitting, C86-inspired look.)

Opening with a track like "Mirrors Image" would leave the listener to believe that the quality would decline throughout the album, but this never happens. "New Ice Age" is a great example of effects and feedback, "Who Can Say?" a twisted fairground song, and the title track could be a lost Joy Division classic. It is the truly stunning closing track though, "Sea Within A Sea", which is the highlight. In fact, it could be classed as one of the greatest closing tracks of all time, so great that it could only be a closing track—nothing could possibly follow this winding, multi-layered soundscape upon soundscape song. Anybody needing a distraction from the nations financial turmoil could simply listen to this seven minute wonder if they were looking for something to completely lose themselves in.

Not that the government weren't taking any measures to try and combat the ongoing financial crisis. On the 2nd April, the 2009 G20 summitt was held in response to the crisis—after all, it was a global crisis, it did not only affect us. Organised at the initiative of German Chancellor Angela Merkel, the leaders at the summit agreed that markets, financial institutions and the wide range of financial assets that they create, and hedge funds, should be subject to appropriate control.

Prior to the summit, on the 14th March finance ministers and central bankers of the G20 met in Horsham. To restore global growth as quickly as possible, the participants decided to approve co-ordinated and decisive actions to stimulate demand and employment. They also committed themselves to maintain the supply of credit by providing more liquidity and re-capitalising the banking system, and to implement rapidly the stimulus plans.

Gordon Brown was also involved in some pre-summit preparation. In the weeks before the G20, he visited several countries on three continents to try and secure backing for his goals at the summit. During this trip Brown was forced to re-clarify his position on fiscal stimulus after criticism from the governor of the Bank of England. Whilst speaking at the European Parliament in Strasbourg, he was challenged by a member of the European Parliament over his spending plans. The problem with summits such as the G20 is they give little consideration to the everyday person and tend to be an orgy of capitalism. Even worse, China were the most influential nation in this one. No wonder the summit led to protests. Even though these protests were peaceful, kettling was used to contain them. The death of Ian Tomlinson, who had been pushed in the back by officers minutes before dying of a heart attack, in spite of appearing to have no active part in the protests, caused waves of controversy. The fact that the security operation cost £7.2million, over a summit to deal with financial collapse, also did little to endear the establishment to the public. In the end, the summit pledged £1trillion to improve trade and international finance, but any realist knew that recovery would be slow. However, as the instance of a formerly derided band making the album of the year in "Primary Colours" it had been shown that a little patience could go a long way.

MANIC STREET PREACHERS—
JOURNAL FOR PLAGUE LOVERS   May 2009

May, 2009 would see the beginning of an issue which was one of the government's biggest downfalls—the publication of MP's expenses.

This issue led to the speaker of the House of Commons, Micheal Martin, resigning after coming under heavy criticism for his handling of the role (John Bercow was elected as his replacement), and the Conservatives were given a victorious benefit—a June 1st MORI poll put them on 40% of the vote. Labour now had just 18%. This seemed decidedly unfair—just as many Conservative MP's had been involved in the expenses row, but people could not see past the expenses spent by the current government.

The emotions of disillusionment and anger felt by the public made a new album from the laureates of this seem timely, but to talk about it in relation to current affairs seems obsolete, as it uses the lyrics left behind by Richey Edwards over fourteen years after his disappearance. As a consequence, it is tempting to simply view "Journal for Plague Lovers" as "The Holy Bible" Part Two—it even uses Jenny Saville artwork again.

But it is not "The Holy Bible." To be blunt, it is not as good. But then again, very little is. It is a great album in its own right, though—their finest *since* "The Holy Bible." Previous album "Send Away The Tigers" had been widely acclaimed, though, which is what made the band feel they were in a position to use Edwards lyrics again—as they explained, if they had done so after the poorly-received "Lifeblood," people would have thought that they were just doing so to win back acclaim.

The biggest challenge was naturally whether they could still write the kind of alive, guitar-driven music which had always enveloped Edwards lyrics. From the minute this album starts, it is obvious that they could—opener "Peeled Apples" is one of the finest songs of the bands career, carried by a central guitar riff and a full-on chorus of *"riderless horses on Chomsky's Camelot/ bruises on my hands from taking my litter out,"* a typical Edwards lyric of the personal and the intellectual.

In July, the last British survivor of World War I, the wonderful and charismatic Harry Patch, died at the age of 111. Sad as this was, nobody could deny that Patch had lived a full life; his death was not a waste. But whilst his death sparked memories of the First World War, our contemporary war was still raging, which was producing many deaths which still seemed such an empty waste—on July 11th, eight British soldiers were killed in 24 hours. Those who had died would no doubt befall the terrible fate of being defined by "their war." Harry Patch had always been determined that he would never be defined by "his war," but a great flaw with Britishness is that we do define people by their tragedies. Edwards is another example of this—yes, of course he was a troubled figure, but his sense of humour, which veers from surreal to self-deprecating, is all over "Journal for Plague Lovers." Surely the most surreal song title of the year was "Jackie Collins Existential Question Time." Meanwhile, the brilliant "Me and Stephen Hawking," spins an entire song out of one old joke—"what did the anorexic say to the paraplegic?" "We missed the sex revolution when we failed the physical." The punchline here forms the chorus of the song, with Edwards imagining it as a conversation between him and Stephen Hawking.

His illnesses, then, still infuse this album. At times it feels actively sick, peppered with bruises and plagues imagery (the album title is also drawn from Albert Camus' novel "The Plague.") As fear over swine flu swept the nation, this seemed rather timely. But how relevant could the lyrics here feel as a whole? After all, most of them were written under John Majors government.

Amy Britton

But, once again we appeared to be veering towards the Conservatives—a Norwich by-election left the Conservatives with a 7,000 majority, in a former Labour constituency. Many Labour constituencies seemed to switching their allegiance. With a Conservative government back on the horizon, the old voice of dissent in form of this band was as relevant as ever.

On the 8th August, it was announced that the Conservatives were studying plans for VAT to be increased by 20% if they won the general election, as part of an emergency package to cut national debt. After all, the financial situation was still dire—unemployment stood at 2, 440, 000. It was a particularly difficult time for the young, who found their qualifications obsolete as there were no jobs to be found.

The young may have bee losing their voice in the wider world, but not in music. That years Mercury Music Prize winner was the beautiful, sensual debut from London teenagers The xx. The name "xx" is drawn from the visual depiction of a peck on the cheek, but as on journalist put it, their sounds doesn't so much give you a peck on the cheek as climb into bed and spoon you hard. Richly comforting and oddly post-coital, but with a suggestion of a nocturnal dark side, this album is classed as shoegaze revival, but it certainly brings something new to the genre; something which makes it seem fresh, relevant, and modern.

It was an increasingly dark age—the number of British Forces personnel killed in Afghanistan had reached 200, and eyebrows were raised over the decision of the Scottish Justice Secretary, Kenny MacAskill, to grant release to the Lockerbie bomber Abdelbaset al-Megrahi on compassionate grounds, stating that he was in the final stages of terminal prostrate cancer. Amidst all of this, The xx were creating a sound so self-contained that it was the closest thing to a musical security blanket—thus, The xx was probably the most worthy Mercury Music Prize winner there could have been this year.

THE CRIBS—IGNORE THE IGNORANT

The expenses scandal continued to hit Labour hard. The latest MORI poll put Conservative support at 43%, 17 points ahead of Labour, and Britain's biggest-selling newspaper, The Sun, withdrew its support for Labour and turned back to the Conservatives.

However, the Conservatives weren't the only ones benefiting from Labour's slide in popularity. As is often the case in times of desperation, a worrying number were beginning to turn to the far-Right as the BNP began a rise in popularity. On 22nd October, their leader Nick Griffin made his first appearance on "Question Time," amidst crowds of protest. The decision to allow him on the programme and thus give a platform to his preposterous views did not sit comfortably—being on "Question Time" was a privilege, not a right. However, once the programme actually aired it turned out to be rather beneficial, as he was exposed for what he was, ignorant and incompetent, thus decreasing, rather than increasing, his support (he later announced his intention to make a formal complaint to the BBC for the way he believed he had been treated by the programmes audience, who he described as "a lynch mob", and the shows other guests.)

For many constituencies, however, this was to late—the BNP had already been voted in. One such area was Wakefield, Yorkshire, home town of the now-established indie band The Cribs.

The Cribs were widely adored in the "indie community"; their previous albums "The New Fellas" and "Mens Needs, Womens Needs, Whatever" bringing them critical acclaim (the NME were particular supporters), but "Ignore The Ignorant" sees them reach a new level of maturity.

Of course, it probably helped that their line-up had made one huge, significant change—having previously just consisted of the brothers Ryan, Gary and Ross Jarman, the former Smiths guitarist, the brilliant Johnny Marr, had joined on the grounds that he was a long term fan. Whilst "Ignore the Ignorant," is still very much a Cribs album (they have a fairly distinctive sound, even though it had been plagiarised to unfairly wider commercial success, by other bands) Marr's guitar adds a new layer to the sound; bigger, louder, but also more competent.

But the step up is not just in the sound. The band were horrified by the victory of the BNP in their hometown and this infuses the album. The title "Ignore the Ignorant" is a direct response to this.

Ignorance was not just limited to the BNP. People opted for "easy" voting options in the wake of disillusionment with Labour, and the last MORI poll of the year pointed to a Conservative landslide with the Conservatives at 43%. Support for Nick Clegg's Liberal Democrats had also increased rapidly. As a consequence of this, the 21st December live televised election debates between the leaders of the three main parties sae Cameron and Brown continually use the phrase "I agree with Nick," as they battled to get him on their side, clearly prepared for the possibility of a hung parliament and necessity of a coalition. It was the most interested Britain had been in politics in years; it also made us all a little to absorbed to notice world issues. On 29th December, Akmal Sheikh became the first EU native to be executed in China in 50 years. Gordon Brown released a statement indicating he was appalled, but the story was barely noticed—maybe the "ignorant" the Cribs are attacking could also be the masses. For all the politics, "Ignore the Ignorant," is very accessible. "We Share The Same Skies," is the albums shiny pop moment, in spite of its rain-infused lyrics of "I know this town has got you down." As unemployment stood at 2.5million and heavy rainfall hit the nation, this could have been any town. The Cribs had always seemed wary of the mainstream, but with this album they showed how many of us they could reach.

AFTERWORD

I suppose any conclusion to this book, looking at the current climate, will rapidly date. As it stands, the "I agree with Nick" situation produced an uneasy combination. Since 2010, the UK has been in the hands of David Camerons Conservative/Liberal coalition. The landscape of harsh cuts imposed on Britain has led to mass dissatisfaction, particularly from the nations young. Earlier this year, riots swept the country.

The artistic world has also been hit by the cuts, but relevant music continues to be made. This years Mercury Music Prize winner was PJ Harvey's "Let England Shake", a great record which reflected on the horror of war. As bloody revolutions have appeared all over the world, it was an album for the time. But light-hearted escapism also has as much a place as ever—the years biggest new British band have been the Vaccines, who convey impeccable indie-pop. New albums from Radiohead and the Manic Street Preachers show a continuing success for our long-term political bands; we are awaiting a new Primal Scream album which, with production by David Holmes, should be an exciting affair.

No matter what the political climate in the UK, its music will always follow. These are dark times once again. Lets hope rock'n'roll can see us through.

Printed in Great Britain
by Amazon